TREKKING IN THE VOSGES AND JURA

About the Authors

Les and Elizabeth Smith originally trained as a scientist and a geographer, and spent many years pursuing sensible careers. Their outdoor interests encouraged them to adopt a less secure but more flexible lifestyle, which allows more time for exploring the Scottish hills and travelling further afield.

Enthusiastic walkers and campers, they have backpacked along many long distance routes, both in the UK and more widely in Europe. Their trips often take them to less publicised areas, where a walking trail can provide an excellent way of seeing the country and meeting local people. They firmly believe that travelling and enjoying the outdoors does not depend on a generous budget.

The Smiths are easily distracted during their walks by efforts to glimpse local wildlife, photograph the landscape, or make some sense of the history of the area. Home is a Perthshire smallholding, where writing finds a place alongside other projects.

TREKKING IN THE VOSGES AND JURA

The GR5, GR53 and Other Treks and Walks

by

Les and Elizabeth Smith

CICERONE

2 POLICE SQUARE, MILNTHORPE, CUMBRIA LA7 7PY
www.cicerone.co.uk

ISBN-10: 1 85284 434 5
ISBN-13: 978 185284 434 9

A catalogue record for this book is available from the British Library.
Photos by the authors.

Advice to Readers

Readers are advised that while every effort is taken by the authors to ensure the accuracy of this guidebook, changes can occur which may affect the contents. It is advisable to check locally on transport, accommodation, shops, etc., but even rights of way can be altered. Paths can be affected by forestry work, landslip or changes of ownership.

The authors would welcome information on any updates and changes sent through the publishers.

Front cover: Joux Castle, misty morning

CONTENTS

Map Key

═══════	road
▬▬▬▬▬▬	GR5/GR53 or short walk route
•••••••••••••••	GR5/GR53 alternative route
ⱶⱶⱶⱶⱶⱶⱶⱶ	canal
⌇⌇⌇	river
▬ ▬ ▬	national boundary
▢	regional park
▲	summit
△	lookout point or named rock
■	other building
○	ruin, or building of historic interest
ⓒ	cave
⚏	castle
⬭⬭⬭	village or town
N66	road number
→	route direction
ⱶⱶⱶⱶⱶⱶⱶⱶⱶ	railway

Contour colour key

	over 1600m
	1400-1600m
	1200-1400m
	1000-1200m
	800-1000m
	600-800m
	400-600m
	200-400m
	0-200m

Contour colour key for overview maps only
Summary map (page 8)
Walking in the Vosges (page 10)
Walking in the Jura (page 11)

	over 2000m
	1500-2000m
	1000-1500m
	500-1000m
	200-500m
	0-200m

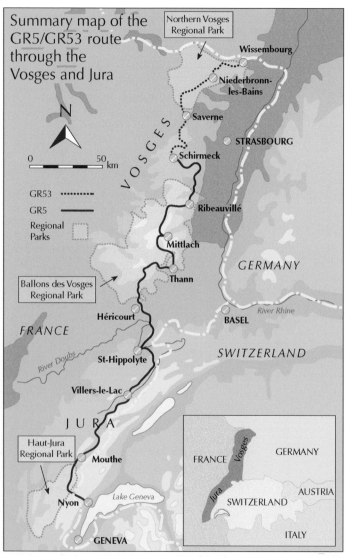

Summary map of the GR5/GR53 route through the Vosges and Jura

Northern Vosges Regional Park

Wissembourg

Niederbronn-les-Bains

Saverne

STRASBOURG

Schirmeck

VOSGES

Ribeauvillé

Mittlach

GERMANY

Ballons des Vosges Regional Park

Thann

N

0   50 km

GR53 ·······
GR5 ——
Regional Parks

Héricourt

River Rhine

BASEL

FRANCE

SWITZERLAND

River Doubs

St-Hippolyte

Villers-le-Lac

JURA

Haut-Jura Regional Park

Mouthe

Lake Geneva

Nyon

GENEVA

FRANCE   Vosges   GERMANY

Jura   SWITZERLAND   AUSTRIA

ITALY

Route profile for the GR5/GR53 route through the Vosges and Jura

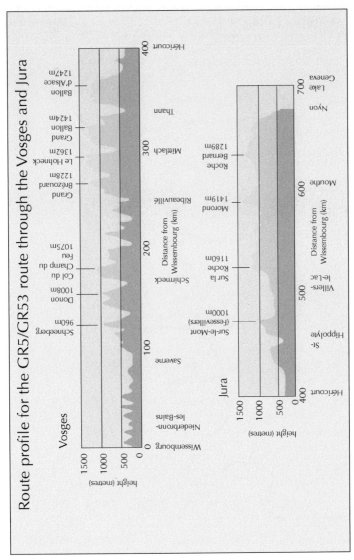

Walking in the Vosges: long distance routes and short walk centres

Long distance routes

GR53 ••••••••••

GR5 ━━━━━

GR531 ━━━━━

GR532 ━━━━━

Short walks centres ●

Wissembourg

Lembach

Lichtenberg   Niederbronn-les-Bains

Soultz-sous-Forêts

La Petite-Pierre

Phalsbourg   Saverne

Dabo

Wangenbourg

Strasbourg

GR5 north to Lorraine

Oberhaslach

Urmatt

Schirmeck   Barr

Villé

Col de Ste-Marie   Lièpvre

Ste-Marie-aux-Mines   Ribeauvillé

Col du Bonhomme

Orbey   Colmar

Col de la Schlucht   Turckheim

Munster

Metzeral

GERMANY

Col de Bussang

St-Amarin

Col des Perches   Thann

Masevaux

Giromagny   GR531 to Leymen

GR5 south to Nyon and Nice   Belfort   GR532 to Mulhouse

N

0   30 km

10

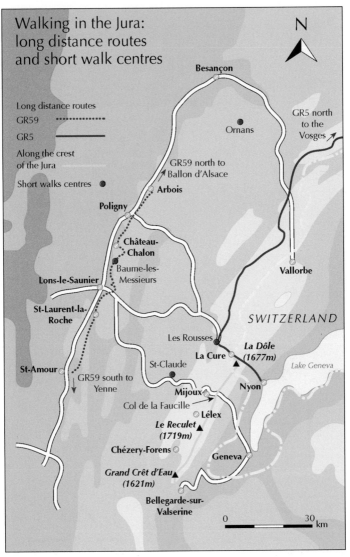

Walking in the Jura: long distance routes and short walk centres

N

Long distance routes

GR59 ·········

GR5 ——————

Along the crest of the Jura

Short walks centres ●

Besançon

Ornans

GR5 north to the Vosges →

GR59 north to Ballon d'Alsace →

Arbois

Poligny

Château-Chalon

Baume-les-Messieurs

Vallorbe

Lons-le-Saunier

St-Laurent-la-Roche

SWITZERLAND

Les Rousses

La Cure

La Dôle (1677m)

Lake Geneva

St-Amour

GR59 south to Yenne →

St-Claude

Mijoux

Col de la Faucille →

Nyon

Lélex

Le Reculet (1719m)

Chézery-Forens

Geneva

Grand Crêt d'Eau (1621m)

Bellegarde-sur-Valserine

0   30 km

Along the Doubs Gorge
(Section 9)

INTRODUCTION

WHY VISIT THE VOSGES AND JURA?

The Vosges and French Jura are areas of mountain country in the extreme east of France, bordering Switzerland and Germany. Compared with the neighbouring Alps these mountains are not high, reaching about 1400m, and perhaps this is one reason why the region is not a major holiday destination and does not have the problems of tourist pressure found in some places. This does not mean that either facilities or a welcome are hard to find.

The Vosges and Jura contain some excellent walking country, made all the more interesting by the huge variety of landscapes found in this small corner of France. A quiet forest footpath can suddenly reveal a castle ruin high on a distant crag, and the exhilarating hilltop views contrast with the sights and sounds of old Alsace villages. Further south, secluded paths wind through deep river gorges before climbing out onto the vast expanse of the high plateau.

In the north of the region the Northern Vosges is a land of tranquil forests where people are few and wildlife is undisturbed. Nature has eroded the sandstone here to leave spectacular rock pinnacles that tower in isolation over the forests. A veritable explosion of medieval castle-building has left the region scattered with an astonishing number of half-forgotten ruins, often perched precariously above rocky precipices.

In the Central and Southern Vosges the forests have their own surprises. The enigmatic ruins of the Mur Païen and the nearby convent of Mont Ste-Odile are shrouded in legend and mystery (see Section 4). Footpaths lead through the age-old winegrowing towns and villages on the edge of the Alsace Plain and up through the trees to open summit pastures. There is so much to discover here - do you linger to savour the charm of old Alsace, with its cobbled lanes and half-timbered houses steeped in history, or do you press on up to the windswept hilltops, where the view over the patchwork plain seems limitless, extending out to the distant Alps?

Further south the limestone of the Jura lends its own unique character to the landscape. Isolated lookout points give stunning views over the seemingly endless blanket of forest below. Elsewhere, rivers have cut down through the limestone to produce

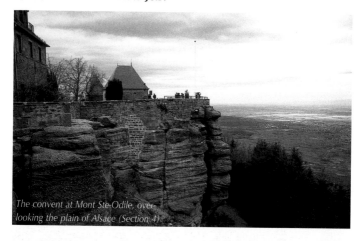

The convent at Mont Ste-Odile, over-looking the plain of Alsace (Section 4)

impressive gorge scenery, with narrow defiles leading between sheer rocky crags. Joux Castle, surely one of the most stunningly sited strongholds in all France, stands guard over one such narrow rocky cleft (see Section 10). The rivers can form gentle backwaters where trout linger in shaded pools, or they can have more dramatic moods – at Saut du Doubs the thunder of rushing water can be heard long before the waterfall comes into sight (see Section 9).

Special mention should be made of one of the real highlights of the whole walk, the airy clifftop path leading up to the summit of Le Mont d'Or (see Section 10). The dramatic wall of towering cliffs at the edge of the plateau forms the border with Switzerland, and the path provides magnificent vantage points over the expanse of the Swiss Jura.

Wildlife enthusiasts will not be disappointed. At dawn and dusk chamois venture out of the forest onto the high pastures, and there is always the chance of a rare glimpse of wild boar rooting among the trees. Kites and falcons can often be seen wheeling overhead, and storks have long been a hallmark of Alsace.

The whole region has an excellent network of footpaths, well within the capabilities of any moderately fit person. These mountains are ideal for walkers, summits being of relatively modest height, and the panoramic views make the breathless ascents worthwhile. When the time comes to rest from walking cross country, the villages and small towns provide distraction in the form of cafés and bars, the occasional museum, wine-tasting in the vineyards, and a friendly and helpful local population.

Cliffs at Le Mont d'Or
(Section 10)

The major part of this book is a practical guide to the principal north–south walking route through this varied landscape, along the GR5/GR53. This 672km (418 mile) waymarked path traverses the entire length of the Vosges, and then climbs up onto the plateau of the Haut-Jura before dropping down to Nyon on the shores of Lake Geneva. We chose to describe a route combining two long distance paths because the GR5 approaches the Vosges from the plains of Lorraine and misses the Northern Vosges completely. The Northern Vosges is a fascinating area with its own unique attractions, so we decided to start the northern end of our route description on the GR53, continuing south through the main part of the Vosges and Jura on the GR5. This has allowed us to describe a route down the full length of the Vosges mountains.

The marked regional differences along the route reflect the contrasting histories of the areas visited. Alsace, on the east side of the Vosges, has long had strong cultural links with the German lands across the Rhine, and this has left its mark on the towns and villages, with their timber-framed houses, local dishes and beers. Although French is spoken universally, the area also has its own thriving Germanic language (Elsässisch). Further south, the French Jura lies within Franche-Comté, also with a history of being separate from the rest of France, and where the

proximity of Switzerland lends a more Alpine influence to the countryside.

If long distance trekking seems to be a rather challenging way to get to know the area, it is certainly not the only option. A more relaxed way to explore the region is to choose one of its many pleasant towns or villages as a base for shorter walks, as described in the latter part of this book.

LANDSCAPE

In the Northern Vosges the low, rounded hills are mostly formed from eroded sandstone, but in places where it is more resistant, prominent rocky outcrops remain. These isolated high points make obvious defensive sites, and the sandstone castles built on them can look like extensions of the rock itself. Further south in the Vosges this layer of sandstone has been eroded away completely to reveal gneiss and granite, harder rock which is responsible for the higher land, the Ballons des Vosges (see Sections 5 to 7), with massive, flat-topped summits and ridges. The east face of the range, which follows the fault line of the Rhine Valley, is steeper than the west and in places forms a line of impressive cliffs. Glaciation has left its mark on these hills. Valleys were widened in some places to form massive, bowl-shaped cirques which are now the sites of glacial lakes. A series of such lakes, including Lac Blanc and Lac Noir, lies just below the cliffs.

One of the sandstone pinnacles supporting Haut-Barr Castle in the Northern Vosges (Section 3)

Above the forest, the tops of the hills are open pasture. The very highest pastures are naturally clear of trees as a result of exposure, but others have traditionally been kept clear by grazing. However, with changes in farming practice, trees are beginning to encroach on some areas again. Below the forest, the lower slopes to the south and east are clothed by vineyards. Winemaking in Alsace dates back many centuries, and has given rise to a whole string of inviting little villages in the valleys.

South of the Vosges the granite is left behind and a mix of sedimentary rocks forms the low land around Belfort. Although the GR5 goes through areas of mixed farming and forestry, this region contains a cluster of industrial towns around Montbéliard.

Just south of Vandoncourt the striking rock arch of Pont Sarrazin (see Section 8) is the first unmistakable sign that the path has reached the limestone that forms the basis of the scenery for the rest of the route to Lake Geneva. The limestone of the Jura creates a landscape distinct from the Vosges, with many fossil-rich sites (the region gives its name to the Jurassic geological period). Rivers have cut deep gorges and often flow underground through caverns. One of the highlights of the GR5 is where it follows the River Doubs as it flows through a series of wooded gorges along the Swiss frontier (see Section 9).

The GR5 then climbs onto the high plateau of the Jura where the limestone extends to great depths. Folded by earth movements and split by faults, the whole region was then

The wooded gorge of the Doubs (Section 9)

Reculée scenery on the western edge of the Jura plateaux (see 'Short walks in the Jura', Baume-les-Messieurs)

scoured by ice so that the resulting plateau is far from flat, instead forming an undulating landscape at about 1000m, now largely covered by forest. Elevated lookout points such as Roche Bernard give expansive views. Farming still continues in forest clearings, but as the rural population declines, trees increasingly encroach onto cleared land.

The path leaves the plateau soon after crossing into Switzerland and descends quite steeply, the final few kilometres crossing the belt of flat fields surrounding Lake Geneva.

Elsewhere in the Jura distinctive flat-bottomed valleys bordered by steep limestone cliffs (*reculées* in French) are a characteristic feature of the landscape. *Reculées* are created when an impermeable layer of marl lies underneath the limestone, and

although not on the GR5 route there are ideas for exploring fine areas of *reculée* scenery under 'Other Walks in the Jura' in the latter part of the book.

HISTORY

Stone tools found in the Rhine Valley are evidence of the presence of man some 600,000 years ago, although these were hunters, not cultivators. Farming only begins to appear from about 5000BC, with the arrival of Neolithic peoples, and occupation was limited to the low lands around the Rhine.

The coming of the Celts in around 1500BC saw metal tools being used to clear much more of the forest. Earthwork defences built during the Iron Age perhaps indicate more trou-

19

The massive Mur Païen dates to prehistoric times (Section 4)

bled times, with large forts, or *oppida*, erected on hilltop sites in the Vosges, including at Le Donon and Hartmannswillerkopf. The enigmatic Mur Païen may also be a defensive enclosure dating from this period. This huge stone wall, over 10km long, is crossed by the GR5 a few miles northwest of Barr (see Section 4).

In 58BC Caesar led the Romans into battle just south of the Vosges and the Romans were to remain for a further four centuries. A series of forts built along the Rhine defended the region and many towns can date their origins to this period. Strasbourg occupies the site of Argentoratum, and Nyon on Lake Geneva was also founded by the Romans. Roads were built through some of the Vosges passes (Saverne and Donon) and a stretch of the GR5 leaving the plateau

and dropping towards Nyon (see Section 11) follows an old cobbled track that dates back to this time.

The eighth and ninth centuries saw the spread of Christianity and the founding of several abbeys, including Wissembourg, Munster and Marmoutier (near Saverne).

The GR53 and GR5 through the Vosges lie for the most part in the region of Alsace, but south from the Ballon d'Alsace to the Swiss border the route runs through Franche-Comté. These regions have very different histories. Alsace, in particular, has a heritage that is part French and part German, and an overview of the various border changes helps to put the region into perspective.

Roman rule collapsed early in the fifth century and Alsace was invaded by the Alemanni from across the

Rhine, an event that was to have long-lasting linguistic consequences. The Alemannic language of these invaders was related to German, differing substantially from the language of the Franks who occupied the regions further west. Although French is now spoken throughout Alsace, local dialects derived from this early Alemannic still thrive.

After the death of Charlemagne in 814 a once extensive empire was divided. The land to the west became France and was separated from the German-speaking lands further east. Alsace lay between these two blocks, and in 870 it was agreed by treaty that it should be joined not to France, but to the German states to the east, and Alsace was to remain a part of this German confederation until 1648.

The region initially prospered as a key part of this empire, but by the 13th century central control was lacking

and local landowners took advantage of the situation, vying with each other for power. Alsace became a mosaic of tiny 'states', and a consequence of this can be seen in the Northern Vosges today, where 30 castles, most of them now ruined, lie within the boundaries of the regional park. A walker on the GR53 will pass a good selection of these strongholds, which are often in picturesque positions on rocky prominences above the forest.

By the end of the 16th century prosperity was returning, with silver mines and wine production generating wealth in the region, but the outbreak of the Thirty Years War in 1618 brought a period of turmoil. The treaty that finally ended this conflict transferred significant parts of Alsace to France, and full integration took place over the following years, so that by 1697 the Rhine was declared to be the official French border.

*First World War fortifications
on the Tête des Faux
(Section 5)*

Alsace was to remain a part of France until the Franco–Prussian War of 1870–71, when invading Prussian forces won a major battle near to Wissembourg and victory quickly followed. Alsace was ceded to the German Reich and the ridge of the Vosges became the new Franco–German border (old frontier stones from this era run alongside the GR5 – see Section 5).

Accounts of the First World War often seem not to mention action in the Vosges. The fighting here between French and German troops took place early in the war, with major battles at Le Linge and Hartmannswillerkopf. Trenches often had to be cut into rock, with the result that they have survived to the present day. The GR5 passes close to these old front lines on two occasions (see Sections 5 and 6).

German defeat saw Alsace pass back into French hands in 1918, but it was an uneasy peace. France soon embarked on building the Maginot Line along the length of the border with Germany and several of these defences are now open to the public. By 1939 this fortified frontier did not extend along the Belgian border, where the Ardennes was felt to be a barrier to any major attack, but these plans did not anticipate the mechanised war that followed, and the Maginot defences were outflanked. The Germans considered Alsace to be a true part of the Reich, not part of occupied France, and declared the inhabitants to be German citizens. As a result, many of the men were conscripted into the German army and sent to the Russian front. Alsace was retaken by the French during the winter of 1944–45.

To the south of Alsace the region that now forms Franche-Comté also has its origins in the same confederation of Germanic states, although this Germanic heritage is less visible in Franche-Comté today, perhaps because other influences have dominated during the intervening centuries. As early as 1295 the region passed into French control, and there followed a period as part of an autonomous Burgundy, a separate state still under French influence.

From 1493 to 1635 Franche-Comté was a Spanish possession, although Spain had little effect on day-to-day life, and during this period France still laid claim to the region, making several attempts to annex it. French control was finally established in 1678 and Franche-Comté has remained a part of France ever since. While the lower lands around Belfort and Montbéliard have attracted industry and a dense population, the more exposed uplands of the Jura have always been sparsely peopled.

WILDLIFE

The wide variety of habitats in the Vosges and Jura supports a wealth of wildlife. Although largely wooded, the region also has open highlands, gorges, river flood plains, lakes and

Storks nesting on an Alsace rooftop (Section 5)

here, had become alarmingly scarce, but now, thanks to captive-breeding programmes and other conservation efforts, the decline has been reversed. There is a good chance of seeing these elegant birds close to the GR5, particularly in the region of Ribeauvillé (see Sections 4 and 5).

Rising into the hills, the extensive woodland cover provides shelter throughout for **wild boar**, with especially high numbers in the undisturbed corners of the Northern Vosges. Often the only sign that boar are nearby is the sound of something large but unseen crashing headlong through the undergrowth. **Roe** and **red deer** are to be found in the woods, but they slip away without creating such a commotion. The trees also provide shelter for **red squirrel**, some of them the much darker form that is not found in the UK. **Dormice**, **beech marten**, **pine marten** and **wild cat** are all present, but you need to be lucky

boggy ground, giving scope for many different plants and animals to thrive.

At the foot of the Vosges the villages on the edge of the Alsace Plain are surrounded by fields and vineyards. **Storks**, the emblem of Alsace and once a common sight

Wild boar are common in the Northern Vosges, but rarely seen (Sections 1 to 4)

to see them. The same goes for **lynx**, which were reintroduced into parts of Switzerland and spread to France from there. Apart from the Pyrenees, this is the only place in France where lynx can be found, but their numbers are low.

The woodlands attract a variety of bird species, although it is not always easy to get good views amongst the trees. The **black woodpecker**, largest of the European woodpeckers, advertises its presence by characteristically loud drumming. You may hear the raucous call of **nutcrackers**, large brown crows that inhabit conifer woods, sometimes perching obligingly on exposed branch tips. The **capercaillie**, largest of the European grouse, breeds in the forests of the Vosges and Jura, but this shy bird is rarely seen, despite its size, as it disappears into the undergrowth if disturbed. Capercaillie prosper in mixed woodland with a high proportion of deciduous trees and many small clearings where they can feed. One bird that may attract attention is the **golden oriole**. Its loud flutey call carries through the forest, with now and again just a glimpse of a yellow-and-black bird flying from tree to tree. The song of the **nightingale** can also commonly be heard in early summer, usually in lowland scrub. The woods also play host to **Tengmalm's owl**, the **goshawk** and the **firecrest**.

The rich growth of small plants can be very attractive in areas of more open woodland, with **periwinkle** and **aconites**, and sweetly scented **lily-of-the-valley** and **daphne**. **Bilberries** too are common, and the annual harvest of berries is used to make *tarte aux myrtilles*, a popular local dish in the Vosges.

Chamois grazing below Joux Castle (Section 10)

The edge of the forests up around the tree-line is favoured grazing for **chamois**. These small, goat-like animals with black-and-white-striped faces are native to various parts of Europe and were introduced to the Vosges in 1956. Since then they have maintained good numbers in the region of the Ballons on the GR5. They tend to seek cover during the day, so early morning and late evening are the best times to see them in the open, with the eastern slope below Le Hohneck a good place to go looking (see Section 5). Chamois are also to be found quite widely in the Jura, particularly near Le Mont d'Or and on the slopes around Joux Castle (see Section 10).

Out of the forests, in the upland regions, there is a chance to see larger birds of prey, including the **golden eagle**, **buzzard** and **kite**, and the sandstone outcrops of the Vosges and the rocky cliffs of the Jura provide excellent habitat for the **peregrine falcon**.

On open pastures the **yellow gentian** is common. This broad-leaved, yellow-flowered plant, often several feet high, is found throughout the region, and extracts made from the roots are still commercially important for making liqueurs and herbal medicines (see Section 11). Above the tree-line a range of Alpine plants can be found, with **pasque flower**, **wild narcissus**, **martagon lily** and **globe flower** giving a delightful splash of colour in season.

Yellow gentians grow in profusion in pastureland

The route of the GR5 in the Vosges crosses the botanically inter-esting areas of Le Hohneck, Le Grand Ballon and Ballon d'Alsace, whereas in the Jura it keeps mostly to the forest. However, although not on the main route, a crest of open summits extends to the south of La Cure, and much of this area is a nature reserve, with some special Alpine plants and the possibility of seeing marmots. This ridge is included under Long Distance Routes in the Jura ('Along the Crest of the Jura') in the latter part of the book.

HOW TO USE THIS GUIDE

The main part of the guide covers the GR5/GR53 footpath through the Vosges and Jura. We have divided this route into 11 sections, each beginning

25

and ending at places accessible by public transport. These sections are therefore of various lengths, the shortest taking two days and the longest about four days.

The outline at the beginning of each section gives an overview, with highlights of what you can expect to see and comments on walking conditions. If you are only planning to walk part of the route, these outlines may help you choose between sections. Some suggestions for where you might make overnight stops are included, although doubtless you will have your own accommodation preferences, and you may well find that it fits your schedule better to break the journey at other points. Each section includes a sketch map and details of the relevant topographical map.

For practical planning of the walk an Accommodation and Food table at the beginning of each section lists places with possibilities for refreshment or breaking your walk, and intervening distances. These possibilities are not exhaustive, but we have tried to include all the budget accommodation (campsites and *gîtes*) likely to be useful. We have also made a special effort to identify accommodation on the more isolated stretches of the route. Up-to-date information can be obtained from regional tourist offices and the internet, and we recommend that you use these sources to supplement this guide. Be aware that village shops may close, and restaurants and hotels cover a range of prices.

Contact information for accommodation and tourist offices can be found in the appendix, and hotels listed are 2 star unless otherwise indicated. Hotel details are not given for places with their own tourist office (where there is usually a wide choice of hotels). In most cases a telephone number is listed, but where *refuges* are not permanently manned we have, where possible, listed an appropriate website for up-to-date contact information. We have also tried to warn of very restricted opening periods.

The detailed route description is divided into shorter subsections, each with an indication of distance and approximate walking time, assuming a fairly moderate walking pace.

The guide also gives an overview of some of the other long distance routes in the Vosges and Jura. These are not described in the same detail as for the GR5/GR53, and are provided to give some ideas for other possible treks. For people who want to get to know a smaller area in more detail, we have chosen some towns scattered through the Vosges and Jura as centres for shorter, day and half-day walks. Each centre is briefly described, followed by some walk suggestions.

WHEN TO VISIT

The altitude and inland position of the region result in a climate of summers that are hot, but not generally too hot for walking, and winters that have considerable snowfalls. Snow cover can be expected from about November to the beginning of April, and unless you are equipped for winter walking it is better not to attempt the higher sections during this time. (The snow does, however, make the Jura an excellent area for cross-country skiing.) As the land of the Jura rises towards the Alps, rainfall increases, and a relatively dry spell in summer can often be followed by a rainier autumn. On the other hand, the glowing colours of the turning leaves and the bright, crisp, frosty mornings can make autumn a delightful time to visit.

The warmer, drier summer can be ideal for walking, but during the period from mid-July to the end of August popular centres can be busy, as this is the main holiday break in France.

LOCATION

The terms Vosges and Jura as used in this guide refer to two general mountain areas. However, because these two names are also used for French *départements* that do not extend over the entire mountain regions, there is potential for confusion.

ACCESS

There are various ways of reaching the region from the UK. The nearest major airports are Strasbourg, Geneva and Basel, but it is also worth checking flights to nearby German destinations.

By rail, Eurostar to Paris with a further connection east is one possibility, although this involves changing stations in Paris. A main-line service links Paris with Strasbourg. TGV express trains serve Geneva, Pontarlier and Vallorbe. In general, French train services are fast and frequent. By road, Strasbourg is about 650km (400 miles) from Calais.

LOCAL TRANSPORT

There are railway stations on or near the GR5/GR53 at Wissembourg, Niederbronn-les-Bains, Saverne, Urmatt, Schirmeck, Barr, Metzeral, Thann, Héricourt, Montbéliard, Morteau, Le Locle, Pontarlier, La Cure, St-Cergue and Nyon. Ribeauvillé has a station, but it is 4km from the town centre, and if the timing is appropriate it is easier to access the town by bus from Colmar station. Check all local railway timetables carefully, as some services may be run by bus (*autocar*) at certain times of the day. Apart from these, local buses are infrequent.

ACCOMMODATION

The area has a wide range of hotels, from the luxury to the inexpensive, although cheaper accommodation sometimes has only basic facilities and hotels in mountain resorts may be

27

geared more for the skiing season. *Chambres d'hôtes* are rooms in private houses, similar to bed and breakfast. When planning a trip it is a good idea to contact the regional tourist offices (Alsace and Franche-Comté, as listed in the appendix), who will send comprehensive lists of accommodation. Local tourist offices (also in the appendix) can answer questions about accommodation in their own area and can generally make bookings if required.

Gîtes d'étape, which provide inexpensive accommodation, are common along the route. Most simply provide dormitories, although some offer almost hotel-like facilities, with meals and private rooms. They are generally open for most of the year. (Note that a *gîte d'étape* is not the same as *gîte rural*, which is a type of holiday cottage, not usually available for single nights.) There are also occasional hostels, either part of the Youth Hostelling organisation or privately run.

Refuges (mountain huts) also provide inexpensive dormitory accommodation, but making use of them is not always straightforward. Walking maps show a high concentration of *refuges* in the Vosges, but many of these have very restricted opening periods. Where such *refuges* are run by walking and skiing clubs they are often only open continuously during the high season. Prior reservation is normally required and preference is given to club members,

so it is as well to check availability before planning a trip that depends on *refuges*.

Finally, *abris* (shelters) may have little more than walls and a roof – useful for anyone caught out in bad weather. There are many *fermes-auberge* in the Vosges – farms offering simple meals based on local produce, but not usually accommodation.

See 'How to Use this Guide' for details of how contact information is organised in the Appendix.

CAMPING

Camping is popular in France and the standard of campsites is often high for a reasonable cost. While many sites are open for the whole season, a few are only open for a limited period, sometimes just July and August.

Campsites close to the GR5/GR53 are given under Accommodation and Food at the beginning of each section of the route, with contact information in the appendix. Comprehensive lists of campsites are available from tourist offices.

Outside restricted areas, wild camping along parts of the GR5/GR53 route is also an option. It is possible to pitch a tent discreetly last thing at night and move on early in the morning, providing it is well away from roads and houses, but remember that all the land is owned by somebody, and if in doubt, seek permission. The aim should be to leave the site looking as though you

A typical ferme-auberge *in the Vosges*

had never been there, avoiding pollution of water courses and guarding against fire. In some forest areas (particularly the Northern Vosges) the use of a flame of any kind is forbidden. There are hazards, however. Hunting is popular in France and you should be aware of the possibility of rifle shooting in woodland. Also, within river gorges water levels can fluctuate widely and quickly, making pitching near to rivers highly dangerous.

There is no general restriction on camping within regional parks, but it is specifically prohibited within nature reserve areas and there are notices (*camping interdit*) to alert you to this. In the regional park of the Northern Vosges visitors are encouraged to leave the forest before nightfall.

FOOD AND DRINK

In Alsace the German style of cooking is seen in the popularity of pork, especially sausages, and dishes such as *choucroute* (based on *sauerkraut*). *Kugelhopf* is a distinctive ring-shaped cake, and *tarte aux myrtilles* is made with the bilberries common on the hillsides of the Vosges.

The Jura has been famous for smoked meats since Roman times. The local products to look out for are sausages and hams, trout from the Doubs, and snails. Both the Vosges and the Jura have fine local cheeses and wines – Alsace is well known for its white wines, and the yellow wine of the Jura is particularly unusual.

A little forward planning of food purchases is required on some stretches of the route. Usually it is sufficient to carry food for a day or two, but it may be necessary to leave the route to visit food-shopping facilities on some stretches. When buying meals there is a wide choice, from village bars to top-class meals in restaurants (although these can be very busy on Sunday lunchtimes, when many French families traditionally eat out). A set meal, usually of local produce, can be bought at one of the many *fermes-auberge* to be found in the Vosges.

When buying food for picnicking and camping, be aware that many shops close for an extended lunchtime, which can cause considerable delay if a potential shopping stop is reached in the middle of the day. Many food shops, particularly bakeries, are open early in the morning, and local markets are good for fruit and salads if you happen to pass on the right day.

WHAT TO TAKE

Although the route does not involve any scrambling or climbing, some sections are rough and exposed, so good footwear and waterproofs are essential. Even in summer, sudden storms can blow up with very little warning. At the other extreme, a hat and sunscreen are wise precautions. The basic walking tools of maps and compass, first aid kit, torch and water bottle are necessities.

For other packing requirements, much depends on accommodation and eating preferences. If using the

many hotels and *chambres d'hôtes* along the route, little is required other than changes of clothing and personal items. If depending on *gîtes d'étape* and hostels, add a sleeping bag. The cheapest and most flexible way of travelling is with a lightweight tent – even if you are not planning to camp every night, a tent gives an alternative if accommodation is a problem. A lightweight stove and utensils are worth considering, but not essential.

Backpackers will be well aware that trips are all the more enjoyable if pack weight is kept down, so ruthlessly weed out any non-essentials at the packing stage. If camping, remember that many French campsites have washing machines and drying facilities, so there is no need to carry too many changes of clothes.

MAPS

The sketch maps in this guide are not meant to be sufficient for navigation – separate walking maps are strongly recommended. Place names in bold capitals in the route descriptions are those included on the sketch maps, and place names in bold are other places of interest that can be found on published maps.

When choosing which scale of map to use, level of detail has to be balanced against expense and weight. The cheapest option is the IGN 1:100,000 (TOP100) series. Three sheets cover the whole GR5/GR53 route (Nos 12, 31, 38). These maps are good for planning and providing an overview of the region. In conjunction with this book they can be used for route-finding, as GR paths are marked, although some people might feel more confident with a more detailed map.

At the 1:50,000 scale, eight sheets cover the route from Wissembourg to Nyon. These maps, at the same scale as standard OS maps, are certainly sufficient for route-finding, and they also give details of many other footpaths in addition to the main GRs, so are preferable to the 1:100,000 if you might want to explore off the route.

The relevant maps are listed under Maps at the beginning of each route section, and details of possible stockists can be found at the end of the appendix.

At a 1:25,000 scale, IGN TOP25 maps can be obtained for the whole GR5/GR53 route, but at least 22 sheets would be needed. These are very detailed and might be worth considering for thoroughly exploring a single centre.

GR SYSTEM AND WAYMARKING

The GR5 and GR53 are part of an excellent network of long distance footpaths in France, the 'Grandes Randonnées'. Primary routes are given low numbers and less important paths have longer numbers, but retaining the initial digit of the parent route in the locality. For example, in the Jura the major path is the GR5, the shorter Vosges–Jura path further west is the GR59, and a shorter path linking the two is the GR595.

Waymarking of GRs is generally with a standard system of marks. A red and white rectangle (white above red) confirms the route. A cross formed by a diagonal red line crossed out by a diagonal white line is used to indicate 'incorrect route'. Warning of changes of direction is often given by the red and white marker being bent to indicate the new direction, and sometimes the marker is attached to a bent white line indicating the new direction. This system is used for the GR5 in the Jura, but the Vosges is an exception. Footpaths were waymarked here before the nationwide system of GRs was developed, and in this area different walking trails have been allocated symbols of various colours. The GR53 and the Vosges section of the GR5 are waymarked with red rectangles.

The standard of waymarking is usually high, but the signs are small, so walkers have to look out for them. If the last waymark was some while ago, consider the possibility that you may have missed the route – retracing your steps to the last waymark may save time in the long run. GR routes do change from time to time, either temporarily, such as to avoid tree felling, or permanently.

Once in Switzerland the waymarking changes to yellow

diamonds. These apply to all footpaths, and this short section of the GR5 is not marked distinctively. The route is followed by looking out for the regular signboards with directions to particular places.

SAFETY AND HEALTH

The chances are that anything that goes wrong will be a minor inconvenience rather than a major calamity, but it is as well to be prepared. UK citizens should apply at a post office for a European Health Insurance Card (formerly form E111) before leaving home. This entitles you to the same services as French citizens, although visits to doctors or hospitals are not completely free. Another valuable source of healthcare is the chemist's shop (*pharmacie*), which many French people use for advice and treatment of minor ailments.

Snake bites are a theoretical possibility as vipers are present in the area – although we have never seen any – but keep a look out, especially when amongst vegetation. Unfriendly dogs might also be a problem, although again we have never been troubled. In the unlikely event of snake or dog bites, seek medical advice. The walker should also be aware of the presence of ticks in France, as elsewhere in Europe, and there is a slight risk of contracting Lyme disease from a tick bite. Current recommendations are to check for

ticks at the end of the day, remove any that you find, and seek advice if inflammation develops.

Your own first aid kit should provide treatment for foreseeable minor problems. In addition, a survival sack or lightweight tent could also prove invaluable if injured, caught out by bad weather, or benighted in the hills. Weather problems can be reduced, but not eliminated, by paying attention to the weather forecast (*la méteo*), which can be found in tourist offices or in newspapers (which can usually be seen in cafés and bars).

Over-enthusiasm at the planning stage can cause problems too. Experienced walkers will already know their own capabilities, but if you are new to long distance walking you may be unsure how far you can comfortably cover in a day, and some trial days out with a full pack before setting off might be a good idea. However, providing your pack is not too heavy it is surprising how quickly you can acclimatise once on the walk. The first few days can be the hardest, so it is a good idea not to attempt too much at the start. As a rough guideline, we base our planning on 15 miles per day initially, and can usually increase this up to about 20, but there is no standard pace – you will soon find what suits you best.

Loss or theft of possessions is always a possibility, but there are some simple measures that can be taken to minimise risks. Money and valuables can be split between several different places to reduce the chance of losing it all, and a routine of checking accommodation or camp-sites carefully before moving on can be helpful.

If the worst does happen, in France the emergency services can be contacted by phoning 15 for medical help, 17 for the police, and 18 for the fire brigade.

Enjoyment of the outdoors will always involve some degree of risk and it is the responsibility of each walker to look after their own safety.

LANGUAGE

Visitors do need some basic French, even if this is just provided by a phrase book. In the absence of French, German is more commonly understood than English, particularly in Alsace. In this region, although the local people are fluent French speakers, many also speak Elsässisch, the Alsatian language.

One effect of the several attempts to incorporate Alsace into Germany, and the subsequent return to France, is that place names may be found in several forms and spellings, as German words are gradually converted into names that look and sound more French. This may explain instances where place name spellings in this book do not correspond to spellings on a particular map or sign.

MONEY

It is suggested that you rely on larger towns for cash-withdrawal facilities. There are several banks in each of the following: Wissembourg, Niederbronn-les-Bains, Saverne, Schirmeck, Barr, Ribeauvillé, Thann, Héricourt, Villers-le-Lac, Mouthe, Les Rousses, and Nyon.

Nearly all of the route described lies in France, but a walker on the Jura section of the GR5 will find it useful to have some Swiss francs as well as euros.

TELEPHONES

If taking a mobile phone, check beforehand with your UK network provider to ensure that it can be used in France. Currently each of the three French service providers has substan-tial but incomplete coverage within the Vosges and Jura. This situation may change. If this is a concern, up-to-date coverage maps can be found on the internet.

Public telephones are quite common, but require a card for use that can be bought wherever there is a sticker indicating *télécarte en vente ici*. Currently you must dial the code number on the card then wait for a connection before dialling the number wanted. To telephone the UK, dial 0044 followed by the rest of the number without the initial zero in the area code.

Section 1: GR53 Wissembourg to Niederbronn-les-Bains

Traditional village houses in Obersteinbach

THE GR5/GR53 LONG DISTANCE ROUTE

SECTION 1

GR53 Wissembourg to Niederbronn-les-Bains

(44.5km/27.5 miles)

The small town of Wissembourg, with its rows of timber-framed medieval houses, makes a pleasant starting-off point, the buildings crowding together along the River Lauter to give the old quarter a picture-postcard appearance. It is known locally as 'la Petite Venise Alsacienne' (the Little Venice of Alsace).

Most of the route from here to Niederbronn-les-Bains is through woodland. The hills are always relatively low, the highest point being at 580m, but as the path follows a succession of hills and valleys, in total there is a good deal of climbing to be done. The high point at the lookout tower at Wintersberg gives views over the Black Forest and the vast undulating forests of the Vosges.

What is remarkable about this section of the walk is the succession of castle ruins that is passed on the way, many of them taking advantage of the isolated sandstone crags that are characteristic of the Northern Vosges. Fleckenstein Castle is perhaps the most visited, its substantial walls standing on a high pinnacle close to the German border. The GR passes close to at least eight other castles before reaching Niederbronn-les-Bains, and there are several more a few kilometres distant. Among them the ruins of Loewenstein and Froensbourg are worth special mention, as both are in spectacularly elevated locations.

The Northern Vosges is never overwhelmed by visitors, so this first sector of the route promises an interesting and relatively undisturbed walk.

A strong walker could complete this section in two days, but this would start the whole journey with a very long day, and there is much to see en route. We suggest a half-day's walk to reach one of the hotels at Climbach, then an easy day would reach Obersteinbach (hotel and *gîte*), with another very manageable day completing the section.

Accommodation and Food

Km	Cumulative km		
		Wissembourg	Hotels, restaurants, cafés, shops
5.0		Scherhol summit	Shelter
0.5	5.5	Col du Pigeonnier	*Refuge*
3.0	8.5	Climbach	Hotel/restaurants, small baker
2.5	11.0	Petit-Wingen	Restaurant
6.5	17.5	Fleckenstein Castle	Café
1.0	18.5		Turn off for Fleckenstein campsite, 1km off route
9.5	28.0	Obersteinbach	Hotels, *gîte*, restaurants
5.5	33.5	Windstein	Hotel, restaurants
11.0	44.5	Niederbronn	Hotels, campsite, restaurants, cafés, shops

Contact details for tourist offices and accommodation are in the appendix.

Maps
IGN 1:100,000 sheet 12
Club Vosgien 1:50,000 sheet 2/8

Wissembourg to Climbach
(8.5km/5 miles, 2hr 30mins, height gain/loss 350m/170m)

The GR53 starts from the railway station in **WISSEMBOURG**. On coming out of the station turn left along the road, following the red rectangle waymarks. Continue past a roundabout and up the D77, passing an information board with a map. After a short distance there is a fork in the road where the GR53 branches right along the Boulevard Clemenceau (D334). It soon leaves to go down to the right along a footpath, with the river and tow wall to the right.

Wissembourg

The River Lauter divides into several channels to flow through Wissembourg, giving the old quarter a unique atmosphere. Considerable stretches of the town wall still survive, surrounding streets lined with handsome half-timbered buildings, and the local museum, the Musée Westercamp, is itself situated in two fine 16th-century houses. As in the rest of Alsace, summer visitors will find balconies and windowsills festooned with flowers, with the gardens in the centre of town adding to the colourful scene.

A footbridge crosses the river to the right, and a short diversion over this bridge reaches the picturesque older quarter of Wissembourg. The GR53 takes the path to the left, climbing up the bank to the road, where the route turns right. Just along this road turn left, up the Rue du Château d'Eau, then left again almost immediately, following the red rectangles towards Col du Pigeonnier. When this road comes out onto a more major one, go left uphill until a waymark indicates a right turn up an unsurfaced track just at the edge of the town.

After about 5mins the GR53 goes left at a T-junction, then right at a fork. Follow this track for about 15mins as it climbs gently to reveal a broad, sweeping view of Wissembourg in the valley below. The track approaches some 18th-century defensive earthworks, which date back to the War of the Spanish Succession, and passes through them to meet a road (D3). The route turns to the right, following a footpath that runs parallel to the road for over 1km.

At the parking area opposite the Maison Forestière Scherhol, turn right along a gravel track, but then almost immediately left up a footpath, the Sentier Edouard Ditenbeck. This path leads into the woods and soon reaches another parking area where a short detour reaches the remains of a *redoute*, an 18th-century banked enclosure.

The GR53 crosses straight over the parking area, heading for Scherhol Sommet and the Col du Pigeonnier, still accompanied by the bank and

The old quarter of Wissembourg

ditch of the old defensive system. Keep on the well-signed woodland path, crossing obliquely over a vehicle track and following the major path to the **Scherhol** junction.

Take the left-hand path, which soon leads past another embankment-and-ditch defensive work and an unlocked Club Vosgien shelter just beyond. Continuing along the path, the *refuge* at **COL DU PIGEONNIER** is about 5mins away. Opening times are restricted, but there is an accessible source of drinking water.

Just below the *refuge* the GR53 takes the Sentier Robert Redslob,

signposted to Climbach. This descends through the trees, turning off sharply left almost immediately to zigzag downhill. After about 15mins it joins a vehicle track. Turn left along here, then when another track comes in from the right, follow it straight ahead. In another 15mins this meets the road just before the edge of **CLIMBACH** (hotel/restaurants, baker).

Turn right along the road and enter the village, passing an information board giving details of a nearby pilgrimage chapel and sacred spring, and a short walking route around the village.

Climbach to Fleckenstein Castle
(9km/5.5 miles, 2hr 45mins, height gain/loss 180m/160m)

Turn right up the Rue de Wingen and follow this road out of the village and round a bend to the left. After about 10mins look out for a vehicle track on the right with a signpost to Petit-Wingen. Take this track to a T-junction and turn left to go downhill into the little village of **PETIT-WINGEN** (restaurant), where the GR53 turns right by the restaurant. Follow the road up beyond the village and then, where it takes a sharp turn to the left, leave by a vehicle track to the right. After only a minute or two, fork left on a more minor track.

This track runs along a valley with a stream down to the left and a quiet lane beyond that. The route drops down to cross the stream and the lane, then takes a path over a wooden footbridge and into the trees to almost immediately join a track, which the GR53 follows to the right. When this emerges onto another track, continue to the right. This track goes along the bottom of the wooded valley with the stream and lane now to the right. Carry on ahead, ignoring orange waymarks to the left, until you reach a large pond. Take a footpath that drops to the right, passing the sign for the Étang du Heinbach.

When the path comes out onto a road, turn left and follow it for about 1km, past the junction at Col du Schaufelshald. The extensive hilltop ruins on the right are Wegelnburg Castle, which lies over the border in Germany.

Continue along the road for a few minutes to the **Col du Litschhof**, with the crag of Loewenstein Castle coming into view ahead. At the col take a vehicle track to the right, then leave this by a footpath to the right, indicated by an information board giving background about Hohenbourg and Loewenstein Castles. Follow this well-made path, crossing one small track and going quite steeply uphill before emerging onto a more level track below the castle rock. Do not be tempted to turn right directly towards the castle, but turn left at this junction. Continue uphill to the **Col du Hohenbourg**.

The GR53 goes to the left here, but a short detour from the route reaches the castles of **Loewenstein** and **HOHENBOURG**. To do this, take the footpath to the right, then immediately fork to the right along the red/white/red waymarked path. The scant remains of Loewenstein are spectacularly sited on a promontory, and Hohenbourg lies just along the ridge to the north.

Returning to the Col du Hohenbourg and the GR53, follow the track for about 100m before forking to the right, downhill towards Fleckenstein. After about 15mins the path reaches the café in front of **FLECKENSTEIN CASTLE**. Turn right along the access road to the castle.

The scant remains of Loewenstein
Castle sit high on a sandstone pinnacle

Fleckenstein Castle to Froensbourg Castle

(3km/2 miles, 1hr, height gain/loss 180m/240m)

The GR53 carries on past the entrance to the castle to follow a well-made footpath into the woods, with the castle rock up to the right. After a few minutes the route takes a right-hand fork and continues ahead to reach the D925 (Fleckenstein campsite is to the left along this road, 1km off route). Cross the road and pass the end of an *étang* (lake) to arrive at a junction where two paths go to the left and two to the right. Do not turn sharply left, but take the second path that turns towards the left, with a sign for Rocher de l'Étang. This climbs steadily through the forest, crossing two tracks then turning left along another track for a short distance before leaving it to the right, as waymarked.

After some 20mins **FROENSBOURG CASTLE** comes into view, standing out above the trees across the valley to the left. Continue along this level track, but look out for a narrow path to the left dropping down through the trees. Both the GR53 and the GR531 (blue rectangles) take this path, but within about 5mins the GR531 leaves to the left as the GR53 continues to the castle. The position of this ruin, high on a sandstone crag, is typical of the castles of the region (access is provided by steps climbing the vertical rock face).

Froensbourg Castle to Obersteinbach

(7.5km/4.5 miles, 2hr 15mins, height gain/loss 50m/110m)

Take the narrow footpath on past the castle, zigzagging uphill to join a broad track where the route goes to the left. After about 100m **look out for** a little path to the right – the junction is not marked by any signs, but there are red waymarks on the trees up to the right. This path scrambles up the side of a sandstone outcrop then rises through the trees, steeply at first, then more gently, and emerges onto a large vehicle track where the GR53 continues to the left.

In only a few minutes leave the track by a footpath to the left. After about 10mins this reaches a more major footpath. Follow this uphill to the right to reach a junction at **Col de Hichtenbach**, where there is a small, open-fronted shelter. Take the track to the left, signposted to Zigeunerfels and Wasigenstein, which goes uphill to reach a crossroads. Go straight on, then after about 100m leave the track by a substantial footpath to the right, signposted to Wasigenstein.

This path meets a track at a T-junction. Turn left towards Zigeunerfels and follow this level track, which has been cut into the hillside. Within 10mins watch for a footpath that goes up the slope to the left. This passes the striking natural sandstone pillars of **Zigeunerfels**, then drops down to join the track again. Almost immediately, turn right at a junction with another track to reach a road.

Follow the road to the right for a few minutes, then at a hairpin leave the road by a footpath straight ahead into the forest. Almost immediately, at a junction with other trails this path turns to the right and soon crosses another track, then continues ahead to reach **WASIGENSTEIN CASTLE**. This is another extensive ruin sitting

high on a sandstone crag, now partially hidden by trees.

From the castle retrace your steps for perhaps 100m. The GR53 route towards Obersteinbach then forks down to the right, where the path joins a vehicle track and the route carries on downhill. At a junction cross another track and go ahead over a footbridge across a small stream. Follow this path as it curves to the left. Keep following the waymarks, which lead across pastureland to join the end of a tarmacked lane at the edge of the village. Continue downhill into **OBERSTEINBACH** (hotels, *gîte*, restaurants).

Obersteinbach to Windstein
(5.5km/3.5 miles, 1hr 45mins, height gain/loss 270m/180m)

Along the main road to the right, the Maison des Châteaux Forts has an exhibition about the many castles of the region, although opening hours are very restricted. The GR53 does not turn along the main road, but carries on straight across and along the road opposite to reach a T-junction. Turn right up the Rue de la Glockengrube and follow this out of the village. Beyond the houses of Obersteinbach the route crosses some pasture.

Wild Boar
Pastures and forest floors in this area often contain obviously churned-up patches where wild boar have been rooting with their snouts for food or

wallowing in mud. Boar are common in the forests of the Northern Vosges and popular quarry for huntsmen. Walkers rarely get a good view of these animals, which are most active at night, and if disturbed are usually quick to move away through the undergrowth. They may hold their ground occasionally, particularly if they have piglets to protect, and the wisest course then is for the people to retreat, as a boar, standing a metre high at the shoulder and weighing in the region of 300kg, is a formidable beast.

Enter the woods and turn right at a T-junction. Continue through open woodland to reach another junction

Approaching Wasigenstein Castle

in a clearing. Take the small footpath straight ahead, signposted towards the ruins of Windstein, and when this meets a track, turn right to reach the **Col du Wittschloessel**.

The route of the GR53 from here as far as Grand Wintersberg uses a multitude of forest tracks and paths. This makes the route description sound complicated, but the waymarking is good and the route is not at all difficult to follow on the ground.

Go straight over the junction at the col, then take the lower, right-hand path at a fork. Turn left when the footpath emerges onto a forest track, which then swings to the right to reach the **Col du Wineckerthal**. At this col the route crosses straight over to take a footpath directly opposite. Almost immediately this path meets another track where the G53 goes to the right. At a broad fork go to the left, and then at the next fork soon after, turn off to the right.

On reaching a T-junction at the **Col du Petit Grueneberg** turn left,

then immediately take a footpath to the right, up into the woods. This path hairpins up to join a track and the GR53 leaves by an uphill path almost opposite. The route skirts the top of the hill and then drops down to meet another track. Turn right at this junction to pass the **Wassersteine** rock.

Where the track forks, branch to the left, and after about 200m look out for a signboard pointing to the right. Leave by this footpath, which goes through the trees and down some steps to join another track. Turn left along it for about 100m, with a fine view of wooded hills to the right, before turning off on a footpath to the right.

At a fork take the left-hand path, following the waymarks to veer to the left downhill. The scattered houses of Windstein appear through the trees ahead. Turn right down a track to a T-junction at the edge of **WINDSTEIN** (hotel, restaurants), with a sign to **VIEUX WINDSTEIN CASTLE** to the right. The GR53 goes left downhill towards the restaurant.

Windstein to Grand Wintersberg
(7km/4.5 miles, 2hr 30mins, height gain/loss 360m/110m)

The route crosses in front of the restaurant 'Aux Deux Châteaux', then turns right just beyond it (a short diversion along the path to the left here would reach **NOUVEAU WIND-STEIN CASTLE**). The GR53 follows the sign to Niederbronn and curves

left after a minute or two, then leaving the track by a footpath to the right going downhill to the Vallon de Gruenenthal.

Cross a road and go up the forest track opposite. About 5mins later take a footpath that drops down the bank to the left then runs along the slope above a road, finally joining the road just outside the hamlet of **Wineckerthal**.

Turn right into the village then leave it by a minor road to the left, following this road as it curves to the left and crosses a small stream. Immediately beyond the bridge turn right onto a footpath into the trees, as indicated by a sign to Grand Wintersberg.

Cross the entrance track to a house, then take a footpath uphill to reach a road – the Route Forestière du Buchwald is opposite. Follow this surfaced lane to the large house at Buchwald and turn half right, following the sign for Col de Borneberg. A track comes in from the left and the GR53 joins it, carrying on straight ahead to very soon take another track up to the left.

After about 200m take a footpath cut into the banking on the left. This path climbs steeply through the woods for a few minutes and crosses two forest tracks. A short while later, where the path emerges onto a third, look to the right for the footpath continuing up

the hill. After the path levels out, it meets a slightly larger track where the route goes to the right.

The GR53 then crosses a junction and meanders amongst beech trees, clearly waymarked, to reach a substantial vehicle track. Turn left to pass an aerial installation at the **Col de Borneberg** and continue to the **Col du Pottaschkopf**, also known as Potashplatz. This is a broad clearing with an information board about the regional park, a picnic area and a small shelter.

Just behind the shelter the GR53 takes a footpath to the right through the trees, leading over to the **Col de la Liese** about 0.5km further on (the Club Vosgien chalet here is open for drinks on Sundays and holidays). Cross the road opposite the chalet and take the footpath out of the car park into the woods, hairpinning upwards to reach the late-19th-century outlook tower on the summit of **GRAND WINTERSBERG**. From the top of this 25m-tower there is a fine view of the Palatinate and the Vosges, and across the plains of Alsace and the Rhine to the Black Forest.

Grand Wintersberg to Niederbronn-les-Bains
(4km/2.5 miles, 1hr 15mins, height gain/loss 0m/400m)

Leave the clearing in the direction of Niederbronn-les-Bains and follow the path down through woods. Cross straight over the next track (the blue circle route), and very soon after this

look out for a sign indicating a small path dropping down to the left. The GR53 takes this route downhill (it does **not** carry straight on following the signs to Niederbronn by Camp Celtique).

The undulating landscape of the Northern Vosges

This route hairpins down, crossing two tracks and turning right down a third, then soon leaving by a footpath to the right. Descend some steps and turn left onto another track, but only for a short distance before taking a path to the right.

At the next junction turn left downhill and continue down the wooded valley.

On meeting a track on a hairpin bend, follow it downhill to the right to join a busy road. Turn left and pass the buildings of Source Celtique (the waters from this ancient spring are now bottled and the brand is widely available).

Carry on along the road towards the town. The route soon leaves by a path up into the woods on the left and reaches another road by a fork. Turn right downhill past the restaurant 'Les Acacias' towards the centre of **NIEDERBRONN-LES-BAINS** (hotels, campsite, restaurants, cafés, shops). (The left fork up the hill is a short cut to the campsite, about 1km away.)

Turn right at the Passage Publique du Parc Grumelius, and where the tarmac ends take the left fork, which leads down to a street. Here the route goes left to reach the centre of town where there is a tourist office and a range of shops.

Local Alsatian Language

In the streets and shops of Niederbronn-les-Bains local people can be heard chatting in a language that is clearly distinct from both French and German. This local Alsatian language is widely used, particularly in the north of Alsace. It went into decline in the years after the Second World War, but more recently has been recognised as making a valuable contribution to local heritage, and people are showing a renewed interest in learning it.

SECTION 2

GR53 Niederbronn-les-Bains to Saverne

(54km/33.5 miles)

Most of this section of the walk is through forest in the heartland of the Northern Vosges regional park. Although not high, the landscape is far from flat, with the route leading over a succession of small hills and valleys, so only at occasional lookout points can the extent of the forest really be appreciated. These quiet woods contain a wealth of wildlife, and it is possible that the walker will glimpse wild boar or marten.

Niederbronn-les-Bains, the starting point, is a spa town with ample facilities and many walking trails close by. The archaeological centre for the Northern Vosges is also located here. Just outside the town the GR53 passes the ruins of Wasenbourg Castle, the first of several castles to be seen on this section. Grand Arnsbourg Castle is a picturesque ruin on an elevated rocky outcrop, with good views over the extensive wooded hills to the north. Later on the considerable ruins of Lichtenberg Castle, set within a huge defensive wall, dominate the village below.

Lichtenberg is one of several villages passed en route, each with its own character. La Petite-Pierre sits on a fortified promontory, and although small, has many tourist facilities. The headquarters of the regional park, situated in the buildings of the restored castle, contains a permanent exhibition giving an excellent background to the history and geology of the area.

In Graufthal some unusual rock dwellings, *maisons troglodytiques*, lie close to the route. These cottages, built into the sandstone cliff, were inhabited until the 1950s. Further on the route skirts a series of crags, including a particularly impressive overhang known as the Saut du Prince Charles.

This section can be walked in three very easy days, with suggested stops at Lichtenberg (hotel and *gîte*) and La Petite-Pierre (hotels and *gîte*). Alternatively, a single stop at Wimmenau (hotel) would complete the section in two days, but be prepared for a longer second day of 29.5km/18.5 miles.

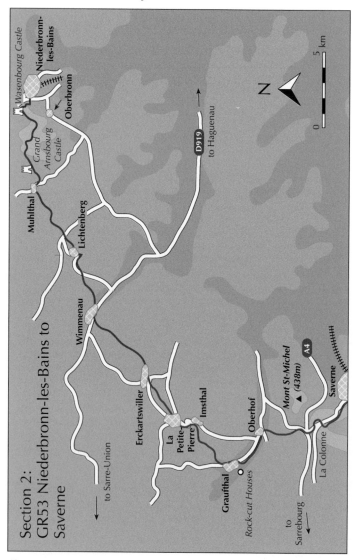

Section 2:
GR53 Niederbronn-les-Bains to Saverne

Accommodation and Food

Km	Cumulative km		
		Niederbronn	Hotels, campsite, restaurants, cafés, shops
11.0		Muhlthal	Restaurant (very expensive)
7.5	18.5	Lichtenberg	Hotel/restaurants, *gîte*
6.0	24.5	Wimmenau	Hotel, restaurant, shop (closed Wed pm)
10.5	35.0	La Petite-Pierre	Hotels, *gîte*, restaurants, cafés, baker
2.5	37.5	Imsthal	Campsite
4.5	42.0	Graufthal	Hotel, restaurants
3.5	45.5	Oberhof	Bar/restaurant
4.0	49.5	La Colonne	Café/restaurant
4.5	54.0	Saverne	Hotels, youth hostel, campsite, restaurants, cafés, shops

Contact details for tourist offices and accommodation are in the appendix.

Maps
IGN 1:100,000 sheet 12
Club Vosgien 1:50,000 sheets 1/8 and part of 2/8

Niederbronn-les-Bains to Wasenbourg Castle
(3km/2 miles, 1hr, height gain/loss 250m/0m)

In **NIEDERBRONN-LES-BAINS** start from the Place de l'Hôtel de Ville, by the tourist office, and cross the bridge over the stream, then immediately turn right through the car park. Walk alongside the stream and continue ahead to reach the public park with a crazy golf course on the right. After passing the amenities block, turn left to leave the park.

Cross the road and follow to the right on a path through the landscaped area opposite. This soon reaches another road just beside a railway bridge.

Turn left to go under the railway bridge, then immediately right along the Allée des Tilleuls. Follow this for about 1km until it passes under a modern concrete road bridge.

49

The De Dietrich Family

Unusually, industry and tourism are interlinked in Niederbronn-les-Bains, as the spa facilities of the town were revived in the 18th century by the De Dietrich family, who pioneered the exploitation and smelting of local iron ore. There is no iron production in the region now, but from these early beginnings a whole empire has developed, and factories that still carry the family name provide employment for about 5000 people locally – one of the De Dietrich sites is passed as the GR53 leaves the town.

Turn sharply left up a track just beyond the bridge – the GR sign indicates Wasenbourg 50mins. Carry on ahead, joining a track that soon runs parallel to a busy main road on the left. After a very short distance turn right at a waymark and follow the path, which then zigzags uphill. Ignore the path off to the right to Source Lichteneck, but continue upwards to reach a junction with a vehicle track. A GR53 sign indicates a turn to the right, but the route does not go along the track. Instead, the sign refers to a footpath on the far side that heads off through the forest.

After about 20mins the path emerges onto another track, close to a sign which describes a charcoal-burners' site. Go to the right along this track for a short distance then branch off left onto another path. Follow this up to **WASENBOURG CASTLE**. Just beside the ruins some Gallo-Roman remains have been reassembled to form a small stone monument.

Wasenbourg Castle to Muhlthal
(8km/5 miles, 2hr 30mins, height gain/loss 100m/330m)

The GR53 turns sharply left just ahead of the castle. Follow this woodland path, signposted to Kreuztannen, and within 10mins it reaches a junction at **Cabane Kohlhutte**. Go right up a broad gravel track, and further uphill the route forks to the left before reaching the little clearing at **Kreuztannen**. Carry on straight across here, but just a few hundred metres beyond, watch out for signs which direct the route off to the right along a footpath. This path winds up through the woods to

reach the lookout tower at **Wasenkoepfel** in about 10mins.

Follow the main path beyond the tower, leading through woods and then along the left edge of a grassy clearing. Keep with this path and it soon reaches a major junction where the GR53 is signposted to the left along a broad track. Within about 5mins this leads to the **Col de l'Ungerthal**, where there is a small shelter and picnic benches.

There are several footpaths on the other side of the road. Leave the col by the path just to the left of the wooden shelter, signposted to Holdereck and Arnsbourg, and leading down to the road at **Col du Holdereck**. Again there is a choice of paths on the far side of the road – the GR53 takes the left-hand path towards Grand Arnsbourg.

Pass straight ahead at the track junction called Grunschaft and soon afterwards the route forks to the left, following a sunken gully as it descends through woods to reach the ruins of **GRAND ARNSBOURG CASTLE**, sitting high on an exposed sandstone crag.

The route passes just to the right of the castle, following the path along the edge of the rock outcrop. Beyond the castle there are splendid open views out to the north. Just downhill the path crosses a vehicle track, then another about 5mins later.

Continue ahead until the path emerges onto a broad track. Follow this to the left, downhill, to the road. Turn right along the road towards **MUHLTHAL** (restaurant). Do not be led off to the right by an unhelpful waymark, but carry on until GR signs take the route off to the left, just before reaching the large Restaurant d'Arnsbourg.

Grand Arnsbourg Castle lies on the GR53

51

Muhlthal to Lichtenberg

(7.5km/4.5 miles, 2hr 15mins, height gain/loss 300m/200m)

Cross the bridge over a stream and follow the path that goes to the right, passing close to the back of the restaurant, then cross another small footbridge. Continue for a short distance, keeping to the left of a stream. The path rises to pass between houses and joins the end of a quiet lane which you follow along the valley to a T-junction. Turn left, then after only about 50m left again off the road onto a track by a lake.

Within minutes the route takes a left fork signposted for Lichtenberg. Only a few minutes later fork to the right on another track that starts to climb, then 50m later look out for the footpath that takes the route off to the left, leading up through the forest for nearly half an hour. As it flattens out it reaches a T-junction where the route turns to the right along a broad track.

This track reaches a junction where Lichtenberg is signed 1hr 30mins ahead, and a route marked by upright green rectangles comes in from the left. Carry on straight ahead here, but be prepared for the next junction, **which is easy to miss**.

Within about 1km a signpost indicates that Niederbronn is 4hrs 50mins behind. The GR leaves obliquely along a footpath to the left, but the sign in this direction is not prominently sited and the path is not obvious. (The route does **not** go on ahead along the track, which is the green waymarked route to Melch.)

Once this turn has been taken the route is easily followed, and Lichtenberg with its hilltop castle is soon visible in the distance. On the way down the path meets a gravel track, the route taking the left-hand, downhill direction and forking left 10mins later. Carry on ahead when another track joins from the right. At **Pulverbruecke** a clear GR sign directs the route left, off the track, over a wooden footbridge and out onto a road.

Cross the road and take the waymarked footpath up through the woods. This joins with a wider track and leads out onto a turning circle with views of the castle ahead. The village of Lichtenberg is up on the hill and the houses below form the little settlement of Picardie. Continue along the track, which passes a large store building to the right and bends right as it climbs into woods and rises up behind Picardie. Follow the sign pointing off left into the village of **LICHTENBERG** (hotel/restaurants, *gîte*).

Lichtenberg to Wimmenau
(6km/3.5 miles, 1hr 45mins, height gain/loss 0m/100m)

Carry on through the main village square, passing the 'Au Soleil' restaurant on the left. At the junction just beyond, a short diversion off the GR route along the road to the left leads to the castle, clearly visible at the top of the hill. However, the GR53 itself turns right at this junction to take the road leading downhill.

Leave this road by the first turn to the left, the Rue du Vogelhardt, which twists between houses. When this road ends, continue along the grassy track beyond, which becomes an earth path dropping down fairly steeply. The path skirts a deep valley to the left and emerges onto a small country road where you turn right, but for only a few dozen metres, then left at a footpath sign indicating that Wimmenau is 1hr 25mins away.

After about 5mins the path crosses a vehicle track and then drops down to join a more major track on the right. Carry on ahead along this track, but **beware** of the next junction, which could easily be missed. Not far along the track the GR53 leaves to the right along a small footpath through open pine woodland. Follow this little footpath, which merges with another path and soon leads out onto a road. Turn left here, but only for a short distance. Just a few hundred metres along the road look out for a GR sign pointing off along the first track to the right.

The track soon reaches a T-junction where the GR turns to the left towards Wimmenau. At the next junction the route carries on along the more minor track straight ahead, rather than following the major track to the right.

Follow on ahead through the forest for over half an hour, eventually reaching a substantial track where the GR route is directed left for just a few dozen metres before leaving on another footpath to the right. The first houses of Wimmenau come into sight through the trees.

The route crosses a road then continues along a footpath. Where this path forks the GR follows the right-hand branch. The footpath is joined by a track coming in from the left. Carry on ahead with the embankment of the railway up to the left.

This track leads out onto a road in **WIMMENAU** (hotel, restaurant, shop – closed Wed pm). Turn left to follow this road over the level crossing and carry on past the station and into the centre of the village. When you reach the D157, turn left and cross over the River Moder to gain the main road (D919).

Wimmenau to Erckartswiller

(6.5km/4 miles, 2hr, height gain/loss 100m/80m)

Turn right along the main road for a few hundred metres, then leave to the left up the Rue Ritti and follow this around to the left. The road ends beyond the houses and is replaced by an earth vehicle track that heads towards the forest. At a junction with a choice of three tracks, where the right-hand track leads to a farm, the GR takes the middle track.

Very soon afterwards the route leaves to the left along another track, with Erckartswiller 1hr 15mins ahead. Soon after entering the forest the path forks – the red/white/red signed route goes on ahead, while the GR53 forks to the right and keeps close to the forest edge with pastureland off to the right. (At the time of writing this junction is easily missed, as a huge fallen tree blocks the turn off.)

Within about 10mins the route crosses a vehicle track and continues along a muddy path. This soon reaches a junction where a GR arrow sends the route to the left.

At a first fork the GR stays with the major right-hand track, but at the next fork, soon after, it leaves on the minor left-hand branch. After 10mins the path crosses another path and soon after meets a crossroads with the blue cross route (Ingwiller left, Wingen-sur-Moder right). The GR

The caves at Ochsental

crosses straight over this junction and, very soon after, forks to the right in open woodland.

The route joins a more major track that is followed ahead to reach the rocks at **Ochsental**, where there are several overhangs and small caves. Beyond the rocks, as the track curves away to the left (signposted towards Château du Meisenbach), the GR leaves on a footpath to the right of the track, signposted to La Petite-Pierre.

The path soon forks, the GR following the right-hand branch going straight ahead. Some 5mins later this joins a forest track on a bend and carries on ahead along the track, leading on past a junction called Vorderkopf to join the lane leading into the village of **ERCKARTSWILLER**.

Erckartswiller to La Petite-Pierre

(4km/2.5 miles, 1hr 15mins, height gain/loss 160m/40m)

Continue along this lane and follow it through the village. At the far end there is a junction where the village street meets a more major road at a bend. The GR turns left along this road (D813), crosses a stream, then very soon after turns off to the right along a gravel track. The track becomes a footpath which follows the edge of a field. After turning the corner of the field a waymark diverts the route into woodland off to the right and the path starts to wind between trees.

Within 5mins there is a confusing fork. The right fork is the more direct, but not waymarked, although it picks up the GR waymarked trail again fairly quickly. The left fork, which has waymarks, swings around to reach the same point.

This broad path is easily followed from here on, crossing one track and forking left at the next junction to lead up onto a short ridge. Towards the end of this ridge the route forks to the right around an outcrop of sandstone. After going through a cleft between two large rocks the path starts to descend, becoming a vehicle track which leads across an expanse of pastureland.

On the far side of the pasture is a junction with a major track. An old Parc Animalier sign points left, and the current GR sign does not give a clear direction. In fact the route turns left along the larger track, which rises to meet a road at a T-junction.

Turn right along the road towards La Petite-Pierre (the signpost to the left currently still points towards the Parc Animalier, which is now closed). The road soon reaches the first houses of **LA PETITE-PIERRE** (hotels, *gîte*, restaurants, cafés, baker). Follow this road downhill for about 1km until you reach a T-junction with the main road in the centre of the village.

La Petite-Pierre to Graufthal

(7km/4.5 miles, 2hr 15mins, height gain/loss 140m/280m)

Turn left along the main road, the Rue Principale, which is flanked by several hotels, restaurants and cafés. Continue through the village, passing the *mairie*, until you reach a fork where the main road goes left to Saverne, but a minor road to the right is signed to the Maison du Parc and the tourist office. Take this road to the right and follow it as it bends around past the war memorial. The GR53 leaves to the left, opposite the tourist office, along a narrow road which leads up alongside the old *redoute* (a simple type of fortified enclosure). This little road runs through a narrow rocky gap, then along a very short elevated ridge before turning to the right and passing the Poet's Garden, which provides a good lookout point over the old fortified village and its castle.

The road becomes a track and soon reaches a fork where the GR takes the slightly downhill track to the right. Another fork follows soon afterwards, and again the GR takes the right-hand, downhill path. In about 5mins this path leads up to the **Rocher du Corbeau**, an elevated sandstone bluff that provides an excellent viewing platform. There are benches here and an open view over the wooded valley ahead.

Coming down from the promontory the route is directed onto a little footpath. Within only 100m there is another rock across the path, but the

route does not carry on beyond this second rock – instead it hairpins down to the left.

At the next hairpin the red disc route leaves to the left, but the GR53 turns downhill and continues to follow a series of zigzags until it reaches the road down in the valley. Turn right along the road, passing the **IMSTHAL** campsite on the left, and a lake then comes into view on the right of the road. The GR leaves the road beside this lake, taking a little lane which branches to the right, skirts the lake and heads across the valley.

The lane goes off to the left towards houses, but the GR route is signposted to the right along a track that leads towards the woods. Almost immediately the route leaves again on a footpath to the left.

This little path gains height through the open beech woods, crossing over a vehicle track on the way up. Follow this clear path for about 1.5km to reach a road near to the brow of the hill. Take the broad earth path that twists to the left on the opposite side of the road. This soon narrows to a footpath and turns to run parallel with the road, which is now off to the left.

Within about 10mins the path winds down to a vehicle track next to a picnic area. The route crosses the track, continuing along a woodland footpath on the far side.

Rock-cut houses at Graufthal

The path soon merges with another vehicle track, but the GR route leaves this track again to the right, only 50m further along. Follow this little path for almost 1km down the hill, with a valley down to the right, to reach a road by some fishponds. Follow this road to the left into the village of **GRAUFTHAL** (hotel, restaurants) a few hundred metres away.

After passing the 'Au Vieux Moulin' restaurant, a short diversion off the GR along the first road to the right reaches the line of rock-cut houses partly built into the cliff face.

Rock-cut Houses

The 70m-high sandstone cliff behind the little village of Graufthal shelters some of the last remaining rock-cut houses in the region. In the Middle Ages several small caves in the rock face were used by the nearby abbey as storerooms for provisions and firewood, and over the years some of these shelters were converted into dwellings. The earliest date of occupation is unclear, but one cottage has a lintel dated 1760, and the last occupant of these cave houses lived here right up until 1958. These primitive dwellings provided the most basic of accommodation and did not arouse much local interest until it was realised that the site was a curiosity for visitors. The houses now form a small museum, and although the opening hours are very restricted they can be viewed from the outside at any time.

Graufthal to Saverne

(12km/7.5 miles, 3hr 45mins, height gain/loss 200m/210m)

The GR53 leaves Graufthal along the road towards Saverne. A few hundred metres beyond the centre of the village the GR route turns off to the right to go along the road that runs alongside the cemetery.

Rock Kate

From the road you can see the headstone of Catherine Ottermann, nicknamed 'Felsekäth' (Rock Kate), the last inhabitant of the rock-cut houses, who died in 1958.

Beyond the cemetery the road soon crosses a stream then turns sharply to the right, and here the GR53 leaves the road along a track to the left which it follows for the next 3km. Staying in the bottom of the valley close to the edge of the forest, it runs roughly parallel with the little stream to the left.

The track reaches a road where the route turns left, crossing a small stream. Just over the bridge follow the road to the left for some 200m. This reaches a signpost where the GR is pointed off to the right along a vehicle track. (A short diversion further along the road from here reaches the inn at **OBERHOF** where refreshments are available.)

A few hundred metres along the track there is a junction where several paths meet. Take the footpath (not the track) to the right, signposted for Saverne and Saut du Prince Charles.

Some 5mins later the path crosses first one track, then a second, and then finally joins with a forest track where the route carries on ahead. Only minutes later this joins with a substantial vehicle track and the route carries on in much the same direction. It then reaches a surfaced lane at a T-junction where waymarks are currently hard to find. Turn left here and be prepared to walk for some time without seeing a waymark.

A major road comes into view on the left, and the lane soon comes out onto a two-lane road – once again there are currently no waymarks or signs here. There is a track on the opposite side of the road, but this is not the correct route. Turn right along the road and follow it for over 1km, crossing a bridge over the busy A4 motorway and continuing as far as a place called **LA COLONNE** (café/restaurant), marked by a sandstone pillar. This stands in front of a junction with the Saverne–Phalsbourg main road, and the large roadside café/restaurant can be seen just along the road to the right.

The GR leaves La Colonne by a small footpath to the left. Within 5mins this path reaches a junction where the route turns right along a track towards Kaltwiller. Very soon after, this leads to a major track junction called **MF Kaltwiller**. Turn right here and cross over the main road.

The Saut du Prince Charles

Go up the surfaced lane on the far side of the road. After only a few minutes turn off left along a little track that heads through woodland and emerges onto another lane. Turn right along the lane, but only follow it for a couple of minutes, leaving it to the left along the indicated footpath.

Within about 5mins this path crosses a section of the **Fossé des Pandours**, which consists of two large banks separated by an obvious ditch. These substantial defences have been dated to pre-Roman times and were probably built by Celtic people. The name derives from the 18th century, when the Pandours – mercenaries fighting for the Duke of Lorraine – used the ditch as a line of defence.

Carry on along the path to meet a vehicle track and continue left along it to reach the picnic area at **Usspann**.

Leave this towards Rocher du Saut du Prince Charles, keeping to the main track until, some minutes later, the route is signed left and crosses a lane, continuing downhill on a path on the far side that drops down the side of a steep valley.

A large rock outcrop is reached on the left, the first of a series of such rocks. The site known as **Saut du Prince Charles** is a particularly impressive overhanging rock about 100m further on. There is an information board, a tiny grotto and steps which divert up to the top of the rock and the *jardin botanique*.

Follow the main path as it zigzags down to a gravel turning area. The GR continues ahead and emerges onto a road.

Go down this road and turn left where it meets a T-junction. Follow

59

this road along, passing factory premises on the right, to finally meet a major road (N4) at a T-junction where there is a bar on the right. Turn right towards the centre of **SAVERNE** (hotels, youth hostel, campsite, restaurants, cafés, shops) and follow the road over the railway. Take the first road to the left after the railway bridge and continue down to the roundabout.

Leave the roundabout up the Grand'Rue, which means turning half right along the busy street lined by shops. Continue up here to reach the canal and the centre of town. The tourist office is further up the Grand'Rue, on the left.

Alsace Townhouses

While villages throughout Alsace contain many traditional half-timbered buildings, Saverne contains examples of more prosperous townhouses. Roofs are sharply pointed, sometimes with ornamented gables and rows of dormer windows. The house façades, often brightly coloured, can expose plain wooden beams or incorporate more richly decorated woodwork, testifying to the skill of local craftsmen. The more opulent houses often have overhanging projections, oriel windows or balconies extending out into the streets. The Maison Katz on the Grand'Rue near to the tourist office is a particularly fine example, where even the beams high above the street are covered in carved decoration.

Traditional townhouses in the centre of Saverne

SECTION 3

GR53 Saverne to Schirmeck

(70.5km/44 miles)

The starting point of this section is the historic town of Saverne, lying in a valley that has long been a gateway between France and the rest of Europe – the town sits right at the edge of the sharp division between the hills of the Vosges and the Rhine plain.

Once again, most of the walking is across wooded hills, but compared with the GR53 sections to the north, this part of the route starts to involve a little more climbing. The path crosses lower hills then rises up to the summit of Schneeberg at 960m. It then drops to the valley of the Bruche before climbing again to cross Le Donon (1008m), where it meets the GR5. The end of this section, the small town of Schirmeck, is once again down in the valley of the Bruche.

Some striking sandstone features are encountered along the way, such as Haut-Barr Castle, sitting on two close crags connected by a bridge, the ruined walls seeming to merge with the rock face itself. Further south the Rocher de Dabo, a huge, steep-sided sandstone rock topped by the St-Léon Chapel, creates a remarkable silhouette. Beyond Urmatt the isolated sandstone arch of La Porte de Pierre is another scenic highlight.

Of the many viewpoints passed along the way, the area by Nideck has two particularly good ones. The lower of the two castles here stands guard at the top of a cliff, dominating the wooded gorge below, while a nearby stream cascades down the head of this narrow valley, forming an impressive waterfall. There are also good all-round views from the summit of Le Donon, which is the site of a Gallo-Roman temple complex and shows evidence of First World War occupation on the lower slopes.

This section can be walked in three days, with suggested stops at Wangenbourg (hotels, *gîte*, campsite) and then the hotel at Urmatt. The third day is strenuous, however, as it is long (30km/18.5 miles) and includes steep climbs, so you might consider a further stop at the hotel at Col du Donon, otherwise accommodation on this final stretch is limited.

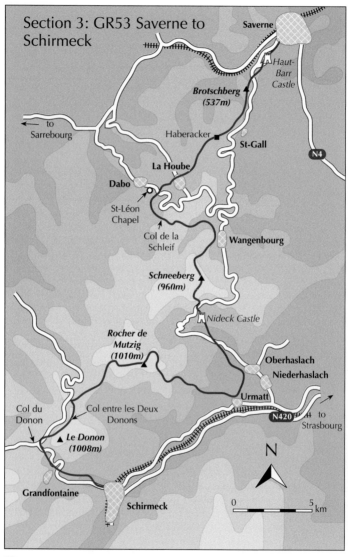

Section 3: GR53 Saverne to Schirmeck

Saverne

Haut-Barr Castle

Brotschberg (537m)

Haberacker

St-Gall

← to Sarrebourg

N4

La Hoube

Dabo

St-Léon Chapel

Col de la Schleif

Wangenbourg

Schneeberg (960m)

Nideck Castle

Rocher de Mutzig (1010m)

Oberhaslach

Niederhaslach

Urmatt

Col du Donon

Col entre les Deux Donons

N420 to Strasbourg

▲ Le Donon (1008m)

N

Grandfontaine

Schirmeck

0   5 km

Accommodation and Food

Km	Cumulative km		
		Saverne	Hotels, youth hostel, campsite, restaurants, cafés, shops
3.0		Haut-Barr Castle	Café/restaurant.
4.0	7.0		Turn off for St-Gall (campsite), 1.5km off route
7.0	14.0	La Hoube	Hotel/restaurant (1km off route)
2.5	16.5	Dabo turn off	*Gîte*, campsite (*auberge* within 0.5km) Turn off for Dabo village, 1.5km off route
		(Dabo village)	Hotel, restaurant, cafés, shop
2.5	19.0	Col de la Schleif	Shelter
5.0	24.0		Turn off for Wangenbourg, 1km off route
		(Wangenbourg)	Hotels, *gîte*, campsite, restaurants, shop (closed Wed pm)
9.0	33.0	Nideck (D218)	Café/possible future *gîte* (on road below gorge)
2.0	35.0	Luttenbach	*Gîte*, campsite (**Note** This is not the Luttenbach near Munster, which also has a campsite.)
2.0	37.0		Turn off for Oberhaslach centre, 1km off route
		(Oberhaslach)	Hotel/restaurants, shops (closed Wed pm)
3.5	40.5	Urmatt	Hotel, restaurants, shops (closed Wed pm)
22.5	63.0	Col du Donon	Hotel, restaurants
7.5	70.5	Schirmeck	Hotel, restaurants, cafés, shops Turn off for Rothau (hostel, campsite), 3km off route.

Contact details for tourist offices and accommodation are in the appendix.

Maps
IGN 1:100,000 sheet 12
Club Vosgien 1:50,000 sheets 1/8 and 4/8

Saverne to Haut-Barr Castle
(3km/2 miles, 1hr, height gain/loss 270m/0m)

Saverne

Saverne's key position, where the Zorn Valley cuts through the Vosges, made it a prosperous trading centre from Roman times. The valley was later used for the route of the Marne–Rhine canal, which now provides a colourful marina in the centre of the town. Many fine buildings may be visited, including the Château des Rohan, the early–17th-century house of Maison Katz and the old castle.

Saverne is proud of the many contrasting gardens found in the locality. A rosary containing over 7000 rose bushes is the centre for a number of rose-based festivities, and the château is set in a park that overlooks the canal marina. There is a botanic garden to the northwest of the town, just off the GR53, and the secluded rock garden by the Grotte St-Vit can be found by taking the GR531 to the southwest.

The walk starts along the towpath from the canal bridge in Grand'Rue. Take the path to the west, walking not towards the *château* and marina, but in the opposite direction, out of town. Immediately after the first bridge over the canal, take the path on the left going up from the towpath to join the second bridge. At the top of the rise turn left, following the GR53 signs towards Haut-Barr, then right along the Rue du Haut-Barr. Keep on this road uphill for over 10mins, and when it meets a more major road, carry on uphill.

Very soon there is a noticeboard for the Forêt Domaniale de Saverne on the left, at a place called Bildstoeckel de la Trinité. Leave the road and follow the GR53 up a footpath through the trees to the left. After about 10mins take the left branch of a fork – the route is following part of a *sentier botanique*. Soon after a clearing with some benches and a display board, take the path indicated to the right. In about 5mins **look out for** a small path leaving at a very tight angle to the left. Continue upwards to **HAUT-BARR CASTLE** (café/restaurant).

Haut-Barr Castle to Haberacker
(7km/4.5 miles, 2hr 15mins, height gain/loss 100m/80m)

The castle and chapel are accessible to visitors and there is a sweeping view from the highest level, especially out across the plain to the east.

Leave the castle car park by a footpath to the left of the road, passing the Chappe Telegraph Tower. The footpath continues parallel to the road, reaches another car park and leaves it by a clear path on the other side.

Haut-Barr Castle

Just before **Grand Geroldseck Castle** the GR53 forks left to follow a broad track round the base of the mound. (A short diversion up the other fork (red diagonal crosses) reaches the castle ruins, which are quite extensive, but there is no access to the tower.) Beyond the castle the path drops down to rejoin the GR53, and a little further on the path to **Petit Geroldseck Castle** goes up to the left. Again the GR53 continues round the base of the mound. Petit Geroldseck is a much smaller castle, with little more than the stump of the tower remaining.

The route meets a road at a clearing known as Hexentisch, where there is an information board. Leave the clearing not by the obvious track opposite, but by a small footpath branching off the track to the left, behind a hexagonal picnic table. Go right at a fork to climb by hairpins through the forest to the clearing at Brotsch. The lookout tower here stands well above the treetops, allowing uninterrupted views in all directions. The GR53 leaves the clearing to the left by a path clearly marked to the Rocher and Grotte du Brotsch.

The route goes downhill through spruce woods, forks left at a junction and merges with a track coming in from the left. This leads to the **Rocher du Brotsch**, a shapely outcrop of sandstone that makes a fine lookout point over a huge expanse of wooded valley. The GR53 is the first path to

the left when descending from the rock (avoid the second path to the left, signposted to Grand Krappenfels). The route hairpins round to pass under the overhang, where there is a large cave – the Grotte du Brotsch. A few more hairpins bring the path down to reach a track that you follow to the right to meet a junction and turn left.

In less than 10mins go straight across a clearing and follow a footpath out at the other side to reach a road. Turn right and follow the road round a bend and past the Maison Forestière **Schaeferplatz**. A few moments later there is a picnic place (turn left here for the campsite at **ST-GALL**), and just beyond it a sign to Maison Forestière Haberacker and Dabo. This points the GR route up to the right along a forest footpath. Go left at the next fork and follow this broad footpath along the side of a slope, parallel to a road, to Lotringer-Baechel.

Almost immediately after leaving this point the route goes left along a forest track, then leaves it again to the right in a few metres and continues to the **Carrefour du Billabaum**. Turn right along the road towards a huge beech stump with a protective roof (this tree blew down in a storm, but the base has been preserved to show its impressive size). Just before the tree stump leave the road to the left onto a footpath through the woods, again signposted to Haberacker. A view opens up across the valley to the right, with a row of rock outcrops on the skyline, one of which forms the base of Ochsenstein Castle. The GR53 turns left onto a road just by the Carrefour du **HABERACKER** and forks left to follow the road uphill.

Haberacker to Dabo Road Junction
(6.5km/4 miles, 2hr, height gain/loss 180m/120m)

Keep on the road for about 5mins, then turn left along a broad earth path into the forest, signposted to La Hardt and Dabo. On reaching a wide forestry track the route does not join it initially, but runs along just beside, dropping onto it for only a few hundred metres before leaving it again to the left by a path up the banking.

When this path reaches another track, cross diagonally over, but at the next one, turn to the right. Where this track meets another at a bend the route carries on straight ahead. At the next fork take the left-hand, slightly uphill branch, which after about 10mins leads to a crossroads at La Hardt.

Turn right towards La Hoube and Dabo, but just as the track curves off to the right, leave it by a path that goes straight ahead into the trees. In a few minutes this crosses a small track, then, immediately beyond, turns left to run downhill beside it through dense conifers.

Cross the stream at the bottom of the valley by a footbridge and turn right up the wooded bank, then left, following an arrow that indicates a stony footpath. The path rises quite steeply between two tumbledown walls towards the village of **LA HOUBE** (hotel/restaurant). The GR53 passes round a house to join a gravel track that emerges onto the road just downhill from the church. (The hotel Des Vosges is up the road to the left here.)

Turn right downhill for about 150m and look out for a grassy lane where the route leaves the road to the left, passing a bench. This leads along the top of a low, broad wall, then crosses a road and enters the forest.

Go across a small track and carry on for about 10mins, curving round the end of a valley and rising through mature woodland. On meeting a major track, cross over to take a footpath almost opposite that descends into a valley. Cross a footbridge then climb up the other bank, initially by some stone steps.

On joining a road, turn right uphill. Follow the road as it curves round to the left then descends slightly to a T-junction, with a magnificent view ahead of the St-Léon Chapel on Dabo rock.

DABO village (hotel, restaurant, cafés, shops) can be reached along the footpath opposite, but the GR53 turns left along this quiet road to reach a junction with the D45.

Rocher de Dabo and St-Léon Chapel, seen from the GR53

Dabo Road Junction to Wangenbourg
(7.5km/4.5 miles, 2hr 15mins, height gain/loss 210m/250m)

The Rocher de Dabo

The intriguing Rocher de Dabo draws the eye from whichever direction it is approached. This strange and imposing flat-topped rock, which may seem so unique, is yet one more example of the effects of sandstone weathering – little wonder that such a site has been fortified for centuries. There has been a castle here at least since the 12th century, and it was enlarged in later years. Invading

French forces laid siege to the rock in 1677 and managed to seize the castle. The strategic strength of the site may have been the cause of the castle's final destruction, because it was blown up by the French two years later and nothing can now be seen of the defences.

Stones from the ruins were used in the building of the current chapel, which dates from 1890. The St-Léon Chapel is dedicated to Léon IX, pope from

1048–54. Léon belonged to the very powerful Eguisheim-Dabo family, local landowners, and he is still celebrated as the only pope to have come from Alsace.

Two roads leave on the far side of the D45. To visit the Rocher de Dabo, visible ahead, divert off the GR53 along the road to the right, but the GR53 takes the Route Forestière du Chat Noir uphill to the left, passing Dabo campsite and *gîte* then taking a footpath to the right. This runs parallel to the road and a little below it, and provides another good position for viewing the chapel and rock.

After a few minutes the route rejoins the road and follows it for a short distance, before leaving by a footpath to the left and passing close to the Auberge du Chat Noir. On reaching a major track a GR53 signpost points along the footpath opposite, which you follow through open woodland. At a T-junction turn left towards Col de la Schleif, following the path as it climbs steadily through thick conifer woods. The path passes Le Rutschfelsen, a stone with a number of curious depressions on its surface.

On emerging onto a road the route goes to the right. After about 5mins leave the road to the left by a broad footpath to **COL DE LA SCHLEIF**, where there is a picnic area, a shelter and an information board.

Leave the col by the Route Forestière du Rosskopf. **Warning** –

the next turn is very easy to miss. The track descends for about 500m, then takes a slight bend to the right followed by a sharp bend to the left. Between these two bends look out for a small footpath dropping very steeply to the left, by rocky steps, down to a tiny stream. There is an arrow and a waymark to show that this is where the GR53 goes, but they are not at all obvious.

The path turns to follow the stream downhill and continues down the valley to reach a wooden bridge. Cross the bridge and climb the path up the bank to meet a track. Turn right and carry on down the valley for just a couple of minutes before taking a footpath to the left. When this meets a road, cross the concrete bridge opposite, just beside a house. Climb the bank beyond and turn left along a broad vehicle track for a few hundred metres, then leave this by a footpath to the right.

Pass the Fontaine Helwig and keep to the main, right-hand path at a fork. Cross a track, then at the next track go left for a few minutes then right. Cross a third track and continue along the hillside with a view to the left of Wangenbourg and its castle and church. At the next track there is a sign ahead to Schneeberg, which is the direction of the GR53. If you want to visit the castle at **WANGENBOURG** (hotels, *gîte*, campsite, restaurants, shop – closed Wed pm), leave the GR here and go down to the left.

Wangenbourg to Nideck Castle

(8km/5 miles, 2hr 45mins, height gain/loss 460m/420m)

The route now climbs steadily for about 1hr 45mins to the summit of Schneeberg at 960m.

Go up the track and keep to the main, right-hand branch of a fork where the GR531 (blue rectangle) branches to the left. At an oblique junction turn left along a track that now levels out. Turn off to the right after a few minutes on a path that rises steadily along the side of the hill and eventually joins a vehicle track.

Take this to the left and continue to a junction where another track comes in from the right. Turn sharply to the right to follow this uphill, then round a hairpin to the left. At the **Col du Schneeberg** take the track to the left, then after about 15mins leave it by a path up to the right. In a few minutes this reaches the summit of **SCHNEEBERG**, a deeply cut block of rock with a *table d'orientation*.

On descending from the rock turn right down a series of steps, then follow a path that goes through conifer forest. Pass straight over a junction with Pl Pandours signposted to the left. When the path meets a vehicle track, turn right for about 50m, then left following a GR sign pointing downhill – with a deep, wooded valley to the left, this rocky footpath descends to meet a track. There are no obvious waymarks, but continue downhill to the right. At the next track cross straight over to take a footpath, still descending through the forest, and at a T-junction take the waymarked downhill track. There is an excellent open view from this section.

On meeting a road the GR53 turns to the right (to the left, beyond a *maison forestière*, there is a car park that also gives access to **NIDECK CASTLE**). Follow the road for about 400m and, just around a bend to the right, **watch out for** waymarks indicating a track to the left and descend past the first, smaller castle at Nideck to reach the second one not far below.

Nideck Castle to Oberhaslach

(5km/3 miles, 1hr 30mins, height gain/loss 0m/240m)

Follow signs along a footpath towards the *cascade* (waterfall). This leads down the side of a deep valley and crosses a very small stream to reach a fenced lookout point. From here there is an excellent view down the Hasel Valley, a wooded gorge with cliffs on both sides. Continue down the steep, rocky path to reach the **Cascade du Nideck**, where a stream plunges down the cliff face from high above, although the water flow can be

The Cascade du Nideck, at the head of the Hasel Gorge

disappointing in high summer. Follow the broad footpath down the valley – the clifftop position of the castle is best appreciated from further down the path.

The path emerges onto a road, with a café off to the right. Turn left, then after a few hundred metres turn right across a little bridge over a stream and immediately left over a footbridge. The path runs parallel to the stream and in a couple of minutes reaches a junction. Bear right, signposted to Urmatt, and continue along the woodland path, still running parallel to the stream on the left with the road visible beyond that. (A spur of the GR53 to the left provides

71

access to the campsite and *gîte* at **Luttenbach**.)

When the path comes very near to the road, turn right, taking a footpath that climbs a bank then winds its way through woodland. This comes out on a tarmac track where the route goes left, then immediately right up a

narrow track that continues along the hillside, still with the river down to the left.

The GR53 enters **OBERHASLACH** (hotel/restaurants, shops – closed Wed pm) by the Rue de la Forêt, then turns left down a more major road towards a pond.

Oberhaslach to Urmatt
(3.5km/2.5 miles, 1hr 15mins, height gain/loss 20m/60m)

The centre of the village and its facilities lie straight ahead here, but almost 1km off the GR53. Just before the pond the GR turns sharply right into Rue du Mittenbach, then left into Rue du Grempil to climb steeply out of the village again. At the end of the tarmac road turn left at an oblique T-junction, then left at a fork, taking the downhill track.

Where a track comes in from the right, follow it to the left for about 10mins, then on meeting another

track again bear left to carry on in much the same direction.

At the edge of **URMATT** (hotel, restaurants, shops – closed Wed pm) do not go straight down the tarmac road ahead, but take the roughly surfaced track to the right that continues around to meet another road. Continue downhill on the Rue de la Forêt, then turn right at the bottom (a left turn here reaches the shops in the centre of the village).

Urmatt to Rocher de Mutzig
(10.5km/6.5 miles, 3hr 45mins, height gain/loss 750m/0m)

At a fork take the right-hand road, by a *fontaine* with drinking water. Pass a crucifix and continue up the road, ignoring a slightly ambiguous arrow by a footpath to the left. Where the road curves to the left, leave it by a footpath to the right into the woods, behind another *fontaine*.

This meets a track at a junction.

Turn right here and keep straight on at the next junction, along the Route Forestière du Kappelbronn. Where a track leaves to the left, take a footpath obliquely left for a few minutes, then at a junction with several faint paths take the distinct path curving to the left and, after passing straight over two tracks, turn right along a third.

*The sandstone arches
known as Porte de Pierre*

After about 5mins go straight on over a crossroads, as indicated towards Kappelbronn and Porte de Pierre, and follow the track as it begins to climb with a stream to the left. Keep straight on, passing the Route Forestière de la Grotte du Loup on the left as the valley begins to narrow. In a few minutes the cave of **Grotte du Loup** comes into view on the opposite side of the stream.

Carry on ahead, then take the left-hand track at a fork – the Route Forestière de la Turbine. Immediately beyond a small turbine shed, follow the track as it curves to the left, ignoring another track straight ahead. At the next sharp bend to the left, take a footpath straight on, uphill, which emerges onto a major track. Turn left for a short distance then take a track to the right with an upright stone beside it – this is clearly marked to Rocher de Mutzig.

By a group of houses on the left there are two tracks on the right. Take the one going on ahead (not the sharp right). This peters into a footpath zigzagging through mature forest. It crosses over a track then, a few minutes later, watch out for a sign to

Porte de Pierre and Rocher de Mutzig, indicating that the route hairpins to the right and does not follow the path straight ahead.

At a forest track turn right, then take a path up the banking to the left to continue zigzagging uphill. After about 15mins watch out for another point where there is a footpath straight ahead, but the route continues upwards as indicated by an arrow painted on a tree. Cross a forest track, leaving it by a footpath almost opposite, then turn right along the next track for a short distance before climbing again, up a footpath sharply to the left, to reach the splendid rock outcrop of **Porte de Pierre**.

Turn left out of the clearing through a woodland section where waymarking is sparse. Take the left-hand, uphill branch of a fork and continue climbing steadily, curving round the side of the valley. Turn left on meeting a broader track and continue for a few minutes before leaving by a footpath to the right. This meets another, deeply eroded track at a T-junction. Turn left to reach the **ROCHER DE MUTZIG**.

Rocher de Mutzig to Col du Donon
(12km/7.5 miles, 3hr 45mins, height gain/loss 270m/550m)

The GR53 is signposted to Le Donon to the right, just before the outlook rock. A few minutes down this path there is a fine view of the valley, perhaps better than the view from the

rock itself. Follow this footpath to **Col du Narion**, where there is a shelter, and carry on straight across the crossroads. On reaching a forest track after a minute or two, do not be tempted by the footpath opposite, but turn left along the main track, despite the lack of immediate waymarks. This track is known as Le Balcon and it gives a broad view of the valley below and the hills beyond, with the two summits of Donon in the distance. Stay on this track for about 25mins until you reach a T-junction.

Turn left along this more major track until it takes a sharp hairpin to the left. Here a lesser track leaves the end of the hairpin, going uphill, but the GR53 takes a footpath to the left of this, going downhill and signposted to Baraque Carrée. This reaches a broad vehicle track where you turn right, but in a few minutes **look out for** a path leaving to the left. The top of this path is quite steep and rocky, but it improves once clear of the track banking. Descend to the clearing at **La Baraque Carrée**, where there is an open-fronted shelter.

Leave by the Route Forestière de la Corrière, which contours around the left-hand slope of the hill for about half an hour, then starts to rise toward the ridge. The mock-Greco-Roman temple on Le Donon comes into view ahead. On meeting another track turn right to come out by the road at **Col de la Côte de l'Engin**.

First World War Bunkers

Just beside the route, under the road, is a First World War bunker, one of a series connected by a walking trail. It is thought provoking to spend a few minutes investigating these underground chambers, although you will need your torch.

The GR53 turns to the left before reaching the road and continues along this track for over 1km to reach a fork. Take the right-hand, downhill fork to **COL ENTRE LES DEUX DONONS**. Turn right past a shelter and a replica marker stone, then take a right fork uphill.

The GR5

From the Col entre les Deux Donons there are signs for the GR5. This long distance route starts on the Dutch coast and comes down through the plains of Lorraine to join the GR53. The two trails now follow the same route into Schirmeck, still waymarked with red rectangles.

Soon afterwards, turn sharply left onto a track and follow it uphill. After a short distance the route leaves by a footpath to the right, which hairpins up through the woods to meet a broad track. Turn right for 100m or so, then take a footpath up to the left. This zigzag path climbs to the summit of Le Donon, on the way up reaching a small First World War shelter and information board. Look out for a red waymark indicating the correct route up from here, which is a steep path to the right.

Le Donon

The Col du Donon has been a route through the barrier of the Vosges for

Near Le Donon

centuries. The Celts, Romans and Franks all used it, and the mountain was chosen as a place of worship from early times.

The most obvious ruin to be seen on the summit today is a Greco-Roman-style temple, but this only dates from 1869. In fact traces of structures from 1000BC have been found, and various Celtic and Gallic gods were worshipped here, but most of the remains are from the Roman period. The Roman temple complex appears to have been sacked in the fourth century, when the empire began to break down, but its final destruction and lapse into obscurity came with the arrival in the seventh and eighth centuries of monks spreading Christianity.

Ironically, it was two men in holy orders, but with an interest in history, who were responsible for the rediscovery of the site in the 18th century. Several archaeological digs have produced a wealth of evidence, and some modern reconstructions mark these sites. One attractive stone to look out for is just to the right of the path below the temple – it shows a bas-relief of a lion and wild boar in confrontation.

The summit was a stronghold of the German army in the First World War, and tombstones of German soldiers can be found on the slopes. There was also fighting here in the Second World War.

On the summit of **LE DONON** go to the left of the temple and down some steps, following the path as it turns and passes under an over-hanging rock. When it meets a more obvious path, turn left and wend your way downhill between the interpretation boards and replica remains. Take a broad footpath that goes to the left of the aerial installation and follow it downhill and over a road. Continue down the well-used path on the other side to cross straight over the next road.

The path becomes a track and then a lane before reaching another road where the GR5/GR53 goes to the left, downhill. Just at the junction there is a large information board with a map and details of the archaeological sites of Le Donon. The road comes out onto the D392 by the Col du Donon (hotel, restaurants).

Col du Donon to Schirmeck
(7.5km/4.5 miles, 2hr 15mins, height gain/loss 0m/410m)

Turn left and follow this main road as it twists to the right downhill. Just before it bends sharply to the left, **watch out for** a footpath dropping down to the right. The route follows this down, crosses a vehicle track and takes a more substantial path on the opposite side.

Stay on this track for about 15mins as it descends steadily through the woods. After bending to the right, look out for waymarks to the left and follow this footpath, crossing one track and joining the next to continue ahead. Shortly after a turning circle in the track, take a footpath that leaves to the right then runs parallel with the track for a short while before descending by some steps to a road. Cross the road and the footbridge opposite to climb quite steeply up the opposite slope.

At the next road turn right and follow it along a short straight section – the houses of **GRANDFONTAINE** are clustered in the valley ahead. Before the road begins to bend to the left, take a footpath rising up the bank to the left. When this joins a track obliquely, carry on ahead to cross two more tracks and continue above the side of the valley with the village of Wackenbach coming into view below.

The path turns left up a side valley, taking the right-hand branch of a fork then swinging round to the right. Beyond a little stream it climbs up to a road where the route goes to the left. Almost immediately it is directed up some steps up to the right to rejoin the road and turn right.

After a couple of minutes take a road to the right as indicated by waymarks on a lamp-post. This ends at a turning circle, but the Route Forestière de la Basse de la Scierie carries on beyond. Follow this for about 150m, then **look out for** a footpath leaving to the left which you follow until it meets a main road. Turn left to reach the edge of **SCHIRMECK** (hotel, restaurants, cafés, shops), then continue down the road to cross the bridge into La Broque. Very soon afterwards turn left by signs to a supermarket, and follow the edge of a large parking area to cross the railway by a footbridge. After coming down the steps on the other side, keep straight on to the station, then turn right down the Avenue de la Gare towards Schirmeck town centre. This street comes out opposite the tourist office.

The GR53

The GR53 ends in Schirmeck, but the GR5 continues to the south, still with red rectangle waymarks.

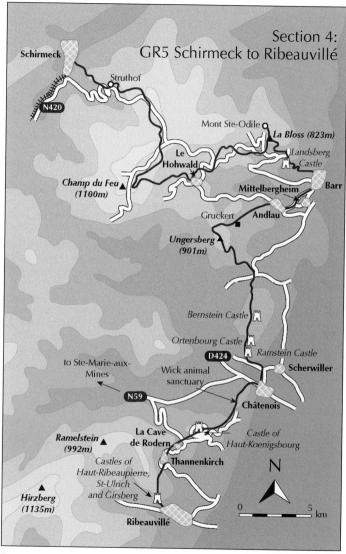

Section 4:
GR5 Schirmeck to Ribeauvillé

Schirmeck

Struthof

N420

Mont Ste-Odile
La Bloss (823m)

Le
Hohwald

Landsberg
Castle

*Champ du Feu
(1100m)*

Mittelbergheim
Barr

Gruckert
Andlau

*Ungersberg
(901m)*

Bernstein Castle

Ortenbourg Castle

D424

Ramstein Castle

Scherwiller

to Ste-Marie-aux-
Mines

Wick animal
sanctuary

N59

Châtenois

*Ramelstein
(992m)*

La Cave
de Rodern

Castle of
Haut-Koenigsbourg

Thannenkirch

Castles of
Haut-Ribeaupierre,
St-Ulrich
and Girsberg

▲
*Hirzberg
(1135m)*

N

0   5
km

Ribeauvillé

SECTION 4

GR5 Schirmeck to Ribeauvillé

(84.5km/52.5 miles)

Historic places form a major theme on this section of the walk. At Mont Ste-Odile the path meets the Mur Païen, a prehistoric wall more than 10km long and said to be the largest megalithic monument in Europe. The convent and chapels on Mont Ste-Odile are also worth visiting. Situated high above the Alsace plain, the view from the terrace here extends beyond the Rhine. A number of castles in varying stages of ruin and reconstruction lie on the route, foremost among them the impressive hilltop castle of Haut-Koenigsbourg, which can be seen from many miles away. The fortified church at Châtenois is another reminder of unsettled times.

An unhappy period of more recent history is remembered at the concentration camp of Struthof. Now partly preserved as a museum, it throws some light onto what went on during the period of Nazi occupation.

While the first part of this section is through forested hills, from Barr onwards the route drops down to the foothills, where vineyards have long been a mainstay of the local way of life. The wealth generated from wine production is reflected in the prosperity of the several small towns and villages, with their many traditional houses. The church at Andlau, just beside the route, has some fine stone carving on the exterior walls.

The walk involves a number of climbs and descents, but the steep stretches do not extend for very long. The final part of the section down into Ribeauvillé passes the three castles of Haut-Ribeaupierre, St-Ulrich and Girsberg. Ribeauvillé is a lively town with a maze of narrow backstreets, possibly tempting GR5 walkers to break their journey.

This section can be walked in four days, with suggested stops at Le Hohwald (hotels, *gîte*, campsite), Barr (hotels, campsite) and Châtenois (hotels and *gîte*).

Accommodation and Food

Km	Cumulative km		
		Schirmeck	Hotel, restaurants, cafés, shops
			Turn off for Rothau (hostel, campsite), 3km off route
5.0		Struthof	Restaurant Chez Dany 0.5km before Struthof site
10.5	15.5	Col du Champ du Feu	Turn off for Champ du Feu (campsite), 1.5km off route
			Turn off for Chaume des Veaux (refuge),1km off route
6.5	22.0	Le Hohwald	Hotel/restaurants, *gîte*, campsite, cafés, shop (closed Tue)
2.5	24.5	Welschbruch	Bar
7.0	31.5	Mont Ste-Odile	Hotel (at convent), café/restaurant
8.0	39.5	Barr	Hotels, campsite, restaurants, cafés, shops
1.5	41.0		Turn off for Mittelbergheim, 0.5km off route
		(Mittelbergheim)	Hotel, restaurants
2.0	43.0	Andlau	Hotels, restaurants, cafés, shops
4.0	47.0	Gruckert	Refuge
18.0	65.0		Turn off for Scherwiller (campsite), 2km off route
1.5	66.5	Châtenois	Hotel, *gîte*, restaurants, cafés, shops
5.0	71.5	Wick	Café
4.0	75.5	Haut-Koenigsbourg	Hotel, café/restaurant, snack-stall
4.0	79.5	Thannenkirch	Hotels, café/restaurants
5.0	84.5	Ribeauvillé	Hotels, campsites (2), restaurants, cafés, shops

Contact details for tourist offices and accommodation are in the appendix.

Maps
IGN 1:100,000 sheet 31 and small part of 12
Club Vosgien 1:50,000 sheet 4/8

Schirmeck to Struthof

(5km/3 miles, 1hr 30mins, height gain/loss 380m/0m)

Cross the square between the tourist office and the *hôtel de ville* and continue across the parking area beyond, with a church off to the right. There is a GR signpost at the foot of some steps opposite. The original GR5 route out of town was directed up these steps, but new road construction makes this impassable at the time of writing. A short, modified (and perhaps temporary) route has been signposted to avoid this obstacle and is described here, but future route changes are a possibility.

Turn to the right from the signpost and follow waymarks past some buildings to take the little backstreet that twists around, passing the fire station. The road comes to an end by the river and there are footpath signs pointing up to the *château musée*. This path is the GR532 (yellow rectangles), but serves as the modified GR5 for this short stretch. Go up this path, turning sharply left further up, following signs to reach the castle. This building, which houses the local museum, is a recent reconstruction (it is worth glancing over the courtyard wall for a good view over the rooftops of the town).

Leave the castle, carrying on to the left along a broad track cut into the side of the hill. This passes an open-sided shelter and soon reaches a signposted junction where the permanent GR5 route is rejoined.

Take the path signposted towards Struthof, and follow this uphill to reach a path junction near several power lines with an isolated cross to the left. Go across the junction taking the track opposite towards Barembach, but only follow it for a few metres. Fork right almost immediately onto a footpath that climbs steeply through the woods.

This narrow path is well signed and crosses three tracks. Very soon after crossing the third, look out for a footpath that peels off to the left. This path leads to a seat at an open lookout point, with the houses of Barembach in the valley below. The route continues along a broad path back into forest, and within 5mins reaches a more major vehicle track where the GR turns left.

Follow this track for the next kilometre as it rises and curves to the left around the head of the valley. At a junction go past the Route Forestière Roquel, which leaves to the right, to reach another broad track just beyond. To the right this is signed as the Route Forestière du Struthof. Off route to the left is a substantial, solid-floored shelter with benches, but the GR leaves this junction by a small footpath to the left of the Route Forestière du Struthof. It runs parallel to the track a short distance below it and climbs back to rejoin it after about 10mins.

The rooftops of Schirmeck

Carry on along the track, passing a house on the right. At the junction called Ici le Struthof go straight on towards Champ du Messin.

Turn left on reaching the road and walk up past the restaurant 'Chez Dany'. Almost opposite these buildings the GR leaves the road to climb a steep little stepped path. This climbs up through the woods, crossing the D130 on two occasions before emerging onto the road just by the **STRUTHOF** camp complex. The route turns left along the road, passing the camp entrance.

Struthof Concentration Camp

Struthof was the only concentration camp to be built on French soil. It was sited here

to provide a labour force to quarry the nearby pink granite, which had been identified as suitable for some of Hitler's grandiose architectural schemes. Initially it was a forced labour camp, using deportees to work the quarries, but it soon became even grimmer, with medical experiments and extermination amongst its goals. About 40,000 people suffered here, 10,000 dying from overwork or disease, or by execution.

Several of the camp buildings remain, and one of the blocks houses a small museum. A memorial to the many thousands who were deported during the Second World War stands by the cemetery. The camp is open from March to Christmas and attracts considerable numbers of visitors.

Struthof to Col du Champ du Feu

(10.5km/6.5 miles, 3hr 15mins, height gain/loss 380m/0m)

Continue along the road, passing the Struthof memorial on the left, with the wartime sand-extraction pit on the right. Just beyond the camp leave the road to the left, following the signposted footpath that drops down into the woods then turns right to follow a woodland path. Within 10mins the route turns right where the path meets a track, and this leads back up onto the road. (On the far side is the *grande carrière*, the quarry where the Struthof prisoners were forced to work.)

There are currently no GR signs at this junction. Turn left along the road, but only for a short distance. **Look out for** the first substantial vehicle track on the left, just a few hundred metres along the road. The GR5 goes down here, but the turn is not indicated – there is no signpost and the first waymark is set well back.

Continue down this track and within about 5mins **watch out carefully for** the route leaving by a footpath that climbs away to the right, indicated by a waymark. This path gains height through thick old forest, and when it meets a broader path carry straight on. This emerges after about 10mins at an extensive open area with a road just ahead. This is **Champ du Messin**, and a signpost on the forest edge points towards Champ du Feu, 2hrs ahead.

There is no clear footpath along the direction indicated, so go forward

to the road then turn left. Follow alongside the road for about 0.5km, passing a small *fontaine* in a stone shelter. There are good views to the south, where forested hills fade into the distance.

As the road starts to bend to the left, the GR leaves to the right down a track heading off through the woods and coming close to the road again in about 15mins, where there is a path junction. Turn right along a little footpath signposted for Champ du Feu.

Within a further 15mins the path reaches another track junction. The road can be seen about 50m away to the left, but the GR turns to the right along a muddy track – the waymarks are infrequent on this stretch. After about 1km a signpost directs the route off to the right towards the **Rocher de Rathsamhausen**, and the rock itself is reached some 5mins later. The rock is not a viewpoint, but it does contrast with the red sandstone that has been so common further north.

The path from the rock soon joins with a track that then emerges from the woods back onto the road. Carry on to the right along the road, and a prominent signpost soon directs the route to the left along a broad forest path that merges with another track. Carry on to the left, downhill, to arrive at a junction with a major track. To the left the signpost indicates La Rothlach, but the GR5 is pointed to the right towards a place known as the **Ancienne Métairie**, only a few minutes distant.

The GR5 does **not** follow the path that goes on past the log-sided shelter. At the junction 30m back from the shelter a signpost indicates that the route to Champ du Feu forks to the right up a footpath. This path gains height and reaches a junction where the path to Champ du Feu Auberge leaves to the right (30mins distant, red disc route). The GR5 carries on along the main path, which is a clear earth path through beech woods.

A few hundred metres beyond this junction the path swings sharply left, around the head of a wooded valley. Follow this clear woodland path, passing the path off left to Chaume des Veaux (*refuge*), crossing a track and then forking right as waymarked. Carry on ahead to reach the road at the **Col du Champ du Feu**.

Col du Champ du Feu to Le Hohwald
(6.5km/4 miles, 2hr, height gain/loss 0m/510m)

Where the path emerges from the trees, turn immediately sharply left to reach a fork where both paths head back into the woods. The path on the right leads to the *tour*, which is an old Club Vosgien lookout tower, now too dilapidated to climb. The GR5 takes the left-hand path, signposted towards Le Hohwald.

The next short stretch was very difficult at the time of writing as there was a great mass of fallen trees across the path. If this situation has not changed, diverting around them and relocating the correct path on the other side can take a little time, as the waymarks beyond are quite widely spaced.

Just beyond this area the path continues downhill to meet a broad track where the route turns left. A few minutes later a clear signboard sends the GR off to the right towards the Source de l'Andlau.

After crossing another track the route soon reaches the *source*, a small spring of clear water. From here the path drops down through woods for the next 2km, crossing straight over several tracks on the way and eventually reaching the **Cascade d'Andlau** waterfall. The GR5 goes to the left over a footbridge that crosses the stream just above the falls. (A short diversion, going down the steps to the right to see the falls from below, is well worthwhile.)

Returning to the top of the falls, take the left-hand, uphill fork just beyond the little bridge, as indicated. This path leads on through the woods to reach, after some 15mins, a footbridge over a second stream, and then heads downhill to soon meet a small road. Follow this down to the right.

After only 50m the route follows a path along the bank to the left.

Cascade d'Andlau

This path leads around the perimeter of the campsite at Le Hohwald to reach a road just by the entrance to the site. Take the left-hand fork in the road ahead and follow this down into **LE HOHWALD** (hotel/restaurants, cafés, *gîte*, campsite, shop – closed Tue).

Le Hohwald to Mont Ste-Odile
(9.5km/6 miles, 3hr, height gain/loss 290m/100m)

Turn left on meeting a more major road, the Rue Ste-Odile. As this road turns to the right, the route carries on ahead up a pedestrian way. Do not follow this left, but carry on past the *salle polyvalente* (community building), which functions as a *gîte d'étape*. Opposite this building the GR takes a footpath that climbs the bank behind a little electricity supply substation.

Not far beyond, the GR5 forks right while the Grande Ceinture path (blue discs) forks left – the arrow here could send GR5 walkers the wrong way.

Continuing ahead, this clear path reaches another fork in about 20mins where the GR goes to the right, downhill to the road. Cross the road and follow the path opposite, signposted for Welschbruch, which soon crosses a small stream. Fork left, uphill, just beyond, and some 5mins later the route takes a footpath that leaves to

85

the left of the track. After a short muddy stretch this path goes along between two banks. Take the obvious path to the left, which climbs the bank and joins a track running alongside.

The track meets a road where you go right and along to the roundabout. Take the D130 to the left, and less than 200m up the road look out for a footpath leaving to the right. Go down this path, which leads past the back of the *auberge* at **Welschbruch**. On reaching a junction of footpaths, take the right-hand, downhill path signposted for Breitmatt. This drops down then turns to the left and runs parallel to the road, which is just down to the right.

The GR signs on this stretch can be confusing. They have been attached so firmly to the trees that subsequent tree growth has caused the signs to split and point in odd directions. The route carries on along this same path, crosses straight over the yellow cross route and reaches the road at **Carrefour de la Breitmatt** after almost half an hour.

Cross the road and continue along the track on the other side. This crosses a clearing then merges with another path. Carry on ahead, following GR signs towards Ste-Odile.

The route goes straight over the next path junction, but soon after meets a major track and turns right along it. Follow this track for about 15mins to reach a bench positioned at a fine viewpoint overlooking the hills towards Barr and Andlau, and

the Plain of Alsace beyond. Very soon after, the path forks and the GR is directed along the left-hand, higher path, with Ste-Odile still 40mins ahead.

This path soon leads out onto a road, close to the junction of **Carrefour de la Bloss**. At this fork the D426 goes left, the D854 goes right, and the GR leaves on a path between these two roads. There is more than one path leaving here; turn along the lesser path that keeps to the left and sets off parallel to the left-hand road (D426). This path follows the curve of the road and soon reaches the substantial remains of the **Mur Païen**.

The Mur Païen

This massive 'pagan wall' is an intriguing prehistoric feature. It is more than 10km long, 1.5m thick and 3m high at its best-preserved sections, but opinion amongst archaeologists is divided as to who built it, when and why. Some suggest that it was a defensive enclosure, others that it was a religious site. What is not in doubt is that it is an impressive piece of work, its huge sandstone blocks carefully fitted together and originally consolidated with wooden pegs.

There is a footpath that follows the circuit of the wall and takes about 5hrs, but the short sections that can be seen from the GR5 give an idea of its scale.

Go through the gap in the wall and continue along the path ahead, crossing over the yellow cross route.

After about 10mins this passes the **Beckenfels**, an outcrop of strangely shaped rocks. Keep to the path ahead, along the left side of the rocks, and avoid the GR5 path to the right to Barr for the time being. Only minutes later a car park comes into view down on the left, and the route takes a little path (waymarked) that branches off left and leads down to it.

Carry on ahead and there is a footpath on the right (marked *piétons*) that leads along to the convent on **MONT STE-ODILE** (hotel, café/restaurant).

Mont Ste-Odile

The legend of Saint Odile tells of her being born blind but miraculously regaining her sight. She founded a convent on the top of this mountain in about 700 AD, and pilgrims still come to Mont Ste-Odile to visit the saint's sarcophagus in the 12th-century chapel, and to seek healing for eye complaints at a nearby sacred spring.

There are fine views from the terrace surrounding the buildings. In one direction is Champ du Feu, and in the other the plains of Alsace and the River Rhine, with the Black Forest beyond.

Mont Ste-Odile to Barr

(8km/5 miles, 2hr 30mins, height gain/loss 70m/630m)

Coming out of the main gateway of the convent the GR5 heads left down a flight of steps. A diversion to the left reaches the sacred spring, but the GR5 turns right at the bottom of the steps to follow the Chemin de la Croix. Now you need to retrace your steps back along the GR5 from the car park as far as the **Beckenfels** rocks. Immediately beyond is a fork – to the right is the path back to Le Hohwald (GR5) and to the left is the route ahead, the GR5 towards Maennelstein and Barr.

After about 5mins the path passes a lookout point a short distance off to the left, with more sections of the Mur Païen nearby. Soon after, the route turns left along a broader track, and then crosses straight over a track junction to reach the summit of **LA BLOSS**, which is totally surrounded by trees.

The path passes a little open shelter before reaching the *table d'orientation* on the top of **Maennelstein**. The ruins of Landsberg Castle are clearly visible on the hill below.

Coming down from this rock the GR5 carries on to the left, then takes a left fork at a faded waymark and continues downhill. After turning left through the Mur Païen the footpath reaches the **Rocher du Wachtstein**. This natural pillar of rock has been joined to the Mur Païen by a short length of wall, and is thought to have been an observation point used by the defenders of the wall.

The path down crosses one track and follows to the left on joining another. This soon leads to the **Kiosque Jadelot**, a wooden shelter with veranda attached overlooking a fine, open view. Soon after, the route forks left then starts to drop down quite steeply to reach a road at a place called **La Handschab**. Cross the road and carry on down the path, forking left almost straight away.

The path passes close to **LANDS-BERG CASTLE**, but you need to divert off the route to the right, just beyond a large old house, to get a closer look. The ruins are considerable, but in quite a dangerous condition.

Carrying on downhill, stay with the main path, which forks right then turns sharply left at a hairpin. Avoid the lesser path straight ahead and keep following signs for Moenkalb and Barr.

The footpath first crosses a vehicle track, then the Sentier des Chameaux. The GR5 passes close to the Kiosque Hartmann, an open wooden shelter, but turns left some 20m before reaching it. Within a further 5mins a GR sign directs the

route off on a path down to the right. This passes the Maison Forestière Moenkalb, which is also an *auberge*, and then joins a lane. Follow this lane to the left and continue along it for almost 1km until you reach a fork. Leave the lane here along the clearly signed path between the two roads.

The path twists down through woods, crossing a lane on two occasions before emerging onto a road close to the Kiosque Emile Muller-Apffel.

The route does not continue along the road here – take the path leaving from the bend just ahead of the *kiosque*. This reaches the Hering monument, where the route takes a track to the right. On the way down into **BARR** (hotels, campsite, restaurants, cafés, shops) this track provides an interesting view over the rooftops of the town and comes out onto a road. Cross over, following the sign towards the town centre. Turn to the left down some broad steps to reach a crossroads where the GR5 carries on ahead along the Rue de l'Église.

Barr to Andlau
(3.5km/2.5 miles, 1hr 15mins, height gain/loss 40m/20m)

There is plenty of scope for exploring the many side streets of the old quarter of the town. The GR5 carries on down the Rue des Boulangers to the junction at the end, where a GR

signpost sends the route ahead towards Ungersberg. This goes along the Rue Taufflieb. Go straight across the Avenue des Vosges, taking the D362 towards Mittelbergheim, and follow this quiet residential street out of the town. The houses are soon left behind, to be replaced by vineyards.

Just before reaching the village of **MITTELBERGHEIM** (hotel, restaurants), follow the GR waymarks along the road that forks to the right. Two towers joined by a curtain wall form the distinctive ruins of Andlau Castle above the vineyards on the right.

On reaching a road junction cross straight over, following the signposts towards Andlau. This leads onto a pleasant lane flanked by vineyards that joins the D62. Turn right to carry on down the main road for about 1km, past a road to the Château de Spesbourg, into the village of **ANDLAU** (hotels, restaurants, cafés, shops).

Andlau to Ungersberg
(7.5km/4.5 miles, 2hr 30mins, height gain/loss 680m/0m)

Turn right along the D425 into a square with a statue of Ste Richarde, founder of the local abbey. Follow the road as it curves right in front of a large building, then left up past the church.

Andlau
Andlau has a particularly fine Romanesque church, much of the building dating from the 12th century. There are some outstanding stone carvings on the west and north sides of the church, and also around the doorway. These show Bible stories, mythical animals, and some cautionary scenes such as people succumbing to temptation by using false weights and measures.

When the major road bears right, just past the church, carry straight on up a very minor road, the Rue Clemenceau. At a fork take the road to the left that climbs sharply uphill,

signposted to Gruckert, and after a few minutes the road becomes a track. Pass a lane to the left and continue ahead through light woodland until the track reaches another road. **Turn left here**, uphill, although there are currently no waymarks (ignore the footpath that continues on the opposite side of the road).

Continue along this road and straight across two crossroads. Where the road hairpins sharply to the right, take the rough stony track straight ahead and follow the GR waymarks on through the forest to the **Col de Gruckert**. The route turns right, then left, to go round the back of the Amis de la Nature *refuge* at **GRUCKERT**, and continues through conifer woodland to reach a crossroads at the **Carrefour du Hasselbach**. The GR5 route towards Ungersberg is clearly signposted ahead.

Keep with the track to reach the Col de l'Ungersberg, a clearing in the forest, then take the track to the left, signposted to Ungersberg, which is the shapely wooded hill visible ahead. Cross a track and continue to a T-junction. Turn left, going uphill a little more steeply on a track that begins to hairpin, and turn left on one of the bends onto another track. Leave it again soon to the right, still following GR waymarks and signs to **UNGERSBERG**, to reach the lookout tower on the summit.

Ungersberg to Bernstein Castle
(8.5km/5.5 miles, 2hr 45mins, height gain/loss 180m/540m)

From the summit follow the GR signs towards Bernstein and Châtenois. The route bends to the right, and after a minute or so follows to the left down a broader path. After another few minutes watch out for an arrow and waymark that point the route off to the left. This obvious footpath goes down through the trees and crosses straight over a track. Follow this path as it zigzags down and eventually emerges at a large clearing with a picnic bench.

At this clearing Sommerain is signposted to the left. Turn left along the vehicle track (**do not** be tempted to leave the clearing by the footpath next to the picnic bench). Some minutes later, leave this track on a small footpath to the left.

On reaching another forest track turn right, but once again leave the track on the left, still following signs for Châtenois, and zigzagging down through beech woods. On joining another track turn left uphill for just a

Looking out from the slopes of Ungersberg

few hundred metres, then take the right-hand, lower fork ahead. After a few minutes the GR5 leaves by a footpath to the right and passes an enclosed water source.

When this footpath comes out at a vehicle track, turn right towards Bernstein. The GR5 leaves by a footpath to the left that merges with another broad path, following it to the left. On joining another track at a T-junction, turn right opposite some houses and in a few minutes this reaches a road.

Turn right to the road junction that is very close by – the sign indicates that this is **Sommerain**. Turn left along the road, but after only about 100m **leave to the right** on a footpath between two forest plantations – there is no signpost here, so you need to be looking out for the waymark.

Continue through the woods, crossing several other tracks and following ahead. Waymarks are scarce on this path, which goes through open woodland allowing views to the right towards the hilltop castle of Haut-Koenigsbourg in the distance. After at least 1km take the left fork where this is indicated and soon reach the junction at **Neue Matten**.

Turn left along a vehicle track and carry on to reach a road junction where the D253 and D203 meet. Cross the D253 and take the footpath that leaves to the right of the D203. At the next road **do not take the path directly opposite**, but turn right for about 30m, then left at a GR5 direction board pointing down a wide path through trees, to reach a clearing at **Teufelsloch**. Leave this by a tarmac lane signposted towards the Château Fort du Bernstein.

After about 100m turn left on a wide footpath that runs parallel to the lane and then rejoins it a few minutes later. Immediately the route leaves the road again along a track to the left. Follow this for 100m, then branch right along a path that leads onto another track. Turn left along this until you reach a junction next to a large and rather odd-shaped rock, the **Rocher de l'Âne**.

Turn right onto the footpath that passes the rock and follow this path ahead to reach the large clearing at **Schulwaldplatz**.

Do not be misled by an ambiguous waymark – the route does not leave by the little footpath to the left of the road just by the clearing, but follows the tarmac road, the Chemin Forestier du Château, which goes steeply uphill.

Follow this road for about 400m, passing a locked shelter and a crucifix, to reach a fork. Take the left fork, which soon becomes a track, and continue ahead to the castle of **BERNSTEIN** – a metal stairway within the tower allows visitors to climb up and look out over the plains of Alsace. In the foreground is the village of Dambach-la-Ville, where the line of the old ramparts can still be clearly seen.

Bernstein Castle to Châtenois
(7.5km/4.5 miles, 2hr 15mins, height gain/loss 0m/350m)

Leave Bernstein Castle in the direction of Ortenbourg to reach the track junction at **Kriegshurst**. Turn to the left here, then immediately right along a second track. After a very short distance take the broad footpath that leaves to the left.

This joins another track on a bend at a place called **Rehhag**. Take this track to the left, and at the next fork branch right along quite a broad footpath. Continue along this footpath, and when it joins a more major track follow it to the left. At a picnic site there is an information board for the geological site of the Massif de l'Ortenbourg.

The substantial white granite remains of **ORTENBOURG CASTLE** lie just beyond. Follow the waymarked path that leads past the castle, and from Ortenbourg take the little rocky path ahead that soon drops down and reaches a small clearing. The GR5 turns to the right, downhill, but a short diversion ahead gives a closer view of **RAMSTEIN CASTLE**, a single tower that is now in a dangerous condition.

The path is clear but quite steep as it winds down though the trees. Follow the GR waymarks downhill to reach a car park. Turn left down the road in the direction of Châtenois, passing vineyards, to reach the main road about 1.5km ahead. (**SCHERWILLER** campsite is some distance to the left from this junction.) Turn right along this road and follow it into **CHÂTENOIS** (hotel, *gîte*, restaurants, cafes, shops), crossing straight over the busy N59 at a roundabout.

Châtenois to Wick
(5km/3 miles, 1hr 30mins, height gain/loss 210m/0m)

Continue down the length of the main street, passing the Rue de l'Église which leaves to the right – a short diversion along here soon reaches the old town gates. The GR continues down the main street, passing the narrowed section of road and leaving along the next road to the right. This climbs up towards the church, passing the entrance to the *gîte d'étape* on the right.

Keep to the Rue St-Georges, on the left of the church, then follow waymarks along a track that leads off to the right. The GR5 follows signs to the right along a concrete road through vineyards. Fork right, then as the track starts to drop back towards the town, follow signs up a track to the left. This enters woods, turning sharply left around a hairpin bend. Continue along this broad track for

The hilltop site of Haut-Koenigsbourg, seen from Wick

about 25mins as it goes along the left-hand side of a wooded valley.

When the main track hairpins to the left (blue ring route), another track carries on ahead with a GR waymark – follow this to Borne Pentagonale, a five-sided marker stone. Just beyond this there is a clearing with a wooden shelter and a meeting of tracks. Turn to the left, following the sign to Wick, and continue ahead with a high wire fence to the left – this is the boundary of the Montagne des Signes sanctuary for Barbary apes. At **WICK** there is a café and information board by the entrance to the sanctuary.

Wick to Haut-Koenigsbourg
(4km/2.5 miles, 1hr 15mins, height gain/loss 330m/0m)

Take a path into the woods on the right to skirt the grounds of the sanctuary, then turn right along a forest track at the Lieu dit La Wick signpost. Follow the route to Haut-Koenigsbourg, soon leaving to the left off the track, and in a few minutes the road to Koenigsbourg comes into view. The GR5 does not join the road, but follows a footpath that runs to the right of and parallel to it, past picnic areas, to Borne Hexagonale. Where the path forks, take the left branch, still parallel to the road. Pass a point called **Kreuzweg**, taking the middle track ahead signposted to Haut-Koenigsbourg.

The path now moves away from the road, climbing quite steeply through the woods. When it meets the road again, cross over, then at a junction with another footpath turn sharply right. The path then meets a higher loop of the road. Cross the road once again, taking the footpath slightly to the left on the other side. This zigzags uphill, past a hotel on the left, following signs to **HAUT-KOENIGSBOURG** (hotel, café/restaurant, snack-stall). The path continues by a series of hairpins, steep in places, until the castle buildings appear above.

Haut-Koenigsbourg

Although it stands on a site fortified from at least the 12th century, much of the building visible today dates from the beginning of the 20th century. The castle was taken by the Swedes in 1633 and substantially destroyed, the ruins eventually becoming the property of the town of Sélestat. In 1899 they were presented to Kaiser Wilhelm II, who conceived the idea of restoring and furnishing the castle in a representation of feudal style. The restoration may not be totally accurate in historical detail, but it is undoubtedly impressive.

Haut-Koenigsbourg to Thannenkirch
(4km/2.5 miles, 1hr 15mins, height gain/loss 0m/250m)

Carry on along a broad footpath with the castle to the right, then continue downhill to cross the road, following the waymarks. Keep on this broad and well-waymarked footpath, crossing a lower loop of the road. This path then merges with a track, still going downhill, and reaches a road junction with a large old house at the corner. Follow the D42 in the direction of Thannenkirch.

After about 100m leave this road by a footpath to the right, and soon the route turns to the left to run parallel with the road. Where this path joins a track, carry on along it to the right to pass behind the houses of the tiny village of **LA CAVE DE RODERN**. Beyond the village, cross straight over a track and follow a footpath through the woods. Keep with this path for over 1km, crossing several other tracks to reach a picnic area where you turn right down the road, passing an information board giving details of the facilities in Thannenkirch. Just beyond this, take the minor road that forks to the left and follow it as it curves up to join the main road. Carry on ahead through the centre of **THANNENKIRCH** (hotels, café/restaurants).

A little beyond the village the road takes a sharp bend to the left, but the GR5 continues on a track straight ahead. Go left at a fork, and after only a couple of minutes take a footpath that climbs up obliquely to the right through the woods. Follow it round the valley side to meet a track. Turn right along this track and carry on until it takes a sharp bend to the left. Just at this turn there is a junction where the GR5 takes the upper path, to the right, towards Trois Châteaux.

On emerging onto a larger track, follow the waymarks to the right. This very soon reaches the place called **Ici les Quatre Chênes**, where there are indeed four oaks. Turn to the left, again towards Trois Châteaux.

After about 5mins leave the forest track for a path on the left, still sign-posted towards *les châteaux*. Continue to a T-junction (with a very minor track opposite) and turn left (currently there are no waymarks here). Very soon there is a path junction and a divergence of GR5 routes. An easier route leaves to the right, going down directly to the castle of St-Ulrich. To visit the hilltop castle of **HAUT-RIBEAUPIERRE** take the path straight ahead and carry on for less than 10mins, although the castle is in a dangerous condition and access is not allowed.

From Haut-Ribeaupierre continue down a steep, zigzagging, but feasible route to reach a small

Girsberg Castle above the town of Ribeauvillé

clearing and the extensive ruins of the second castle, **ST-ULRICH**, just beyond. The route continues downhill, giving an excellent view of the third castle, **GIRSBERG**, on its rock promontory. **RIBEAUVILLÉ** (hotels, two campsites, restaurants, cafés, shops) is reached in less than half an hour by following a distinct, wide path that hairpins down through the woods. The route passes beside vineyards with a good view of the town below, then turns right to drop down beside the town wall to reach the Place de la République.

The tourist office and the many facilities of the town are down the Grand'Rue to the left.

Ribeauvillé

Ribeauvillé lies at the edge of the Plain of Alsace, surrounded by vineyards and overlooked by the three ruined castles on the nearby slopes of the Vosges. The history of the town is strongly linked with the Lords of Ribeaupierre, one of the most powerful families in Haute-Alsace. They came to prominence in the 13th century and their lands included Ste-Marie-aux-Mines, where exploitation of silver mines generated huge wealth. Some evidence of this age of prosperity can be seen in the museum situated in the mairie.

The town has long been associated with travelling musicians (ménétriers), and a traditional festival, the Pfifferdaj, is still held every September.

The Grand'Rue and the little backstreets on both sides are flanked by old buildings. Timber-framed houses dating to the 16th and 17th centuries are much in evidence, and the sole surviving town gate, the Porte des Bouchers, still stands astride a narrow cobbled street.

SECTION 5

GR5 Ribeauvillé to Mittlach

(52km/32.5 miles)

This section includes one of the most popular stretches of the route in the Vosges. While the landscape is generally one of rounded hilltops, the high ridge that forms part of this walk has a rugged, east-facing cliff line, with views over glacial lakes set in imposing cirques in the valley below.

The lively little town of Ribeauvillé, with its narrow streets, traditional buildings and flavour of old Alsace, provides a pleasant start to this section. The footpath leaves the town to climb through extensive woodland, and it comes as a surprise in this peaceful landscape of trees and mountain to stumble over reminders of wartime conflict. The remains of trenches and blockhouses, and rusting tangles of barbed wire surrounding the summit of Tête des Faux, are relics from the First World War.

Beyond Col du Calvaire the path emerges from the cover of the trees onto the *hautes chaumes* (high pastures), with excellent views. The GR5 crosses the Réserve Naturelle de Tanet–Gazon du Faing, an area of forest, bog and grassland. From here the landscape of the central Vosges can be appreciated, dominated by forested ridges with a scattering of villages in the valleys between.

For many kilometres between Col du Calvaire and Col de la Schlucht the path runs along the top edge of cliffs that drop down steeply to the wooded valleys below. A series of lakes, including Lac Blanc and Lac des Truites, is situated just to the east. Although there are some short, steep climbs, the walking along the ridge is easy. Le Hohneck, at 1362m, is the highest point reached on the GR5 so far, and an abrupt final descent reaches the Wormsa Valley. The two tranquil lakes of Schiessrothried and Fischboedle, set in the wooded hillside, offer places to linger on the way down.

This is a good section of the walk for spotting chamois, but any disturbance will see them disappear. Other attractions include the ruins of Bilstein Castle and the botanic garden at Haut-Chitelet (near to Col de la Schlucht), both just off route.

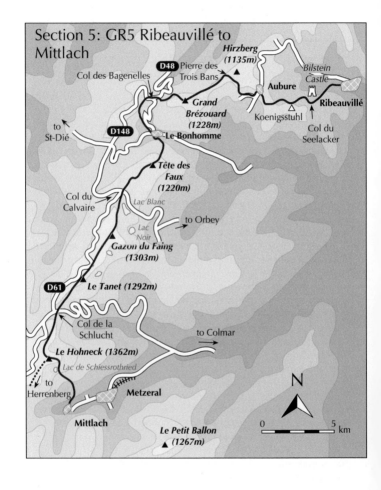

Section 5: GR5 Ribeauvillé to Mittlach

Col des Bagenelles
D48 Pierre des Trois Bans
Hirzberg (1135m)
Bilstein Castle
Aubure
Grand Brézouard (1228m)
Koenigsstuhl
Ribeauvillé
to St-Dié
D148
Le Bonhomme
Col du Seelacker
Tête des Faux (1220m)
Col du Calvaire
Lac Blanc
Lac Noir
to Orbey
Gazon du Faing (1303m)
Le Tanet (1292m)
D61
Col de la Schlucht
to Colmar
Le Hohneck (1362m)
Lac de Schiessrothried
to Herrenberg
Metzeral
Mittlach
N
Le Petit Ballon (1267m)
0   5 km

This section can be walked in two fairly strenuous days, with a suggested stop either at Le Bonhomme, where there are hotels, or the hotel/*gîte* at Étang du Devin. The second day could be broken into two very short days by stopping at Col de la Schlucht, where there is a hotel.

Accommodation and Food

Km	Cumulative km		
		Ribeauvillé	Hotels, campsites (2), restaurants, cafés, shops
10.5		Aubure	*Gîte*, campsite, restaurant, baker
5.0	15.5	Pierre des Trois Bans	Shelter
8.0	23.5	Col des Bagenelles	Hotel, *refuge*, *gîte*, *ferme-auberge*
2.5	26.0	Le Bonhomme	Hotels, campsite, restaurants, café/bar, shop
2.0	28.0	Étang du Devin	Hotel/*gîte*
5.5	33.5	Col du Calvaire	Hotel, *refuges*, café/restaurant
4.0	37.5	Gazon du Faing	*Ferme-auberge*, 0.5km off route
2.0	39.5		Turn off for Schanzwasen (*auberge*/hotel), 1.5km off route
4.0	43.5	Col de la Schlucht	Hotels, restaurant
1.5	45.0	Trois Fours	*Refuge/gîte*, *ferme-auberge*
1.5	46.5		Turn off for Chaume du Haut-Chitelet (*refuges*), 1km off route
0.5	47.0	Le Hohneck	Restaurant, *auberge*/hotel, just off route
1.5	48.5	Schiessrothried	*Refuge*
2.5	51.0		Turn off for Metzeral (hotels, shops), 3km off route
1.0	52.0	Mittlach	Hotel, restaurant/bar, shops (closed Mon pm)
			Turn off for campsite (2.5km off route)

Alternative Route from Le Hohneck

	Le Rainkopf	*Refuge*

Contact details for tourist offices and accommodation are in the appendix.
Note Wild camping is not allowed in the nature reserve at Gazon du Faing.

Maps
IGN 1:100,000 sheet 31
Club Vosgien 1:50,000 sheet 6/8

Ribeauvillé to Aubure

(10.5km/6.5 miles, 3hr 15mins, height gain/loss 700m/140m)

Storks

Ribeauvillé is one of the places on the GR5 where storks are most likely to be seen. These elegant birds are symbols of prosperity and the emblem of Alsace. By the early 1970s the fall in numbers of this popular bird was so marked that in 1976 the Centre for the Reintroduction of Storks was set up in Hunawihr, 2km south of Ribeauvillé. Storks migrate to Africa for the winter, and a huge proportion of them were not returning – hunting, accidents with power lines, heavy use of pesticides, and drought in the countries where they over-wintered all took their toll.

The solution was to keep some of the birds in Alsace over the winter. Before being allowed to fly free, young birds are kept in captivity for two years until they lose their instinct to migrate. Food has to be provided over the winter, as it is lack of food that makes migration necessary. From a low point of two breeding pairs in the whole of Alsace in 1982, numbers have increased to over 200 pairs.

These large black-and-white birds, with long red legs and beaks, are quite distinctive, and their nests on towers and chimney stacks are also obvious. Massive constructions of sticks and mud, the nests are 1.5–2m in diameter, 0.6–1m high, and weigh up to 500kg. Despite the mess and risk of structural damage, having a stork's nest on the roof is considered lucky, and platforms are sometimes provided to encourage them.

In Ribeauvillé a stork's nest can usually be seen on the old tower in the Rue du Rempart de la Streng, not far from the tourist office.

From the Place de la République go up the Route de Ste-Marie-aux-Mines, following a GR5 signpost for Aubure. On reaching a traffic island turn sharply left and follow the road for several hundred metres. Turn right along the Rue St-Morand, and at the end of this short road continue up an earth footpath through open woodland.

This path climbs steadily, and within a few hundred metres reaches an oblique path junction where the GR5 turns along a path branching off sharply to the left. (Although the path ahead is signposted as the yellow cross route towards Hôtel Pépinière, there are currently no GR5 waymarks pointing off to the left, so **this turn could very easily be missed**.)

Follow the path as it hairpins up the hill, emerging onto a broader vehicle track where the route carries on to the right for about 20m, then leaves to the left up a footpath.

The path then reaches another track just beside a junction. Cross over and go up the track opposite, signposted towards Col du Seelacker and Aubure. In a very short distance take the woodland footpath up to the left. Cross straight over a path that leads down to Vallon du Bilstein and continue ahead, with hardly any waymarking, until you reach the **COL DU SEELACKER** about 20mins later – the small clearing and pond that lie at the col are entirely surrounded by woodland. Turn right to reach a slightly staggered crossroads. The route goes uphill, almost straight ahead, following the sign to Aubure. Continue along this forest track, ignoring a path on the left signposted to Riquewihr, until you meet a more major track. Ahead is a sign to Château de **BILSTEIN**, 300m off the route. The GR5 swings round to the left, towards Koenigsstuhl and Aubure.

In a few minutes the path reaches a large tree labelled 'Sapin des Français'. Leave the main vehicle track here and take the footpath to the left through the forest to reach a gravel track. Turn right past a memorial cross, and immediately beyond take a left fork.

Branch to the right, uphill, at the next fork. The track hairpins sharply to the right, but the route leaves at this point, following a sign to Koenigsstuhl. Follow this woodland path uphill and after about 15mins a large rock comes into view on the right. Close inspection reveals an inscription, confirming that you have indeed reached the **KOENIGSSTUHL** (King's Seat).

Koenigsstuhl

The rock at Koenigsstuhl has two indentations, which with a bit of imagination can be used as seats. Nowadays the surrounding trees considerably restrict the view out across the valley.

The path levels out now. At a division in the track keep to the more major, left-hand branch. Follow this to a clearing and take the footpath opposite down through the trees. Pass over another little track and carry straight on, through younger woodland, to reach a picnic site where there is a Club Vosgien memorial. The footpath goes slightly to the right of the picnic area. On reaching a major track, turn left.

At the next junction turn right, but almost immediately drop down off the vehicle track onto a very broad earth path. At a clearing with a fork take the left path, signposted Aubure. This comes out onto a road which you follow to the right down into the village of **AUBURE** (*gîte*, campsite, restaurant, baker), the highest village in Alsace. Head along the left fork, towards the church, for the village centre.

Aubure to Pierre des Trois Bans
(5km/3 miles, 1hr 30mins, height gain/loss 330m/0m)

On reaching the church and the *mairie*, turn sharply left, following the road uphill. At a road junction there are various marker signs, but the GR5 goes straight ahead, continuing up the road towards the Col de Fréland. Just over 5mins later turn right at the col along a road past a *belvédère*. Ignore the first vehicle track to the right and continue along the road for a further 200m. The route then forks up a vehicle track to the right, the Chemin Militaire, which has an arrow to Pierre des Trois Bans. At a junction where another track crosses diagonally, take the higher track ahead, effectively straight on.

After about 15mins the route leaves the track by a minor fork to the right, with a sign indicating the direction of **PIERRE DES TROIS BANS** (shelter). Almost immediately, fork right and continue uphill to a junction and take the lesser used, less steep track to the left.

Pierre des Trois Bans to Le Bonhomme
(10.5km/6.5 miles, 3hr 15mins, height gain/loss 100m/540m)

'Pierre des Trois Bans' is painted across a shelter in a triangular clearing at a crossroads. From here a diversion of a couple of hundred metres reaches a viewpoint where there is an outlook across the valley to hills beyond, but the view is quite closed in by trees.

From the clearing the route goes to the left and drops downhill to reach a broad forestry track coming in from the left. Follow it ahead and continue past another track coming in from the right. The view gradually opens up on both sides of the ridge. Keep to the track as it curves left, signposted to Brézouard. Leave the main track by a footpath to the right, following the signs to Brézouard and Col des

Bagenelles. Less than 10mins later **watch out for** a little path leaving to the left – this goes uphill onto the granite top of Petit Brézouard, where there is a broad view of the surrounding hills.

The path dips down, past a rather dilapidated Club Vosgien shelter, then rises onto another summit which, although higher, has its view restricted by trees. Take the narrow path through the woodland opposite, climbing up to the summit of **GRAND BRÉZOUARD** (1228m). Slightly to the right of the summit clearing there is a path heading steeply downhill. The GR5 soon turns off to the right and reaches a car park situated on a col.

Climbing Grand Brézouard

The route crosses the car park and continues uphill between the trees almost directly opposite. After about 200m turn left at a fork and follow the forest track to **COL DES BAGENELLES** (hotel, *refuge*, *gîte*, *ferme-auberge*). A road to the right (D148) goes to Col du Bonhomme and one to the left (D48) leads down to the village of Le Bonhomme. It is possible to follow this road down into the village, but the GR5 takes a more complicated but shorter route that avoids some of the hairpins.

Leave by a footpath ahead, between the two roads, across a field. This path then meets a tarmac lane. Turn left and follow the lane round a corner before leaving again on the right, down a track between fields. The route joins the D48 at a bend. Turn right, and very soon turn right again, off the road down a footpath through young woodland. After crossing the road again, the path becomes a more pronounced vehicle track. Fork right from this onto a footpath that turns into a vehicle track as it reaches the first few houses of **LE BONHOMME** (hotels, campsite, restaurants, café/bar, shop).

103

Le Bonhomme to Col du Calvaire

(7.5km/4.5 miles, 2hr 30mins, height gain/loss 540m/90m)

Follow the road into the village, cross the main road and continue along the path opposite, beside a bus shelter. This climbs quite steeply through a field to meet a lane at the top. Turn left, uphill, and this quiet lane rises up into woodland. Follow the road for nearly 2km up to the hotel/*gîte* at Étang du Devin. Leave the road here and carry on in the same direction along a broad vehicle track, signposted to Étang du Devin and Lac Blanc.

Étang du Devin is a quiet lake surrounded by woodland – a good spot to stop for a break. Leave the vehicle track here and follow the footpath, marked to Tête des Faux, opposite the First World War concrete shelter. This climbs quite steeply through conifer woodland.

Former Munitions Depot

The path passes another large concrete military building, a former German ammunition depot where munitions were winched up to be ready for use on the lines at the top of the ridge. A few old photographs inside the building give an idea of how things once looked.

The route climbs up to pass the Roche du Corbeau on the right. Beyond this, at a fork in the path bear right, signposted to Tête des Faux and Cimetière Duchesne, along a footpath that dips down through the trees.

The path soon rises again to reach the Panorama des Alpes, where a panorama board identifies the towns below and the mountains in the distance, as far as the Eiger. At the summit of **TÊTE DES FAUX**, on the high point of this section of the ridge, the route passes the remains of battle lines from 1914–18, with obvious trenches and rusty barbed wire entwined in the undergrowth.

Tête des Faux

Soon after the outbreak of war in 1914, the Germans established an artillery command post on Tête des Faux, a summit with commanding views in several directions. The French saw the nearby Col du Bonhomme as a potential approach route for their assault on Colmar and needed control of the heights alongside. On 14 September the French attacked in strength, using two battalions of crack mountain troops, the Chasseurs Alpins, together with a battalion of infantry. They seized the area and dug in. The Germans counterattacked on 24 December and pushed the French back, but could not retake the summit. These front-line positions effectively became fixed for the rest of the war.

On the hillside today the trenches remain, often hewn into the underlying rock, with opposing front lines sometimes approaching within a few dozen metres. Two fortified strong points can also be identified, and there is a memorial to the Chasseurs Alpins.

If you are interested in learning more about the First World War in the Vosges, there is a museum at Le Linge, 5km off the GR5, between Orbey and Munster, where front-line trenches have been preserved. There is also a small museum at Hartmannswillerkopf (see Section 6).

The route descends to pass a junction where the GR532 branches off to the right. Continue on to the **Carrefour Duchesne**, where the mili-

tary cemetery gives a further reminder of the area's history. An information board maps the progression of the battle front in this area, with photographs from the period. The GR5 passes the cemetery and continues straight on through the woods.

A more major forest track comes in from the right and the route follows it to the left. This leads eventually to the quite sizeable Refuge Tinfronce on the right of the track, a few minutes before reaching the **COL DU CALVAIRE** (hotel, *refuges*, café/restaurant).

Col du Calvaire to Col de la Schlucht
(10km/6.5 miles, 3hr 15mins, height gain/loss 170m/170m)

At Col du Calvaire the GR5 path reaches the D48, where there is a chalet-style café/restaurant. Cross the road and turn left, but after going only a few metres along the side of the road look out for a sign leading off to the right, along a footpath. Initially this leads down through woodland, and after just a few minutes reaches a clearing where the path turns to the right and begins to climb steadily uphill, still surrounded by trees.

Lac Blanc can be glimpsed between the trees to the left and far below. The path continues uphill and within about 1km there is a fork, with the correct route clearly marked as the right-hand path. A few minutes later the footpath leaves the forest cover behind and reaches the open

hilltop. An information board confirms that you are entering the Réserve Naturelle de Tanet–Gazon du Faing (a list of restrictions includes the requirement to keep to paths through the reserve).

The path still rises, climbing up onto a very broad ridge with views opening out to both east and west.

Boundary Stones
Occasional boundary marker stones can be seen to the left of this section of the path. They are quite eroded, but have an 'F' on the west and a 'D' (Deutschland) on the east, marking the border fixed at the end of the Franco–Prussian War in 1871. The land to the east remained part of Germany until the end of the First World War.

Lac des Truites from Gazon du Faing

The route follows a broad, worn path (a side path to the left offers a two-minute detour for a view over Lac Blanc, but the main route carries on). Within half an hour this reaches a prominent signpost at a junction where the path to the left goes to **LAC NOIR**. This lake is now joined to **LAC BLANC** by a subterranean pipeline as part of a hydroelectric scheme. The GR5 continues straight ahead, signposted to Col de la Schlucht. A few hundred metres further on the route bends right where it meets a wire fence, and the land just beyond the fence falls steeply away. Continue along the marked route to reach the signpost at **GAZON DU FAING** (*ferme-auberge* 0.5km off route).

Turn right to follow the signs indicating Le Tanet and Col de la Schlucht. The next few miles provide excellent walking as the path follows the crest. The land to the left drops away in a series of cliffs and rocky headlands, and the views extend towards the valley of the Rhine in the east. Route-finding over the following stretch should give no problems, except when misty. The path passes a series of prominent signboards that are clearly visible in this open landscape.

Pass an impressive rock, identified by a nearby sign as the **Taubenklangfelsen**, and continue along the clifftop path. After passing a final high point at Ringbuhlkopf, the route drops down to meet a minor road (D61) at a car park. This road is the Route des Crêtes, originally built for military purposes, but now providing a fine tourist drive along the crest of the Vosges. The road twists off to the right, but the GR5 carries on through the car park, leaving it on the far side where a prominent sign indicates that Col de la Schlucht is now 1hr 20mins distant.

The path ahead climbs over a rocky prominence at **ROCHE DU TANET**. Carry straight on, ignoring paths to left and right (and passing a sign to the left indicating the route to Schanzwasen Auberge). Pass the junction at **Haut de Baerenbach** and descend though woods to meet the D417 at **COL DE LA SCHLUCHT** (1139m) (hotels, restaurant). This col has more in the way of tourist developments than any passed so far, the result of its popularity as a winter skiing station, and in summer many of the facilities are still open.

Col de la Schlucht to Mittlach
(8.5km/5.5 miles, 2hr 45mins, height gain/loss 220m/830m)

Turn right along the road for a short distance, then left up a lane beside a shop. The lane soon becomes a rough track going to the left of the church. Continue uphill through woods, with glimpses of the valleys and lower hills of the Vosges through trees on the left. The path emerges into open meadows with the Alps on the skyline to the southeast. At a junction with a road there is a signpost indicating that Chalet des Trois Fours (*refuge/gîte, ferme-auberge*) lies to the left. Take the road to the right, following the sign towards Le Hohneck and Metzeral. **Look out for** a footpath that leaves the road to the left within a couple of minutes – this is the route of the GR5, although at the time of writing there is no red rectangle, only a blue triangle. Follow this path as it rises steadily up the ridge, with steep-

ening cliffs to the left, until you reach the **Col de Falimont**. There is a signpost here giving a variety of options, and the path slightly to the left of straight ahead, signposted to Sommet du Hohneck, is the one to choose (turn off here for the *refuges* at Haut-Chitelet).

Chamois

The slopes around Le Hohneck are favourite haunts of chamois, introduced into the Vosges in 1956. While chamois may well have roamed the Vosges in former times, there is no evidence to confirm this, although across the border in the Black Forest it is known that the native chamois were hunted to extinction in the 15th century. Reintroduction to the Black Forest took place in 1938, and it was 11 descendants of these animals that were released at Ranspach, near Le Markstein, in 1956, since when the population has grown substantially, with some 800 to 1000 animals in the Southern Vosges today. To avoid tree damage the forest authorities allow carefully controlled hunting, first permitted in 1975, to try to limit numbers to these levels.

Before the early 1980s chamois had no natural predators in the Vosges, although since then introduced lynx may take a few animals, but increasing disturbance from people is also an issue, and may have an influence on local populations.

From Col de Falimont there is a clear path to the top of **LE HOHNECK** (1362m) (restaurant, *auberge*/hotel just off route). This is the highest point in the immediate vicinity and has a summit restaurant and terrace, giving an impressive 360° panorama.

Alternative Route
An alternative GR5 route leaves here and takes the path that goes south from Le Hohneck. It skirts Le Kastelberg and Le Rainkopf (*refuge*) to follow the ridge before rejoining the main GR5 at Col du Herrenberg (see Section 6) after 7.5km.

The main GR5 route descends in the direction of Schaeferthal, leaving the summit by the path that starts a little to the right of the telescope, and

there are currently no red rectangle waymarks. Follow the red/white/red path signposted to Schaeferthal and drop fairly steeply to reach the **Col du Schaeferthal**. From here the GR5 follows a very rocky path to reach a VTS *refuge*. Take the footpath that drops quite steeply below the building, with Lac de Schiessrothried visible down in the valley. The route continues down a series of hairpin bends through the forest.

Turn right to reach **LAC DE SCHIESSROTHRIED** (*refuge*) and cross the dam. Immediately beyond this, turn left, following the sign for Fischboedle, and descend steeply through the trees, crossing another track (the stream from the lake is on the left). On reaching Lac de Fischboedle, cross the small dam at the outlet. This little lake is known for its picturesque setting, surrounded by steep, wooded slopes.

Follow a stony path down through the woods, turn left where this meets a vehicle track, then look out for a right turn off the track onto a forest footpath very soon afterwards. This has a GR5 signpost to Vallée Wormsa, Metzeral and Mittlach. The path follows a ledge in the hillside going down through woodland. When the route meets a small track, it veers to the right along it. The woods open out and the track crosses pastureland.

The GR5 diverges here – to the right the primary route goes to Mittlach and Herrenberg, while the left fork forms a spur to Steinabruck and **METZERAL** (hotels, shops, 3km off route). To stay with the main path, turn right to reach a vehicle track a few minutes later and keep right, following the signs, to reach the village of **MITTLACH** (hotel, restaurant/bar, shops – closed Mon pm).

Lac de Schiessrothried

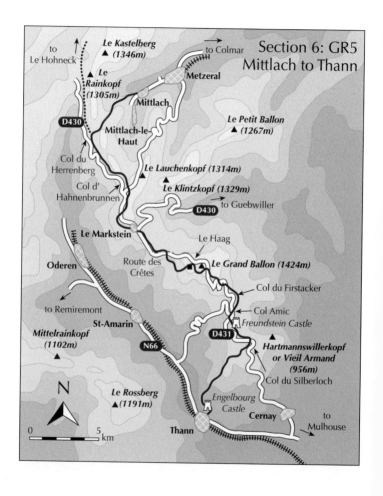

to Le Hohneck

Le Kastelberg
▲ *(1346m)*

to Colmar

Section 6: GR5
Mittlach to Thann

▲ *Le Rainkopf (1305m)*

Metzeral

Mittlach

D430

Le Petit Ballon
▲ *(1267m)*

Mittlach-le-Haut

Col du Herrenberg

▲ *Le Lauchenkopf (1314m)*

Col d' Hahnenbrunnen

Le Klintzkopf (1329m)

D430

to Guebwiller

Le Markstein

Le Haag

Oderen

Route des Crêtes

▲ *Le Grand Ballon (1424m)*

Col du Firstacker

to Remiremont

Col Amic
Freundstein Castle

St-Amarin

D431

Mittelrainkopf (1102m)
▲

N66

Hartmannswillerkopf or Vieil Armand (956m)
▲

Col du Silberloch

N

Le Rossberg
▲*(1191m)*

Engelbourg Castle

Cernay

to Mulhouse

0   5
└────────┘ km

Thann

SECTION 6

GR5 Mittlach to Thann

(41.5km/26 miles)

This section includes Le Grand Ballon, highest point of the Vosges, and easy road access means that the summit region may be busy, although elsewhere along the ridge the path is left to hikers.

Most of the climbing for this stretch of the walk is tackled soon after leaving Mittlach, when about 600m is gained over 4km. At the top of this ascent the route leaves the forest behind. Along the ridge the GR5 runs roughly parallel with the quiet tourist road of the Route des Crêtes, but only rarely along the road itself. There are many good lookout points over the wooded valleys below, and *fermes-auberge* provide refreshment opportunities at several of the cols.

Le Grand Ballon is worth visiting to see the immense view (a 360° panorama board names points of interest out to the horizon). The descent is mainly through forest, passing the ruins of Freundstein Castle. Further on, the First World War cemetery and small museum at Hartmannswillerkopf lie alongside the GR5. About 1km off route a large cross now marks the site of the battlefield where it is possible to see the remains of trenches, dugouts and shelters dating back to 1915.

On finally dropping down into the valley, the path passes Engelbourg Castle and the unusual Oeil de la Sorcière (Witch's Eye). A great deal of height is lost over the final few kilometres, to reach the small town of Thann, lying in the valley of the Thur.

This section can be walked in two days, with a suggested stop at Le Markstein (choice of hotels and *gîtes*) after a short day, leaving a longer second day.

Accommodation and Food

Km	Cumulative km		
		Mittlach	Hotel, restaurant/bar, shops (closed Mon pm)
			Turn off for campsite (2.5km off route)
6.5		Col du Herrenberg	*Ferme-auberge*
4.0	10.5	Col d'Hahnenbrunnen	*Refuge, ferme-auberge*
4.5	15.0	Le Markstein	Hotels, *gîtes, refuge*, café/restaurants
7.5	22.5	Col du Haag	*Ferme-auberge*
1.5	24.0	Le Grand Ballon	Chalet-hôtel, restaurants
1.5	25.5	Ferme du Ballon	*Ferme-auberge*
3.5	29.0	Col Amic	*Ferme-auberge*
1.0	30.0	Freundstein	*Ferme-auberge*
2.5	32.5	Col du Silberloch	Restaurant
1.5	34.0	Molkenrain	*Refuge, ferme-auberge*
7.5	41.5	Thann	Hotels, *gîte*, campsite, restaurants, cafés, shops

Contact details for tourist offices and accommodation are in the appendix.

Maps
IGN 1:100,000 sheet 31
Club Vosgien 1:50,000 sheet 6/8

Mittlach to Col du Herrenberg
(6.5km/4 miles, 2hr 15mins, height gain/loss 660m/0m)

Mittlach

Mittlach dates back to the 16th and 17th centuries, when it was settled by Tyrolean lumberjacks and iron miners, giving it a shorter history than many of the other villages in the region. Forestry continues to be important in the district today, but the iron deposits are no longer exploited. Mittlach escaped major damage in the First World War, although nearby Metzeral was right on the front line and was totally destroyed.

From the centre of the village of **MITTLACH** go uphill past the church and across a stream. The GR5 leaves the road to the right just beyond a noticeboard for the Forêt Domaniale du Herrenberg.

The footpath climbs a bank into the woods, signposted to Herrenberg. This forest is crisscrossed by a number of paths and tracks, which can make the route appear complicated, but it is well waymarked. After a few minutes cross straight over a major track, then a second, more minor track soon after. Continue through an area that, at the time of writing, had just been felled.

On reaching a broad track, turn left and follow it as it hairpins to the right, uphill. About 100m further on,

leave the track by a footpath turning sharply left and follow this ahead as it crosses other tracks.

Keep climbing this path for about 40mins, then follow the waymarks up a steep verge. This joins a broad forestry track on the outside of a hairpin bend. From here there is an excellent viewpoint looking back down the valley to **MITTLACH-LE-HAUT**. Take the forest track uphill, passing a crossroads at the Chemin des Italiens. Pass the Chemin des Souilles on the left and go straight over the next junction, passing the Chemin Renault. The route continues upwards, following a stony track, to leave the forest at an access gap. Turn left and follow the path across open pasture.

Col du Herrenberg

Vosgienne Cattle

On the high pastures in summer the GR5 walker will see many herds of cattle. The little Vosgienne is one breed worth noticing, as it is unique to this part of France. A small cow, it is usually black and white, with a continuous white line down the top of its back, and often with some black and white speckling. Vosgienne were introduced into France in the 17th century and were once widespread in the Vosges, but numbers dwindled after the last war and its future looked insecure. Plans to develop the breed were put in place in the 1970s and numbers have now increased significantly. These cows are valued for their hardiness and ability to thrive in hill conditions, and for the quality of their milk. The many local cheeses, including the well-known 'Munster' cheese, owe a great deal to the little Vosgienne.

Carry on along the path for about 15mins, currently without waymarks. It curves to the right and leads to a gate where it meets a vehicle track. Turn left to reach the **COL DU HERRENBERG** (here the high-level alternative route from Le Hohneck (see Section 5) rejoins the main GR5 from the right). The Route des Crêtes (D430) and the *ferme-auberge* of Huss lie just ahead.

Col du Herrenberg to Le Markstein
(8.5km/5.5 miles, 2hr 45mins, height gain/loss 20m/0m)

Do not join the road, but turn left on the signposted footpath out of the col. Carry on along the path for about half an hour and cross straight over a path junction, then a tractor track. Turn right at the next junction, following the signs for **COL D'HAHNENBRUNNEN** (*refuge*, *ferme-auberge*). Join the road and turn left along it for a short distance to pass the *refuge* on the left and reach the col itself. Leave the road by a footpath on the left, signposted to Le Markstein.

At Le Breitfirst cross the D27 and take the footpath opposite. When it comes out on the D430 cross the road and continue along the path, which cuts off a bend then follows the curve of the vehicle road.

The GR5 skirts **LE MARKSTEIN** (hotels, *gîtes*, *refuge*, café/restaurants), just above the road, descending to join it beyond the village.

Le Markstein

Le Markstein is a small, modern ski resort, functional rather than picturesque, but it does provide a useful centre for accommodation, snacks and meals, although there is no shop for provisions.

Le Markstein to Le Grand Ballon
(8.5km/5.5 miles, 2hr 45mins, height gain/loss 230m/20m)

On the far side of Le Markstein continue to a crossroads. The road to the left goes to Lac de la Lauch (D430), but take the one straight on, signposted to Le Grand Ballon (D431). The footpath starts off along the left-hand side of this road, which you follow for about 3km.

The path then reaches a signpost with alternative routes to Le Grand Ballon. Ahead is a route via Lac du Ballon, but the GR5 follows the route to the right, via Col du Haag. This involves leaving the **ROUTE DES CRÊTES** and passing through woodland to approach Col du Haag from the south. Cross the road and drop downhill. The route leaves the road along a track, but after only a few minutes forks up to the left. Ignore further paths to the left and right until reaching the road again in about half an hour.

Temperature Inversion

From the slopes of Le Grand Ballon the effect of temperature inversion is sometimes an impressive spectacle. When a layer of colder air is trapped in the valleys, the result is a sea of cloud across the lower ground, with the hilltops of the Vosges appearing as islands breaking through to the sunshine above. Most frequently seen on cool autumn mornings, the cloud layer can extend right across the Rhine Valley as far as the distant Alps.

Turn left uphill to reach the junction at the **COL DU HAAG**, where the Ferme-Auberge du Haag is to the left and the GR5 goes to the right, alongside the road. As the road curves to the left, the route follows a footpath up the hill ahead, climbing steadily, curving round to the right. Follow this stony path for about 0.5km around the south side of the summit. It then turns sharply around to the left, and it is a short climb from here to the top of **LE GRAND BALLON** (1424m) (chalet-hotel, restaurants).

Le Grand Ballon to Col Amic
(5.5km/3.5 miles, 1hr 45mins, height gain/loss 0m/590m)

Le Grand Ballon

The radar dome on the top of Le Grand Ballon is visible for a considerable distance, and the detailed panorama board on the surrounding terrace is worth a visit. In clear weather it is possible to see the Alps and the Black Forest, as well as the hills and valleys of the Vosges. Slightly down the hill is the Diables Bleus memorial, commemorating a light infantry division of the French army who fought here in the First World War. Further down the hill you pass the scant remains of the old hotel on the way to the present Hôtel du Grand Ballon. This hotel is run by the Club Vosgien, a long-standing organisation for walkers, so despite the rather grand marble flooring and wood panelling, walkers are welcome and a reasonably priced set meal is usually available. Opposite is a more recent restaurant, and between the two is the car park where there are stalls selling souvenirs and local produce to the many tourists who come to enjoy the views.

Descend from the summit to meet the road at the Hôtel du Grand Ballon. Follow the road to the right, signposted to Vieil Armand, and just beyond a ski lift on the left, look out for a GR waymark indicating a foot-path to the left downhill. Follow this path down a ski run (this may involve passing through gates in an electric barrier). Ahead is the plain of Alsace with its scattering of towns and villages.

Waymarking is scarce at this point. **Do not** be tempted to follow a path to the left towards the ski lift, but continue for over 1km down the ski run. The path heads down to a large building with a red-tiled roof, the **Ferme-Auberge du Ballon**.

At the *ferme-auberge* the route crosses the road and follows the GR5 sign indicating Col Amic via Firstacker. It continues downhill across open grassland with broad views of wooded hillsides. The path meets the road again, having cut off a hairpin bend, but crosses straight over to descend into beech wood. Carry on in the direction of Firstacker.

The path reaches a T-junction where the left-hand route is sign-posted to Judenhut, but the GR5 waymark is to the right. In a few minutes this comes out at a clearing at **FIRSTACKER**. Looking across to the hillside opposite, there is a First World War memorial chapel, the Chapelle du Sudel, with a *tricolor* flying beside it.

The route drops down to a vehicle track where there are a number of direction signs. Turn right for only a few metres, then left to follow an earth track uphill, which curves round below the chapel. Very soon the GR5 takes a small footpath to the right that drops down through conifer woods.

This path soon runs parallel to the Route des Crêtes again, then goes down to meet it at the road junction at **COL AMIC** (*ferme-auberge*).

To the left the roadsign points to Vieil Armand, and the site of this battlefield is marked by a large cross visible on a hill ahead. Another sign gives directions to a nearby *ferme-auberge* at Kohlschlag, and on both sides of the road are picnic areas with substantial stone tables and benches. The GR5 leaves the road through the picnic area on the opposite side, following the GR waymarks.

A few minutes later the path comes out on another road. The route to Chapelle Sicurani, marked with a yellow triangle, is opposite. This is not the GR5, which turns to the right along the road for about 50m. **Look out for** a footpath going up the bank on the left and continue along this path to reach the ruins of **FREUND-STEIN CASTLE**.

Freundstein Castle

At 984m Freundstein is the highest of the many castles of the Vosges. In the ownership of the same family from at least the 13th century, it was severely damaged by lightning in 1526, and soon after abandoned as the family home for more comfortable premises. As a military building it was last used as an observation post in the First World War, and heavily bombarded as a result.

The GR5 dips downhill again, through hazel wood and into a field. It comes within sight of the road, but bears left past a sign for the Ferme-Auberge Freundstein and climbs into the woods.

Once in the woods the footpath cuts into the side of the hill, for a short distance following a rocky ledge. The route comes round the head of the valley to reach a junction where a minor path goes straight ahead – the GR5 turns off to the left as indicated by the waymarks. Within 10mins this reaches another path, crossing diagonally. Turn left along here, and the route climbs steeply round the head of a little rivulet and carries on along the side of this deep, wooded valley. Between the trees it is possible to look back to the obvious landmark of the dome on Le Grand Ballon.

The footpath climbs to join the D431. The entrance to the museum and memorial of **HART-MANNSWILLERKOPF** or **Vieil Armand** is within sight to the left.

Hartmannswillerkopf Museum

The museum at Hartmannswillerkopf is a low, grey, stone building with the main door flanked by two massive statues. A rock-cut crypt contains the remains of 12,000 unknown soldiers, and a cemetery and memorial area lie behind. An information board with maps and photographs illustrates the history of the battlefield of Hartmannswillerkopf.

There was fierce fighting in the area as both sides attempted to hold the high ground overlooking the Belfort Gap. During various offensives in 1915 and early 1916 the summit changed hands eight times. Neither side was able to claim a decisive victory, and the battle lines remained static until the armistice. The name Vieil Armand was given to the hill by French soldiers, who found the local Germanic name of Hartmannswillerkopf difficult to pronounce.

The land dips down beyond the cemetery, then rises up to the hilltop battlefield, now marked with a 20m-tall cross. This area may be visited by taking a short detour from the GR5, and the trenches and bunkers, dug through solid rock, are particularly well preserved. Volunteers provide guided tours in July and August, and the museum is open from Easter to October.

The GR5 continues down the road outside the memorial, past the Auberge du Silberloch. On the right is an information board with a map showing sites in the region where traces of the 1914–18 conflict can still be seen. Also on the right is a *fontaine* (not drinking water). Leave the road to go up the track immediately beyond this to reach the **COL DU SILBER-LOCH** (restaurant).

Col du Silberloch to Thann

(9km/5.5 miles, 2hr 15mins, height gain/loss 160m/720m)

After about 200m a signpost indicates that the GR5 takes a footpath on the right. After a steady climb, turn left at a stone post and follow the path between a hedgebank and a field fence. This comes out into pasture and soon meets the end of a road. Follow the right fork uphill towards the Ferme-Auberge du **Molkenrain**. This *ferme-auberge* serves refreshments and has tables outside on the terrace, and from here the sweeping view across the valley includes Hartmannswillerkopf in the distance. Immediately past the farmhouse follow the footpath to the right, up a bank into a field – it heads straight up the hillside behind the farmhouse.

At the top of the field an access gap through the fence leads onto a track. To the left the track serves a large aerial installation, but the route goes downhill to the right, towards a *refuge* belonging to Les Amis de la Nature. On reaching the *refuge* **do not** follow the track as it bends round it to the left, but **look out for** a wooden water trough on the right. The GR5 follows the footpath that goes down to the right by this trough, signposted to Thann.

The path drops into woods again, but the view across the plains is visible between the trees to the left. When a track crosses the path, turn right along it for a few metres, then leave it again to the left. At the next, more substantial track, again turn right for a very short distance before taking a track to the left, downhill.

Camp Turenne is an open, flat clearing in the forest, surrounded by trees, and a memorial commemorates soldiers who died in the vicinity in the First World War. (A short diversion down the path to the viewpoint at Rocher d'Ostein is well worthwhile.) The GR5 continues to the right of the memorial on a clear track signposted Thann par ruines d'Engelbourg.

Further down the track is a picnic area with a view out across the valley, but climbing the outcrop of rock beside it gives an even more spectacular outlook point.

At the clearing called **Camp des Pyramides** go straight across the cross-roads, following the signpost for Thann – this earth path is quite stony underfoot at points, as it descends steadily through the forest. The next clearing offers another choice of paths. Go straight on, and after a few minutes reach the clearing of **Col du Grumbach**.

From here there are two possible routes to Thann. One, marked by a yellow cross, leaves to the left to descend by Kattenbach, but the GR5 takes the longer route via the ruins of Engelbourg Castle. Follow the Route Forestière du Rosenbourg out of the clearing, and a short way down this broad track there is a sharp turn to the right, still following the signs to Thann and Engelbourg down a well-made track.

After about 10mins turn off to the right along a woodland footpath to descend by a series of hairpin bends to **ENGELBOURG CASTLE** ruins, set on a high mound. The GR5 turns sharply left, but the easiest way to visit the ruins is to carry on round the bottom of the mound, past an information board with a plan of the fortifications, and take the path up to the castle from the south.

Engelbourg Castle

The ruins of Engelbourg Castle, dating from the 13th century, are quite extensive, although none of the walls have survived to any great height. The most notable feature is the Witch's Eye. When the castle was demolished in the 17th century, a massive piece of tower landed intact on its side – the result is a huge vertical circle of stonework with a round hole through the middle. It has been heavily repointed to keep it intact, but it is quite striking nevertheless.

From the terrace in front of the castle there is a fine outlook over Thann and the valley of the Thur to the wooded hills opposite. Down the valley there are vineyards on the lower slopes, and the plains of the Rhine in the distance. Thann is the southern starting point for the Route des Vins motor trail, which meanders through the vine-growing areas of Alsace.

Looking down on the town of Thann reveals a mixture of old and new, with a large Gothic church, a tower, and some traditional steep, tiled rooftops.

The Oeil de la Sorcière at Engelbourg

On returning to the GR5 beyond the information board, turn right. This gravel track goes down the side of a valley, initially turning away from **THANN** (hotels, *gîte*, campsite, restaurants, cafés, shops), but then swinging round past orchards to reach the edge of the town.

Follow a residential street down to a T-junction and turn left along the Rue du Rangen. Cross the River Thur and carry on along Rue Anatole to

reach the town centre. A right turn towards the church leads into an area with shops, cafés and other facilities. The tourist office is on the Rue de la Première Armée, just beyond the church, and the museum, which tells the town's story, is on the Rue St-Thiébaut, which runs from the church towards the river. To the left of Rue Anatole are more facilities and the railway station.

SECTION 7

GR5 Thann to Héricourt

(64km/39.5 miles)

This section of the GR5 crosses areas of the Western Vosges that are less accessible, and so less visited, than the more popular regions north of Thann. The exception is the area surrounding the summit of Ballon d'Alsace, where easy road access does attract visitors.

Much of the route up from Thann is wooded, with a sprinkling of remote *fermes-auberge* on the high pastures, where a refreshment stop can make a welcome break. While height has to be gained to climb out of the Thur Valley, the climbing is for the most part gradual. Deep, wooded valleys and isolated lakes make this a very attractive area, and the view over Lac des Perches, a magnificently sited glacial lake, is particularly memorable.

The high point of this section is the crossing of Ballon d'Alsace itself, at 1247m. The last few hundred metres of the climb to the summit are quite steep, but the effort is rewarded. Less developed than Le Grand Ballon, and in a wilder setting, the view from the top is excellent. South from the Ballon the route descends from the Vosges to the village of Giromagny, which has a full range of shopping and dining facilities and an interesting mining history.

The GR5 onwards from Giromagny to Brévilliers crosses the flatter land of the Belfort Gap. The route climbs up to the hilltop site of the Fort du Salbert, built in the 1870s and now largely ruined. Much of the structure of this fort is below ground, but the site allows good views over the Belfort region and beyond.

The nearest railway link is at Héricourt (3km off route), and we have used this town to define the end of the section rather than the tiny village of Brévilliers, which has few facilities.

This section can be walked in three days, the first of which is quite long. Suggested overnight stops are at the hotel at Ballon d'Alsace and the *gîte* in Évette.

Accommodation and Food

Km	Cumulative km		
		Thann	Hotels, *gîte*, campsite, restaurants, cafés, shops
6.0		Col du Hundsruck	*Ferme-auberge*; turn off for Bourbach-le-Haut
		(Bourbach-le-Haut)	Campsite, 1.5km off route
2.5	8.5	Le Rossberg	*Fermes-auberge*, 0.5km and 1km off route
2.0	10.5	Vogelstein	Turn off for Gsang (*ferme-auberge*), 1km off route
1.5	12.0	Belacker	*Ferme-auberge*
6.0	18.0	Col des Perches	Turn off for Rouge Gazon (*auberge/hotel/gîte*), 1km off route
7.0	25.0		Turn off for Boedelen (*refuge*), 1km off route
1.5	26.5	Ballon d'Alsace (road)	Hotel, *ferme-auberge*, restaurant
2.5	29.0	Plain de la Gentiane	*Refuge*
5.5	34.5		Turn off for Auberge Stalder (*gîte*) just off route
3.0	37.5	Giromagny	*Gîte*, campsite, restaurants, cafés, shops
5.5	43.0	Lachapelle-sous-Chaux	Small café/bar
4.0	47.0	Évette	*Gîte*, restaurant, café/bar.
2.0	49.0	Salbert	Shop (closed Mon)
5.5	54.5	Châlonvillars	Small shop
9.5	64.0	Brévilliers	Supermarket on main road, small shop in village
			Turn off for Héricourt, 3km off route
		(Héricourt)	Hotels, restaurants, cafés, shops

Contact details for tourist offices and accommodation are in the appendix.

Maps
IGN 1:100,000 sheet 31
Club Vosgien 1:50,000 sheet 7/8

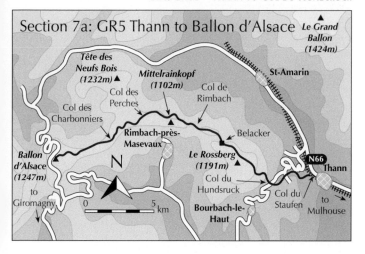

Thann to Col du Hundsruck
(6km/3.5 miles, 2hr, height gain/loss 410m/0m)

Thann

People have been walking to Thann for far longer than the GR5 has existed, as the church of St-Thiébaut was a popular destination for pilgrimages in the Middle Ages. This church, which dates from the 14th to 16th centuries, is one of the most richly decorated in all of Alsace, and its west doorway is particularly striking. The multitude of carved figures, over 450 in all, form a series of narratives which tell familiar Bible stories.

Other attractions in Thann include several fine Renaissance houses and two medieval towers, the Tour des Sorcières (Witches' Tower) and Tour des Cigognes (Storks' Tower), which once formed part of the town wall. The survival of these historic buildings is remarkable, as the town was heavily bombarded during both world wars.

Another survival from the past is the annual festival of the Crémation des Trois Sapins, held on 30 June. This half-pagan, half-Christian tradition, in which three fir trees are set alight, dates back to 1161.

Starting out from the *hôtel de ville* take the Rue Kléber (a continuation of the approach route along Rue Anatole) and cross the N66. Go over a railway level crossing, continue along the Rue Kléber and take the first road on the right (Rue des Jardins).

Turn right at the end, along the Chemin du Staufen, and follow it as

123

Beside the River Thur in Thann

it curves around to the left, heading out of town. The road begins to rise as the climb out of the valley of the Thur begins.

On the right the road passes a small block of flats – this is at the very edge of the town and the road ends here. The GR5 continues up the hill along a pleasant little woodland track and the view of the valley behind is soon lost.

Less than 1km along this path watch out for a GR waymark where the route leaves the main path by a

footpath to the right. It arrives very quickly at a triangular clearing with some wooden benches, the **COL DU STAUFEN**.

Turn left from the clearing, uphill along the Route Forestière Roi de Rome. This passes a sign for the Croix de Mission, and later reaches a bench giving a good view over the valley to the right and Le Grand Ballon in the distance. A little further on the path, now a vehicle track, enters the large clearing of **Place du Roi de Rome**.

The GR waymark here is ambiguous – do not take the false path past the picnic benches, but leave the clearing along the vehicle track. Within a couple of kilometres this broad track passes an unusual oak tree – it has six very substantial trunks – on the right.

The track emerges at a road. Turn left, passing a road junction in a clearing called the **Plan Diebolt Scheurer** on the map. There is a little wooden shelter here and a route board. The GR5 is signed as leaving to the left of the road, just beyond the junction, before taking a path immediately to the right through the forest, zigzagging steeply upwards through beech woods. It then crosses another track, which forms a narrow clearing, and carries on through the woods, still climbing steadily. After about 1km the path joins the road at the **COL DU HUNDSRUCK**. There is a small *auberge* here and signs to a second 1km away.

Col du Hundsruck to Belacker
(6km/3.5 miles, 1hr 45mins, height gain/loss 430m/200m)

Cross the road and take the gravel footpath with clear GR waymarkings, which soon climbs back into woodland and follows along the side of a steeply wooded valley. Within 1km the path reaches the edge of open pasture on the left and there is a junction where the GR5 divides. An alternative route leaves to the right, signposted 'GR5 par ferme-auberge du Thannhubel' (Thanner Hubel), indicated with a red triangle and also a red rectangle. This alternative route, not described here, rejoins the main route in about 2km. The main GR5 route is signposted ahead to Le Rossberg with the familiar red rectangle.

Cross a major track within a few metres of the last junction – the path becomes very stony as it continues through woods. When this footpath merges with a more major track, keep going ahead in roughly the same direction. The view to the left opens out over the tree-covered summits on the southern edge of the Vosges.

The track finally leaves the woods and crosses onto the high pastures. On leaving the wood, turn left along a vehicle track that is a few metres ahead (do not follow the little path that runs to the left immediately alongside the woodland boundary fence).

Ahead on the skyline is a chalet-style building – the Ski Club Rossberg *refuge*. The track leads past this chalet and immediately reaches the **Col du Rossberg**, where a fence crosses the track. (The *fermes-auberge* of Le Rossberg and Thannerhubel both lie off the route from this point.)

Go through the access point in

The lookout rock at Vogelstein, high above the Doller Valley

the fence and turn left. Follow along-side the fence to reach a signpost indicating that the GR5 branches obliquely to the right. Just below to the right is the Ski Club Mulhouse *refuge*, which has an accessible water supply.

Within only 15mins the track forks, the left fork signposted to 'Wegscheid par Sattel, Fuchsfelsen'. Take the right fork, even though GR waymarks are not apparent. This track passes isolated clumps of beech trees, and soon an odd-shaped rock comes into view on the skyline ahead. This lies just to the left of the route and gives an excellent view over the whole area. The Ballon d'Alsace is visible far ahead, but is difficult to distinguish with certainty.

The path from these rocks soon crosses a belt of beech wood. The *ferme-auberge* of Gsang is signposted off to the right (15mins), but the GR5 continues ahead. Another prominent lookout rock, known as the **Vogelstein**, is passed on the left. The view this time is over the Doller Valley to the south-west. The path loses height now and meets another track at an oblique T-junction. The route turns right along this track (the left arm leads to Masevaux via the GR532).

The buildings of the *ferme-auberge* of **BELACKER** soon come into sight, the path winding down towards them. This very traditional establishment is an excellent refreshment stop where you can enjoy coffee and home baking on the terrace.

Belacker to Col des Perches
(6km/3.5 miles, 1hr 45mins, height gain/loss 260m/180m)

Past Belacker the path immediately joins a vehicle track at a hairpin bend. Take the left-hand, uphill direction of the hairpin, but only for a short distance. The GR5 leaves by a gate on the right of the track with open grassland beyond. The blue triangle route to Wegscheid turns off left here, while the sign for the GR5 points ahead. Take the main path, which curves to the left, keeping to much the same level – it can be seen for a considerable distance ahead along the hillside.

Over the next kilometre this footpath provides fine views over the hills and valley to the south. The woods start to close in again before reaching the **COL DE RIMBACH**, a path junction where the GR5 goes straight on.

A short distance beyond the col there is a turn that needs watching out for. The GR5 leaves the track by a footpath to the left going up into the woods – there is a sign on the tree opposite, **but it could easily be missed**. This becomes a well-worn little path through dense woods. After

about half an hour the path swings sharply to the left around a headland, identifiable on the map as **MITTEL-RAINKOPF**. There is an extensive view to the right just before this.

Beyond here, **watch out carefully**. A point is reached where the path hairpins sharply to the left, then zigzags up the hill. Unfortunately the GR waymark at the very first hairpin is ambiguous, and it is very easy to carry straight on along a false trail that becomes ever fainter. The correct path keeps fairly high through the woods, not too far below the ridge of the hill. If the path you are following is losing height and there are no GR waymarks to be seen, then it may be time to backtrack.

Once past the zigzags the path is easily followed towards the junction at **COL DES PERCHES (Col du Sternsee)**. On the approach to the col a brief open area allows an appreciation of the steeply wooded face of the cirque ahead, before the final steep little descent just before joining the col.

Col des Perches to Ballon d'Alsace
(8km/5 miles, 3hr 15mins, height gain/loss 240m/50m)

At the col a signpost indicates that refreshments can be obtained at Le Rouge Gazon (*auberge*/hotel/*gîte*), 20mins to the right, while the GR5 carries on straight ahead. The col here

is surrounded by trees, but an open area of scree is soon reached where there is a view over Lac des Perches. The path continues around the wooded bowl forming the backdrop

*Lac des Perches and the forested
slopes of the Southern Vosges*

to the lake, passing another viewpoint later on.

The path leaves the cirque and soon crosses a stretch of open pasture before merging with another track coming from Rouge Gazon, with the GR5 carrying on ahead. Within minutes the route is back into woodland and soon passes a point where a small stream flows across the path.

About 5mins later, while the main track twists down in an S-bend, the official route of the GR5 takes a gravel path that follows a direct line, cutting off two of the corners. The gravel path first leaves to the left, then crosses the same track twice before leaving to the left. The point where the path finally leaves the track has a very prominent signpost.

The path crosses a clearing then heads into steeply sloping woods to emerge at the **COL DES CHARBON-NIERS**. The GR5 crosses another track and continues along the footpath opposite. Although this is a high col, there is no view beyond the woods. About 15mins after this col, look out for a GR waymark leading off to the left while the original path continues on ahead.

Another kilometre further on and the route is joined by a yellow/white/yellow waymarked route coming in from the right. The GR5 keeps with the main path, curving left. Almost half an hour later look out for the next junction, which has GR waymarks but no signpost. The route turns off to the left down a woodland path, while the original path forks away to the right.

The surrounding woodland begins to become noticeably rockier over the next stretch, and at the **Col de Morteville** the trees are in amongst tumbles of rocks. The route continues in the same direction with a path joining from the right. Within a few minutes the footpath starts to snake its way around rocks and zigzag up a steep section.

A further kilometre along the path there is a fork, the left branch signposted to Boedelen (*refuge*) and Sewen. The GR5 takes the higher fork, to the right. Continuing along here, the Ballon d'Alsace comes into view – steep sided with an extended flat top. The path to La Jumenterie leaves to the right, but the GR5 continues on ahead. In a few minutes a much closer view of the wooded eastern slope of the Ballon is revealed, close enough to see figures up on the summit. This looks encouraging, but in fact there is still a steep uphill section to tackle before getting there, and that climb starts straight away. The path takes a zigzag line up between rocks and tree roots and is hard going with a heavy pack.

The climb reaches a level footpath on the summit plateau of the **BALLON D'ALSACE** (hotel, *ferme-auberge*, restaurant). Given that there is a car park a short distance away on the far side of the Ballon, it is quite likely that there will be other visitors

129

up here, at least during the summer. To reach the main path down towards the road, turn left and walk on past several information boards. The summit plateau covers a wide area and you may wish to divert across to the *table d'orientation*, and beyond it to the statue of Joan of Arc.

The Ballon d'Alsace

The Ballon d'Alsace is an excellent vantage point for looking out over much of the Southern Vosges and beyond. There is a *sentier découvert*, with ten information boards covering such topics as geology, plants, animals, bird migrations, life on the high farms and other background. There is a theory, for example, that all the hills named 'Ballon' or 'Belchen', and there are quite a number in the region, were places of particular significance in Celtic times, owing to possible alignments between them. You may be sceptical of theories of ancient astronomical observatories, but it is an interesting idea and is described on one of the boards.

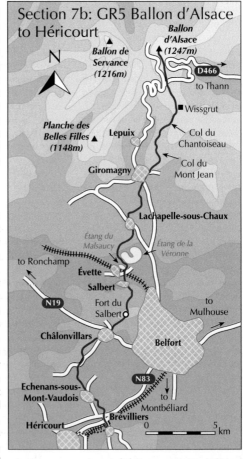

Section 7b: GR5 Ballon d'Alsace to Héricourt

The patriotic statue of Joan of Arc dates back to 1909. Alsace was still part of Germany at that time, and the Ballon was right at the edge of France, so the statue was erected to symbolise the attachment that France had for the lands of Alsace.

Ballon d'Alsace to Wissgrut
(4.5km/3 miles, 1hr 30mins, height gain/loss 50m/220m)

Coming down from the plateau, several *auberges* can be seen ahead alongside the road. At a point where the path takes a sharp right-hand turn (about 300m before reaching the road), the GR5 leaves to the left on a footpath signposted towards Giromagny.

The footpath crosses the pasture ahead, roughly parallel with the road, but well separated from it. At the far end of this large field there is an access way through the boundary fence, and the path beyond leads through a narrow belt of woodland. On the far side it passes a ski lift and continues alongside a ski run before joining a gravel track. Over to the left a break in the trees allows a clear view of the craggy south face of the Ballon.

The track soon joins the main road. The GR5 takes a footpath that runs parallel with the road and to the left of it. The path goes around the back of a *gîte rural*, then continues along the side of the road as far as a junction where the road to Masevaux leaves to the left.

Across the road is an information board at the area called **Plain de la Gentiane** (*refuge*). The signpost here currently gives contradictory information – the direction to follow is the red rectangle, which points across the road and is shown as heading towards Belfort. There is a second red rectangle sign on the same post which points

down the road to the right, apparently to Wissgrut, and is best ignored.

From this signpost cross the road and follow the vehicle track through open pasture opposite, past several ski huts. The path leads alongside a ski run. The trees begin to close in on both sides, but a wide gap to the left provides a good view over Langenberg farm and the valley below. The path leads on past the top of the ski run and there are huge numbers of yellow gentians in the open areas here. For the next kilometre the route keeps to a band of open grassland, skirting to the right of a hilltop with a statue of the Virgin. Just beyond are the old farm buildings of Wissgrut.

The signpost at **WISSGRUT** is an important one for GR5 walkers. It marks the point where **the waymarks change from red rectangles (used to the north) to red and white rectangles (used to the south)**. The system also changes, since from here on 'do not go this way' signs, in the form of crossing red and white lines, are used. The one disadvantage of the change is that the red and white waymarks are used for all GRs in France (except in the Vosges), so in regions where several GRs come into close proximity you can find yourself hiking off along the wrong trail. (**Note** Red rectangles are still used as waymarks south of Wissgrut, but they no longer mark the GR5.)

Wissgrut to Giromagny
(7km/4.5 miles, 2hr 15mins, height gain/loss 0m/600m)

From the Wissgrut signpost **do not** carry on following the red rectangle route along the vehicle track that keeps to the grassy ridge – the GR5 follows the smaller footpath (not a vehicle track) which drops down to the right of the ridge and heads towards some beech trees. The first of the red and white GR5 waymarks can be seen as you enter the beeches, and just into the trees the path meets a vehicle track. Almost immediately the first of the red and white crosses appears ahead and the route turns off to the right. Go down this path to a signpost at **Le Gros Hêtre**.

Turn left, taking the path heading down through the trees to arrive at the **COL DU CHANTOISEAU** where there is an open-sided wooden shelter. The GR5 carries on ahead on the uphill path, without much change of direction, leading directly to a short, steep section. Where the path meets an obvious fork, follow the waymarks along the right branch and continue on along the ridge ahead through dense forest. This path then leads down to the right of the ridge to a signpost at **La Grande Roche**, although it is disappointing that there is no prominent lookout rock here.

Further on the route reaches a path junction where it turns left on the uphill path (the Auberge Stalder is down the path to the right) leading to the **COL DU MONT JEAN**. Take the

path left here, towards Giromagny, (the suggested time of 1hr 30mins is surely overestimated). The route descends via a lane between hedge-banks, passes two ponds and eventually reaches a gravel track. Turn right, downhill, passing orchards. The track becomes a surfaced lane and passes houses on the edge of **GIROMAGNY** (*gîte*, campsite, restaurants, cafés, shops).

Follow the lane down to a road junction close to a Colonie de Vacances. Go straight on along the Rue des Sources, which reaches a T-junction with the D14 where you turn right for about 400m to reach a T-junction with the Rue Maginot. Turn right again here and follow this road as it curves left, passing the entrance to the campsite before reaching the Grande Rue. The tourist office is a short distance to the right.

Giromagny

Giromagny lies at the heart of a mineral-rich region of the Southern Vosges. Mining began in the 14th century, but the golden age was in the later half of the 16th century, when silver, copper and other metals were extracted from ever-deeper excavations. Mineral extraction ended by 1800, when alternative local industries developed using the water power of the River Savoureuse. The Mining Museum in the heart of the town tells the story of this once important industry.

The Fort de Giromagny, situated a few kilometres southwest of the town, is easily reached on foot. It dates from the 1870s and, like Fort du Salbert (see later in this section), was built by the French to defend the Belfort area. The fort is only open to the public on limited occasions, so views are usually restricted to the outer perimeter. To the south the Belfort Gap is mostly flat, but the wooded hill with hilltop mast in the distance is the site of the next fort in the chain, Salbert, reached after a further 13km along the GR5.

Giromagny to Lachapelle-sous-Chaux
(5.5km/3.5 miles, 1hr 45mins, height gain/loss 0m/80m)

From the T-junction where the Rue Maginot meets the Grande Rue, turn left along this busy main street. Continue until the *gendarmerie* (police station) can be seen ahead on the left and a supermarket is just across the road. Turn right along the Rue des Prés Heyd, pass some small blocks of flats on the left, then turn left into Rue sous la Côte.

This road curves left, gradually leaving the houses behind and becoming a country lane. Continue along this lane as it takes a very sharp left-hand bend. The tarmac ends and the GR5 is signposted along a rough track straight ahead.

This track becomes a footpath and after 5mins appears to fork, but both branches soon rejoin. The path then reaches a junction where the route is signposted left along a roughly cobbled path. The GR5 waymarks become a little scarce on this next section, being outnumbered by red disc marks referring to the Randonnée des Forts path, which follows the same route.

Stick to the main footpath through the woods, which eventually emerges into open country and passes a sports field on the left. Carrying on in the same direction, the route then follows a short section along a surfaced lane, the Rue des Oiseaux. When this lane turns off sharply left, the GR5 continues ahead along a rough vehicle track towards Lachapelle-sous-Chaux.

The countryside hereabouts is a patchwork of small woods and fields, and the route makes use of several different paths. After following the existing track for several hundred metres, it reaches a T-junction and turns right along a cobbled vehicle track. Just a few minutes later this track swings away to the left and the GR5 continues straight on along a wide footpath that very soon passes between two lakes (although on our second visit one lake was drained and the other was very low).

Just beyond the lakes turn left at a T-junction along a broad vehicle track that crosses open grassland to reach a road. Turn left, but look out for a GR sign pointing to the right after only about 100m. The GR5 leaves along a footpath through farmland, soon passing a pond off on the right. The church spire in **LACHAPELLE-SOUS-CHAUX** (small café/bar) is visible ahead and within 10mins the village itself is reached.

Lachapelle-sous-Chaux to Évette
(4km/2.5 miles, 1hr 15mins, height gain/loss 0m/0m)

On entering the village carry straight on ahead to reach a T-junction and turn right along the Rue du Moulin, a quiet road with houses on both sides. After a few minutes the GR5 turns off to the right along the Rue de Bellevue. Follow this road for the next kilometre.

At the point where the road forks the GR5 takes neither fork, but leaves along a track to the left. Ahead is a distinct wooded hill topped by a mast, the site of Fort du Salbert, still two hours' walk away. Just a few hundred metres along this track a signpost indicates that the route forks left along a gravel vehicle track. To the left a series of lakes comes into view.

Follow this same track for about 1.5km, ignoring side tracks. It curves left and then runs alongside the **ÉTANG DE LA VÉRONNE**. On the way it passes an information board about the **Site du Malsaucy** and its environment centre. Stay on the track until you reach a traffic barrier and turn right onto the road just beyond, heading away from the lake now. Within about 100m a second lake is reached, the **ÉTANG DU MALSAUCY** (the *gîte* listed under Évette is situated here). The GR5 keeps this lake on the right and passes round the end of it. Turn right to walk towards the village of **ÉVETTE** (restaurant, café/bar) on a path that runs between the lake and the road.

Leaving the Vosges behind

134

The defensive ditch at Fort du Salbert

Évette to Fort du Salbert
(3.5km/2 miles, 1hr 15mins, height gain/loss 250m/0m)

Pass the Auberge du Lac on the right and carry on over the level crossing ahead. Do not turn right along the minor road after the railway, but keep with the more major road that curves to the left. Within about 100m turn left along the Rue du Val, which becomes an unsurfaced track and changes name to become the Chemin du Verboté.

A signpost is reached at a track junction. Straight on is the GR533 and right is the E2 to Fort du Salbert. Turn right here, as this is also the route of the GR5. The gravel track becomes a little tarmac road, and after passing house number 8 take the left-hand fork, and in a very short distance the road meets a T-junction where you

turn right. Within 100m this leads to a second T-junction with a rather more major road (D24) where the GR5 turns left (turn right here to reach the village shop (closed Mon) at **SALBERT**). Pass a bus shelter on the right and very soon after turn to the right along the D8, Rue de la Vierge, signposted to Châlonvillars.

Walk past the Rue de la Fontaine on the left, and immediately afterwards leave the road and take a track to the left.

The track starts off parallel to the road then curves away to the left into the woods. Stay on this path, ignoring the first side paths to left and right. After a few hundred metres there is a junction with a crossing path and the

135

waymarks indicate a sharp left turn, this path heading straight up the side of the hill at an uncomfortably steep gradient. A first crossing track is ignored, but on meeting a second the GR5 is signed to the right. After a short level section, this then climbs up to meet a vehicle track just next to an information board about the geology of the area.

The footpath leaves on the other side of the vehicle track and continues uphill. A multitude of minor paths crosses the hillside here, but the waymarks indicate the way up this final short stretch to the top. The path carries on upwards, briefly turns left along a flat section, then resumes its upward progress, eventually emerging next to the large ditch that surrounds

FORT DU SALBERT. Access to the upper part of the fort is over the wooden bridge and up the steps, and there are good views away to the south from there. The GR5 route does not cross over this bridge, but takes the obvious path to the left.

The Fort du Salbert

Built in 1875, this fort is one of a chain of a dozen similar forts that encircle Belfort. All date from the 1874 to 1914 period and were raised following the shock of the Prussian victory in 1871. Each fort sheltered infantry and artillery and provided an interconnecting defensive shield around the town. These forts are now mostly overgrown and decayed and access to the underground areas requires special permission.

Fort du Salbert to Châlonvillars
(4km/2.5 miles, 1hr 15mins, height gain/loss 30m/290m)

Follow the path from the access bridge down to a large, grassy, terraced area surrounded on two sides by stone walls. Walk through this part of the fort as far as the road beyond and turn left towards the car park. The route now branches off on a footpath to the right of the road, almost opposite the car park entrance, dropping down through woods to join the road at a hairpin bend. Turn right and take the vehicle track that immediately leaves to the right, off the bend.

The track soon passes a sign to a viewpoint on the left that once offered

an extensive view over Belfort, but is now getting blocked by trees. Back on the original track the route continues steadily down through dense woods. It is crossed by another track, then curves left and follows along the top of a raised embankment, once part of a railway that supplied the military. Further on the overgrown remains of another old military site are passed on the left.

From here keep to the same track for about half an hour. It emerges from the woods and continues with hedges and fields on both sides as the buildings of **CHÂLONVILLARS** (small shop) come into view.

When the track meets a minor road, follow this over the canal bridge ahead. Continue to the junction with the N19 and cross straight over to go down the road opposite, the D218 signposted to Chagey. This road leads down through the village, past the war memorial and into the main square.

Châlonvillars to Echenans-sous-Mont-Vaudois
(6km/4 miles, 2hr, height gain/loss 20m/30m)

Turn right at the *tabac-presse*, taking the road signposted to Châtebier. Within 100m turn left up a little green lane beside a house. This climbs steeply uphill and joins a road near to the church. Turn right up the road and follow it out of the village.

As the houses are left behind, the road becomes a track with views east over Belfort, soon leading into woods. Stick to the main track for about 10mins, ignoring side paths, to reach a fork. This might cause a momentary hesitation, but the upper path has a GR cross, so stay on the lower path. Very soon this arrives at a little spring (*fontaine*) and marker stone (*borne*) with an information board, all just to the left of the track.

Continuing along the path turn left at a junction ahead, where other paths to right and straight ahead are both less distinct, and carry on to reach the D218. Turn right along here for several hundred metres. After going round a right-hand bend, look out for a substantial gravel track leaving on the left, signposted to Echenans-sous-Mont-Vaudois.

The track heads into dense beech woods. After 5mins look out for the junction where the GR5 is signed off to the right. Turn along this narrower track, heading towards the Croix des Femmes, situated close to the path on the left and reached within a few minutes. The cross is dated 1792 and marks the place where a mother and her two daughters were killed by lightning when caught in a storm while working in the fields.

Shortly after leaving the cross the route follows the main track when it swings 90 degrees to the left (ignore the other minor tracks here).

There follows a stretch of at least 1km along this vehicle track through the forest before it emerges onto a country road with a village visible to the left. Turn left and follow the road into **ECHENANS-SOUS-MONT-VAUDOIS**. There is no shop or café here, but drinking water is available (see below). Keep to the road until it meets a more major road at a T-junction, then turn left for about 50m, then right along the Rue du Levant.

Echenans-sous-Mont-Vaudois to Brévilliers
(3.5km/2 miles, 1hr, height gain/loss 0m/20m)

This road leads out of the village to a turning circle, then continues as a track. Just beyond there is a labelled drinking water tap on the side of a building.

The track bends right between woods then takes a turn to the left, at which point the route leaves to the right along a gravel track. Within about 5mins the track reaches a junction where the path to the right is signposted to Héricourt (1hr 45mins), but the GR5 carries straight on.

Very soon after, where the track forks, take the right hand-track, although the waymark may be a little ambiguous. Carry on to reach the edge of the woods and go across a large field with sight of a busy road off to the right. The track takes a bridge over this dual carriageway then passes the first few houses of the village of **BRÉVILLIERS** (supermarket on main road, small shop in village). Cross straight over another major road (N83) and take the lane opposite, the Rue de la Barrière, crossing the railway and continuing along to the village square.

Clochers Comtois

The curved dome of the church belltower in Brévilliers is an indication that the route has now passed into Franche-Comté. This region, which extends from Belfort down to the Jura, has a distinctive style of belltower often simply called a clocher comtois. The graceful domes on these towers are

sometimes decorated with coloured tiles to form geometric patterns. There are over 650 clochers comtois within Franche-Comté, and several can be found near to the route of the GR5. Of these, the most colourful are at Héricourt, Les Fourgs and Pontarlier.

The style is said to have reached Franche-Comté from Florence in the 16th century. Much rebuilding was necessary after the French conquest of the region in 1678, and many church domes date back to this period.

Turn right here if you wish to leave the GR5 to go to **HÉRICOURT**, where there is a railway station and other facilities (hotels, restaurants, cafés, shops). (2km to the station, 3km to the town centre.)

From Brévilliers to Héricourt
To reach Héricourt turn right at the *lavoir* (washing area) and fork left along the Rue des Chalets. Follow this track to pass a series of ponds off to the right, then turn right onto a side track and follow yellow triangle waymarks through an access gap to the left. Cross the meadow, going over a footbridge and passing into the woods beyond. Keep on this yellow triangle route, which soon turns off along a path to the left. This route may then be followed to the edge of Héricourt.

SECTION 8

GR5 Héricourt to St-Hippolyte

(46km/28.5 miles)

Although the Montbéliard region is one of the more heavily populated parts of France, with a concentration of industrial towns, the GR5 is skilfully routed through woodland and small villages to provide an attractive link between the Vosges and Jura.

The initial part of the route crosses the lowlands of the Belfort Gap, with few significant gradients – indeed, many parts are practically flat. Just outside Nommay it passes two large lakes with a leisure centre and then continues through the countryside using canal towpaths and quiet rural tracks. In early summer there is a good chance of hearing nightingales along this stretch. The landscape varies as the path crosses onto limestone country, passing an impressive natural rock arch at Pont Sarrazin. The route then rises to run beside the Swiss frontier, where border marker stones become common features along the way.

Finally the GR5 descends to the hillside chapel of Chapelle du Mont, where the view over St-Hippolyte is revealed. The town lies enclosed in the winding valley of the Doubs, overlooked on all sides by steep, wooded hillsides and cliffs.

This section can be walked in two easy days, with a suggested stop at Vandoncourt, where there is a *gîte*. (The choice of accommodation is limited in this area.)

This section of the GR5 starts from the village of Brévilliers, accessible from Héricourt railway station by a 2km route waymarked with yellow triangles (not part of the GR5), described below.

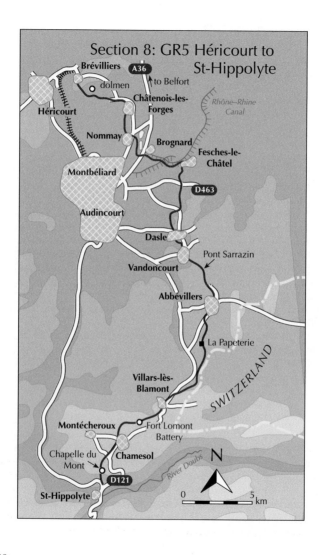

Section 8: GR5 Héricourt to St-Hippolyte

Accommodation and Food

Km	Cumulative km		
		Brévilliers	Supermarket on main road, small shop in village
			Turn off for Héricourt, 3km off route
		(Héricourt)	Hotels, restaurants, cafés, shops
7.0		Châtenois-les-Forges	Restaurant, café, shops
7.5	14.5	Fesches-le-Châtel	Restaurants, cafés, shops (all 2km off route)
7.0	21.5	Dasle	Restaurant, shop (closed Wed)
1.5	23.0	Vandoncourt	*Gîte*, restaurant, shop (closed Mon, open Sun am)
4.5	27.5	Abbévillers	Café/bar, shop (closed Mon, open Sun am)
3.0	30.5	La Papeterie	Bar/restaurant
12.0	42.5	Chamesol	Restaurant
3.5	46.0		Turn off for St-Hippolyte, just off route
		(St-Hippolyte)	Hotels, campsite, restaurants, cafés, shops

Contact details for tourist offices and accommodation are in the appendix.

Maps
IGN 1:100,000 sheets 31 and 38
IGN 1:50,000 Le Doubs No2 Zone Est

From Héricourt to Brévilliers
Turn right from the railway station and at the first junction turn right across a level crossing. Follow the vehicle track as it curves to the left, then take a way-marked, lesser track which leaves to the left. Fork right, then cross almost straight over a major forestry track. Turn right onto a smaller track which becomes a footpath. In less than 5mins turn right at a T-junction. Keep to the path through meadowland and across a footbridge. Carry on almost to the corner of the field and leave by an access gap to join a narrow track. Turn right uphill, then very soon left at a T-junction. This gravel track leads into Brévilliers.

Brévilliers to Châtenois-les-Forges
(7km/4.5 miles, 2hr 15mins height gain/loss 50m/70m)

From the centre of **BRÉVILLIERS** go uphill and follow the road round to the right of the church. For the next short stretch the GR5 coincides with signs indicating the way to a dolmen. Turn left up a short, steep pedestrian way between two houses. On reaching the top, turn right along the Rue de la Chevrette to a T-junction. Turn left up the Rue de Vô and left again along a road between fields. At the next junction the way to the dolmen is signposted to the left, but the GR5 takes the right-hand fork. (The dolmen is reached by diverting off route for about 1km. It has been excavated and is protected by a large shed, which allows viewing, but not access.)

This road winds its way through fields and copses, rising gradually to a ridge with a sweeping view of the wooded valley beyond. Drop down to reach the trees and carry straight on down the track along the woodland edge to enter the woods ahead. After a few minutes take a broad footpath to the left, signposted to Nommay.

For a little while the GR5 now follows part of a trail based on the historic border markers of the Principality of Montbéliard, which was a separate entity until the end of the 18th century. These stones, with their worn markings, appear along the track for the next few minutes.

At a slight clearing the history trail leaves to the left and the GR5

Crossing the flat countryside of the Belfort Gap

goes straight on, following a GR waymark. At the next clearing follow the track round to the right, where it becomes more defined, with broad grass verges.

Follow this track to a staggered crossroads and take the route almost straight ahead, which skirts a large clearing. The surface of the track gradually improves until it leaves the forest as a tarmac lane and meets a road coming in from the left at a picnic area. Carry on in the same direction along this road and enter **CHÂTENOIS-LES-FORGES** (restaurant, café, shops) on the Rue Maréchal Foch. Continue down this residential street to reach a round-

about, bright with bedding plants in season. Turn sharp right, taking the Rue Kléber, which is the higher of the two roads to the right. Follow the waymarks all the way along this road and then turn left at the T-junction into the Rue de Villars. (**Note** The route has been altered – the old GR waymarks are still visible at points, but do not follow them up the Chemin du Vrai Bois to the right.)

At a road junction with a large sandstone cross it is possible to go on downhill into the village centre where there is a range of shops, but the GR5 turns right to leave the village by the Rue de Lieutenant Bidaux. Follow the road for a short distance.

Châtenois-les-Forges to Nommay
(1.5km/1 mile, 30mins, height gain/loss 0m/0m)

When the road turns sharply to the left between houses, the route carries straight on, becoming a gravel track between fields. From this track the broad view now includes glimpses of industrial works in the valley below. The route enters **NOMMAY** by the Rue du Cimetière. On reaching a junction with the N437, cross the road, turn right, then turn left almost immediately into the Rue des Jardins. Follow the road until you reach a T-junction, then turn left. When this small street comes out onto the D424, turn right and cross the bridge over the River Savoureuse.

Immediately beyond the bridge, turn right along a rough lane. When it reaches a turning circle, turn right to join a broad gravel track along a raised bank. Pass a lake to the left and carry on along the embankment. Do not take the broad track to the left that goes between two lakes, but keep straight ahead with the second lake on the left – there is a leisure centre on the far bank. The GR5 curves round the beach at the far end of the lake then climbs a set of steps to the right leading over a footbridge to a car park. Turn left and head for a path leading up to a bridge over the major road (A36).

Nommay to Fesches-le-Châtel

(6km/3.5 miles, 1hr 45mins, height gain/loss 0m/0m)

Cross the bridge and **BROGNARD** is immediately ahead, but the route does not enter the village. Turn right and go down the path onto the tree-lined canal towpath (access to the canal is forbidden at night for safety reasons).

On reaching a basin where two canal spurs meet, follow the towpath to the right, across the aqueduct spanning a river. Beyond another canal basin keep following the towpath to the right. Just beyond a lock there is a footbridge over the canal. Turn left

across it, then left again along the towpath on the far side to walk along the other side of the canal towards Fesches-le-Châtel.

After about 1km there is a road bridge. Leave the canal here and turn right along the Rue du Canal into **FESCHES-LE-CHÂTEL** (restaurants, cafés, shops, all 2km off route). On reaching a church turn right, then left up the Rue de l'Égalité towards the cemetery. (A left turn at the church would reach the village centre, but the facilities are still some distance away.)

Fesches-le-Châtel to Dasle

(7km/4.5 miles, 2hr 15mins, height gain/loss 60m/50m)

Where the road forks, take the left-hand, lower fork. This quiet lane passes between the cemetery and an orchard, then becomes a track which the route follows as it turns to the right to enter woods. Carry on along an obvious vehicle track in open, deciduous woodland, cross straight over the D463 and follow the track ahead. Continue following the GR waymarks through the trees.

At a small clearing with a marker stone, cross a more major track and take the path ahead – the route follows a winding footpath through the woods.

On reaching a road, cross over to a small but clearly marked footpath on the other side. This reaches a

broad forestry track, but a GR cross blocks the path on the opposite side. Turn left up a footpath just before the track and enter the Forêt Communale d'Exincourt.

The footpath curves to the left while the track leaves at an angle to the right. Follow this footpath for a little over 1km until the GR5 turns sharply to the left – look out for a GR cross warning that the path straight ahead is not the route. The GR5 almost reaches the forest edge and follows it around to the right before coming out between two fields.

The village of **DASLE** (restaurant, shop – closed Wed) is just ahead. Turn left towards the cemetery and carry on onto a tarmac road going downhill into the village. On reaching the T-junction at the bottom, just by the old village water trough, the GR5 turns right (a left turn then a right would reach the village shop). At the war memorial go down to the left and curve round to reach the D126. Turn left here and very soon turn right into the Rue des Aiguillottes.

Dasle to Vandoncourt
(1.5km/1 mile, 30mins, height gain/loss 50m/0m)

This road goes between allotments with fruit trees then passes to the right of a depot with storage tanks. Beyond the depot the road ends, but a vehicle track carries on through the fields, rising towards a ridge.

Where the vehicle track, now fainter, turns to the left, follow it to come out between two hedges. Turn left along the road past a cemetery, with the rooftops of the village of **VANDONCOURT** ahead (*gîte*, restaurant, shop – closed Mon, open Sun am), to meet the Rue du Piquet. Turn right into the village.

Vandoncourt to Abbévillers
(4.5km/3 miles, 1hr 30mins, height gain/loss 190m/10m)

At the bottom of this road go straight across the D253 and down the Rue des Damas, then along the Rue du Pont Sarrazin, which has a signpost to Pont Sarrazin. A few hundred metres later take a right fork that once again follows the Pont Sarrazin signs. Carry on along this road until it ends at the creeper-clad restaurant 'La Cachette'. A rough track signposted to Pont Sarrazin goes to the right of the buildings and soon reaches an information board.

The Legend of Pont Sarrazin

There are several versions of the legend of Pont Sarrazin. According to one, a band of marauding Saracens was camped in the vicinity and one of them carried off a local maiden. Rather than allow herself to be captured, she threw herself from his horse into the ravine, but her fall was stopped by the miraculous appearance of this bridge of rock. When her abductor tried to follow on horseback, the bridge was too narrow and he fell to his death. There is also a more prosaic explanation for the origin of the arch, involving the erosion of limestone by water trickling through the rock.

Climb some steps through the woods and follow the side of a small

Pont Sarrazin, a natural limestone bridge

gorge. The path comes out in front of **PONT SARRAZIN**. This impressive arch links the sides of the rocky gorge to form a natural bridge.

Just to the right of the arch, climb up the side of the valley by a footpath indicated by a green arrow. It zigzags almost to the lip of the gorge, but where another green arrow indicates a path to the right, follow the main path round to the left, leading towards the top of the arch. A small path branches off to the left onto the bridge itself, but this is not part of the route.

Just beyond this, turn left where the route meets a narrow vehicle track. At a T-junction with a more major track, turn right. (There could

be confusion at this point – a minor alternative route of the GR5 joins from the left, so there are waymarks in that direction too.) Follow the track as it veers to the right through gradually thinning woodland. At the end of the woods it snakes on through fields, becoming a tarmac lane.

After about 45mins go over a small crossroads then turn right at the next junction, heading towards **ABBÉVILLERS** (café/bar, shop – closed Mon, open Sun am) and reaching a road junction on the village main street. The GR5 takes the road almost opposite, signposted to Meslières (down the road to the right from this junction is the café/bar and a shop).

Just before the sign indicating the edge of Abbévillers, turn left up a lane through fields. This track passes pastureland and leads back into woods, gradually descending into a small gorge where shelves of limestone across the way may make the going slightly awkward at points. After a few minutes the route reaches a dilapidated wooden footbridge at the bottom of the valley. Across the streambed turn right and descend by the left bank

When the woodland path comes out onto a track, turn right (signposted to La Papeterie). A small river soon flows alongside on the left and some buildings come into sight beyond the riverside fields. At a junction the GR5 takes a track to the left towards these buildings. **Be alert for this**, as at the time of writing the waymarkings would be easy to miss. The track crosses a bridge over the river and curves to the right.

LA PAPETERIE is a bar/restaurant with a covered terrace. **Look out for** a stony track to the left before reaching these buildings – the GR5 takes this track into the woods, where it becomes quite steep, climbing a fern-filled gorge.

Almost at the top of the slope there is a T-junction. Turn right along this woodland path, which roughly follows the border with Switzerland – there are border stones along the next stretch of the route. Within about 40m climb some steps to the left and turn right at the top.

Border Stones

The border stones beside this section of the path have an 'F' on the French side, and a shield with a bear – for the Canton of Bern – on the Swiss side. On the top of the stones a groove indicates the line of the border, and many of them are dated 1817. After many years of turmoil in Europe, Napoleon was finally defeated and France was forced to agree to give up all territorial gains. These issues were all discussed at the Congress of Vienna in 1815 and many central European boundaries were rationalised as a result.

Cross a vehicle track and leave it by the footpath on the other side. The path, still following the border, loses some height, but regains it by climbing up steps to the left. Continue along the path ahead, which still follows the border.

Cross another vehicle track, keeping on the path and following the border stones. The path continues between the woods and a pasture, passing a picnic table amongst trees to the left and crossing another vehicle track. At a fork take the path twisting sharply to the left. About 100m further on it takes a short, steep climb up a bank to the left before turning right.

Follow the path for a short distance further, passing a point where the border turns off to the left. A small track runs along the border, but the GR5 goes straight on to leave the woods at a metal stile. Cross a pasture, but look out for another yellow metal stile on the left. Climb the stile and turn right to join a substantial vehicle track.

To the right a series of small villages spreads out towards Montbéliard and its surrounding towns in the distance. The track becomes a tarmac lane, and after passing a farm on the right-hand side there is a T-junction where the GR5 goes left, downhill, into the village of **VILLARS-LÈS-BLAMONT** (there is a farm here that demonstrates the use of the *tuyé*, the traditional huge chimney for smoking meats). Take a left fork in the village and go down past the church to reach a roundabout. Keep on the main street to enter the Place de la Mairie, with the *mairie* and then the war memorial on the right, and continue ahead to meet the D73 at a junction.

Villars-lès-Blamont to Chamesol
(5km/3 miles, 1hr 30mins, height gain/loss 210m/140m)

Cross this road and take the Rue du Lomont uphill, passing an ironwork cross at the corner. Pass a lane going to a house to the right, but very soon after turn right along a footpath marked by a GR waymark.

At a fork take the left branch and in a few minutes the route meets a road and follows it uphill for some distance. The road hairpins sharply to the left, but the GR5 leaves it at the bend, carrying on roughly straight ahead. Follow the GR waymarks into the woods, taking the uphill track on reaching a fork.

The path becomes narrower, contouring along the side of a hill and negotiating a small rocky cleft, then climbing through the woods, quite steeply at first, but then more easily. This arrives at a deep, rock-cut ditch with ramparts above which form part of the **FORT LOMONT BATTERY**. Follow the signs to the viewpoint on the top of the battery, although the growth of trees is beginning to block the view of the wooded hills beyond. The platform gave a commanding position for artillery, with munitions being stored in the galleries underneath.

Returning to the path from the viewpoint, go past a tumbledown shed, turn left and carry on along a woodland track. This track soon runs along the top of an artificial embankment that was part of a network of supply routes for the fortifications in the area.

A large farm track joins from the right. Continue ahead along this more substantial track, then leave it by a footpath to the left through the trees, just before the track bends to the left at a junction – the footpath simply cuts off a hairpin and rejoins the track very soon. Keep to the vehicle track as it skirts to the left of an area of pasture. At the far side carry on along the track, now with the forest to the right and a field to the left. Beyond there is a fine view of an undulating landscape stretching into the Swiss Jura.

The track comes out onto a road where you turn right and cross a cattle-grid. When this road joins another on a hairpin bend, go left downhill. Pass a house on the right and the remains of another cattle-grid

on the left. Not far beyond the cattle-grid **look out for** a turning on the left where the GR waymark might easily be missed. The route turns off the road to the left, down a vehicle track and across a pasture to enter some woods. Amongst the trees the track passes a rusty old tank, and then a large barn on the left with a house ahead. At the barn there is another turning **which could easily be missed**. The route follows the path going at right angles to the right that comes out, in little more than a minute, on a road. Turn right downhill, then left at the first road junction, going down this road towards **CHAMESOL** (restaurant).

Chamesol to St-Hippolyte, Chapelle du Mont

(3.5km/2 miles, 1hr, height gain/loss 20m/250m)

The GR5 does not go through the centre of Chamesol, but turns right, uphill, on the road towards Montécheroux. After about 300m a restaurant, 'À Mon Plaisir', stands on a corner. Turn left just before the restaurant and follow a quiet road to a T-junction with the D121, where roadsigns indicate Montécheroux to the right and St-Hippolyte to the left.

Take a footpath immediately opposite, through fields, to enter woodland again. The path goes down the side of a wooded gorge, twisting around hairpin bends at a steep section. It then meets a more major track where there are metal

gates to the right, but the route goes left, downhill.

Further down is a signpost left to the **CHAPELLE DU MONT**, where there is a clearing giving a fine view over St-Hippolyte. Take a stony footpath from the front of the clearing, going down in a series of zigzags to meet the road.

The route reaches the D121 beside a cemetery – turn left here. Turning right almost immediately after joining this road gives access to **ST-HIPPOLYTE** with its range of facilities (hotels, campsite, restaurants, cafés, shops), but the GR5 continues along the D121.

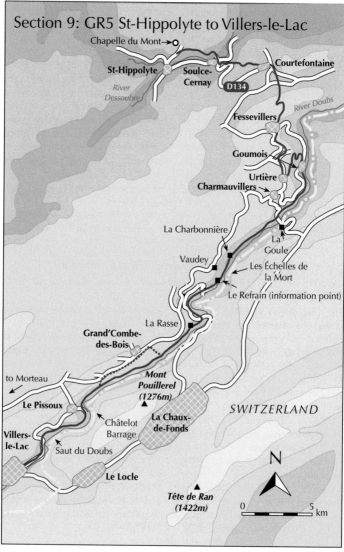

Section 9: GR5 St-Hippolyte to Villers-le-Lac

SECTION 9

GR5 St-Hippolyte to Villers-le-Lac

(65km/41 miles)

This section of the walk is quite unlike any of the others, as much of the way follows the limestone gorge cut by the River Doubs.

Starting above St-Hippolyte, a town that sits low down in the Doubs Valley, the GR5 route follows the river to Soulce-Cernay. It then short cuts over higher ground to take off a loop of the valley before rejoining the river at the village of Goumois.

Beyond Goumois the route follows the Doubs closely and includes some spectacular stretches of river gorge. While in places the sides of the valley slope gently down to the quiet river below, along other stretches the river has produced a deep, narrow pathway between steep cliffs. There are particularly impressive viewpoints close to Les Échelles de la Mort. These 'ladders of death' are hardly as frightening as their name might suggest, and they do add extra interest to the walk.

A couple of centuries ago all sorts of industries were drawn into the area to make use of the power of the river. Today these workshops are gone. One of the attractions of the path through the gorge is that this is for the most part isolated country, long stretches of the route being without sign of habitation.

Towards the end of the section the Saut du Doubs waterfall, seen at its best after heavy rains, is a popular destination for riverboat cruises from Villers-le-Lac. Other points of interest include the little chapel at Urtière, with traditional wooden *tavaillons* cladding the belltower, and the excellent information display at Le Refrain, illustrating past and present life in the gorge.

This section does not involve much climbing, but it does include three places where fixed ladders form part of the route.

This section can be walked in three days, with suggested stops at Goumois (hotels, *gîte*, and campsite), and either the hotel at La Rasse or off route at the *gîte* at Maison-Monsieur in Switzerland (otherwise you have to climb out of the gorge to reach alternative accommodation).

Accommodation and Food

Km	Cumulative km		
		(St-Hippolyte)	Hotels, campsite, restaurants, cafés, shops
4.0		Soulce-Cernay	Restaurant
5.5	9.5	Courtefontaine	Bar/restaurant
7.5	17.0	Fessevillers	*Gîte*, restaurant
7.0	24.0	Goumois	Hotels, *gîte*, campsite, restaurant, café, shop (closed Thur)
5.5	29.5	Bief d'Etoz	Restaurant ('La Goule', Switzerland, closed Wed)
5.0	34.5	La Charbonnière	Shelter
2.0	36.5		Turn off for Le Vaudey (*gîte*), 2km off route
0.5	37.0		Turn off for Bois de la Biche (hotel), 1.5km off route
0.5	37.5	Le Refrain Parking	Shelter (old chapel)
7.0	44.5	La Rasse	Hotel/restaurant (closed Tue/Wed)
			Turn off for Maison-Monsieur (*gîte*), 1km off route
3.5	48.0	Bistrot Bonaparte	Refreshments, high season only
4.0	52.0	Abri du Torrat	Shelter
3.0	55.0		Turn off for Le Pissoux (café), 1km off route
4.0	59.0	Saut du Doubs	Café restaurant, snack-stalls (beyond falls)
1.0	60.0		Turn off for Le Cerneux Billard (*gîte*), 3km off route
5.0	65.0	Villers-le-Lac	Hotels, *gîte*, campsite, restaurants, cafés, shops

Contact details for tourist offices and accommodation are in the appendix.
Note If wild camping, be aware of warnings about water-level fluctuations along the Doubs.

Maps
IGN 1:100,000 sheet 38
IGN 1:50,000 Le Doubs No2 Zone Est

The GR5 skirts just north of **ST-HIPPOLYTE**. Pick up the route on the D121, the main road, beside the walled cemetery. If approaching from the Chapelle du Mont direction, turn left along this road (turn right if coming up from St-Hippolyte). Follow the road uphill, passing a road off to the left to Pleinchamps. After about 1km watch out for a waymarked track to the right going down a bank beside trees, with the road soon curving away from it.

Follow this track across the corner of a field. It then drops down, with trees on either side, to reach a signpost indicating that Soulce-Cernay lies ahead.

The route skirts along the edge of a field with a scrubby hedge to the left. Keep to the main track to reach a substantial building, once the farm of La Grosse Roche. A sign points ahead towards *vestiges du château*. Only 30m beyond the old farm another sign indicates that some caves and a waterfall all lie straight ahead, but the GR5 turns off to the right, going down the side of the field.

The route again enters trees and follows a stony footpath. Losing height, the path becomes a grassy track cut into the slope. It crosses a plank bridge over a small stream and then leads past a small house. The route turns downhill, with the stream on the right. More buildings lie ahead and the track curves to the left,

becomes tarmacked and carries on between fields. A small road from La Saulnerie comes in from the right. Join this road and continue straight ahead with the River Doubs off to the right between tree-lined banks.

The River Doubs

The River Doubs will become familiar to GR5 walkers over the course of the next few days. Rising on the Jura plateau close to Mouthe, it is known for its particularly convoluted course. While the straight-line distance between the source and the end of the river is only 90km, the river flows for 435km to achieve this. From Mouthe, where the Doubs emerges from a cave as already a sizeable stream, it flows northeast, defining the Franco-Swiss border for many kilometres. There follows a huge meander into Switzerland before the river turns back to the west, then southwest, finally flowing into the Saône.

The Doubs has lent its name to one of the four départements of Franche-Comté and is an important fishing river. The origin of the name is open to question, but one possibility is that it derives from the Celtic word 'dubh', meaning black. The same word is still found in Scotland, where a dubh lochan is a dark, peaty pool.

A sign here, the first of many along the river, warns that water levels can rise very suddenly because of dams and power plants upstream.

The road arrives at a bridge spanning the river. Cross over to reach the junction on the far side, and to the right lies the small village of **SOULCE-CERNAY** (restaurant).

Soulce-Cernay to Courtefontaine
(5.5km/3.5 miles, 1hr 45mins, height gain/loss 420m/20m)

The GR5 turns left from the bridge then almost immediately right, going up a minor road between houses. This leads up the hillside, becoming a gravelled track. After a few minutes this track turns very sharply away to the left, and the GR5 leaves on a second track that carries on straight ahead at the bend and continues into woods.

After just a few minutes this joins the D134. Turn left and follow this uphill around a long curve to the right. When the road starts to take a left-hand bend, the route leaves by a footpath on the left up the bank.

Only a few minutes later the path skirts an area of pasture then carries on uphill through more woodland. A point is reached where a grassy vehicle track comes up from the left. Do not go down the track, but just beyond there is first an obvious worn footpath, then a fainter path over a little clearing. Take the obvious path which leads away between trees.

The path continues up to join the D134 again. Turn left and follow it for ess than 5mins. The GR5 leaves to the left, down a footpath into the woods.

The path is joined by a forest track that comes up from the right. Continue straight ahead along this track and there soon follows a quite steep little uphill section. The track emerges close to the farm of La Joux. Turn right to go around the front of the building. Pass the farm then follow the vehicle track across pasture with woods up to the right. The view is opening out now, with a line of limestone outcrops marking the upper levels of the Doubs Valley away to the left.

About 0.5km from La Joux the track swings around a second small farm, La Race. The track becomes a tarmacked lane and continues uphill. Follow this lane for another kilometre to reach **COURTEFONTAINE** (bar/restaurant). On entering the village the road rounds a hairpin bend to the left and passes below the church. At a crossroads go straight on along the Rue du Lavoir.

Courtefontaine

Like many villages in the north of Franche-Comté, Courtefontaine has an imposing and prominently sited *lavoir*. A miniature Greek temple may seem an over-the-top way of embellishing the local water supply, but a reliable source of water was something to be valued in a limestone landscape where surface water can be scarce. These ornate lavoirs date from the late 18th and early 19th centuries, a time of relative rural prosperity when villages would compete with their neighbours to build more impressive structures. The buildings contained the water source (*fontaine*) that supplied the washing area (*lavoir*), and usually a nearby animal drinking trough (*abreuvoir*). Long since out of use, some have been demolished, but others are valued as a surviving link with the past.

Courtefontaine to Fessevillers
(7.5km/4.5 miles, 2hr 15mins, height gain/loss 190m/130m)

In the centre of the village is a road junction with the colonnaded *lavoir* on the right and an *auberge* beyond. The GR5 goes straight ahead at this junction, along the road opposite, beside the war memorial. Turn left at the T-junction reached soon after.

Follow this quiet road for about 0.5km until it joins the main road. Turn right along the D134, passing the Rue les Vareilles on the right. About 300m further on look out for a gateway on the right where the GR5 leaves the road. Although there is no obvious path beyond, the route heads across the field. Walk first towards a waymark on a power-line post, then make for a gate on the far side. From here look ahead across the next field. A road runs alongside the far field boundary and a second road can be seen to join it at a T-junction. Head across the field towards this junction, in much the same direction as previously.

Once out of the field take the road opposite, signposted for La Mine. This quiet lane leads up past a farm on the right and reaches some farm buildings ahead. The GR5 follows the road as it turns to the right in front of these buildings. (There is a large painted sign on the wall to emphasise that walkers should not take the track straight on past the farmhouse.)

Keep following this lane for the next 2km as it rises steadily, passing the house of Le Creux on the right and curving up through woods. The tarmac eventually ends beside an isolated farm. Carry on along the vehicle track ahead.

Very soon afterwards the track goes around the edge of a block of woodland with an area of open grassland to the left. **Look out for** a GR cross on a tree ahead and an arrow pointing left, although the route to be taken may not be apparent. There is a faint vehicle track across the field, but by the time you reach the arrow you will have gone past it. Retrace your steps for a few metres and follow this faint track as it crosses the field to a gate through the hedge on the far side.

155

The path cuts across the corner of the next field, goes through a small copse and emerges onto a lane in front of the farm of Montassier-dessous.

Turn right and follow this lane for about 1km until it takes a hairpin bend to the left. On the right of the bend the GR5 leaves by a grassy track that curves away and soon joins a vehicle track.

The track leads on through rough pasture, then some woodland, then more pasture. When a path forks off left, stay with the right-hand, waymarked track. The route leads on through a gate and up to the side of some woodland. On entering woods the GR waymarks divert off on a path to the right, cutting off a corner before rejoining the track.

Very shortly afterwards the track turns sharply right, but the GR5 leaves by a footpath to the left. Cross a tiny stream then climb a series of steps. At the top turn right along the track towards the church, then left on reaching a road. This leads past the *gîte d'étape* to reach the main road in **FESSEVILLERS** (restaurant).

Fessevillers to Goumois
(7km/4.5 miles, 2hr 15mins, height gain/loss 140m/490m)

Turn right along the main road. There is an *auberge* ahead, but the route turns left up the Rue d'Urtière. Climb out of the village, turning right at the junction where the Rue de la Fromagerie leaves to the left. A sign then indicates the way to a viewpoint over the village, off the route, along Rue sur la Côte. The GR5 turns left just before this, along the road that passes in front of a farm.

Follow this road as it steadily gains height. After about 0.5km a road to the right is signposted to Les Seignes, and the GR5 takes the road to the left towards Mont-de-Fessevillers.

Continue along this little road for another kilometre as far as the buildings of the farm at **Sur-le-Mont** on the right. Soon after, the road bends sharply to the right, and at this point go down the track that carries on straight ahead. (**Note** This section of the GR5 route has changed, and older maps will show the route leaving to the left here.) On reaching a road turn right and continue for about 2km, passing the little settlement of **URTIÈRE** to reach the chapel just beyond.

Turn off left and pass in front of the chapel to reach the lane beyond. Turn left, following the sign towards Goumois, and then right at the next junction.

Within a few minutes ignore the road off to the right, signposted to Charmauvillers, and carry on ahead. The route is soon directed off to the left, leaving the lane by farm build-

Goumois lies on the border of France and Switzerland

ings, crossing a stile and following a footpath through the woods. After about 20mins this leads onto a lane. Turn left, following this lane downhill.

Shortly afterwards the lane hairpins to the right and a track carries on ahead. The GR5 continues following the lane around the bend, but a possible short diversion up the track gives access to a huge rock with a bird's-eye view over Goumois, the Doubs and across into Switzerland.

A few hundred metres down the lane beyond the hairpin, turn left following a GR waymarked gravel track signposted to Goumois. On the way down this track hairpins right and joins another track coming from the right. Continue downhill to the D437. Turn right until a sign opposite the Hotel Taillard sends the GR5 down a minor road to the left. Turn left at the next road junction and continue downhill to reach the small exhibition centre in **GOUMOIS** (hotels, *gîte*, restaurant, café, shop – closed Thurs. The campsite is about 1km to the north, close to the river.).

157

Goumois to Bief d'Etoz
(5.5km/3.5 miles, 1hr 45mins, height gain/loss 20m/0m)

Turn right at the exhibition centre and follow the Route du Jura out of the village. Opposite the Chalet Muller a *sentier d'interprétation* signposted to the left is also the GR5. It passes through woodland and emerges after a very short time onto a minor road.

Turn left, following the road along the valley with the River Doubs to the left. After about 20mins this reaches a picnic area and the tarmac road ends. The GR5 continues along a gravel track.

Within only a few minutes there is an unofficial sign pointing uphill to the right for Les Échelles de la Mort. The path indicated goes diagonally upwards and is unconvincing. Stay with the major footpath here, which keeps low down by the river – normal GR waymarks will be found further on.

Only a few minutes later some buildings come into sight on the opposite (Swiss) side of the river. The main path drops down towards the edge of the river here, but there are GR5 waymarks leading off to the right on a narrower path through the woods. This leads over a rocky section as the path negotiates a route along steep ground between trees and boulders, but this does not last long and the path then drops back closer to river level.

Continue along this riverside path, ignoring the nearby vehicle track and following occasional waymarks – one rough section is crossed using a short fixed ladder. Soon afterwards the path reaches a fishing hut with a vehicle track leading to it. The signpost indicates that this track has come down from Goumois, and the GR5 follows it in the other direction.

A hydroelectric generating station comes into view on the Swiss bank, and a few minutes later the path passes the little chapel of **Bief d'Etoz** and joins a road.

Bief d'Etoz to La Charbonnière
(5km/3 miles, 1hr 30mins, height gain/loss 70m/0m)

There are steps off down to the left, but the GR5 continues ahead along the road. Very soon after, a restaurant – 'La Goule' – comes into view on the Swiss riverbank. To visit it, stay on the route until the road takes a hairpin bend down to the left, and **LA GOULE** can be reached by following the road down and crossing the dam. The GR5 leaves the road at the hairpin bend and takes a vehicle track that carries straight on ahead.

After about 10mins this reaches a turning area. Continue on the track

In the depths of Doubs Gorge

beyond, which has a vehicle barrier. As this track swings a short distance from the river an ambiguous waymark might tempt you to take a small path down to the grassy area on the left, but the correct route still stays with the main track.

Approximately 25mins after leaving the road above the dam the GR5 leaves the track, taking a footpath to the left – there is a clear GR cross on a tree ahead to emphasise this. The path leads past **La Verrerie de la Bouege**, the site of a long-abandoned glass-making workshop – a few ruins built into a cliff are all that remain. Immediately after this there is a junction where you carry straight on up a steepening slope.

Within 10mins the route emerges once more onto a vehicle track. Continue ahead, but the next turn is easily missed. **Look out for** a path leaving to the left. There is a waymark, but the GR5 arrow (to La Charbonnière du Haut) is hardly visible when walking in this direction. If this turning is overshot and the waymarking appears to have stopped, it might be worth backtracking. Alternatively, miss a short section of the route by carrying on along the vehicle track, then turning left on reaching a road and going downhill to pick up the GR5 again at La Charbonnière.

The little woodland path reaches a signpost at Les Champs du Doubs. Carry on ahead to emerge on a road. Turn left to arrive moments later at **CHARBONNIÈRE DU HAUT**, an old farm now converted into a shelter. The shelter (*abri*) is open-sided, but equipped with benches and tables.

La Charbonnière to Le Refrain (information point)
(3km/2 miles, 1hr, height gain/loss 120m/110m)

There are two possible routes from here. The main GR5 route, which includes the descent of the ladders at Les Échelles de la Mort, is described below. An alternative route, which avoids these ladders, keeps more closely to the riverbank and rejoins the main route at Le Refrain.

Despite the name, Les Échelles de la Mort should not present too many problems. There are three fixed metal ladders, each very sturdily built, and each with handrails, so climbing

down can be done reasonably safely, even with a weighty pack, although one of the ladders is quite a long way from the cliff face and some people may feel a little exposed here.

The low-level alternative route branches down towards the river just in front of the shelter and is signposted GR5 Le Refrain par le bord du Doubs.

To continue with the main route, carry on along the vehicle track past the shelter, following the sign to GR5 Le Refrain par Les Échelles de la Mort.

The middle ladder at Les Échelles de la Mort

Follow this track straight ahead, passing the signpost at Les Chazeaux. Beyond is the small shelter of Les Neux de Aulx, a shed with a tin roof, but it does have a sleeping platform. A path leaves to the right to the *refuge* of **Le VAUDEY**, but the GR5 goes straight ahead.

Within a further half an hour the path passes a turn to the right to Bois de la Biche (hotel), then leads out onto an open lookout point above the gorge. A steep, rocky path leads down from here, very soon reaching the top of the three ladders of **LES ÉCHELLES DE LA MORT**. After the last one the rocky path below passes a fork where a GR cross warns against taking the lower, right-hand branch. Keep with the main path as it hairpins to the left and travels for some distance in what is apparently the wrong direction, back along the river.

Minutes later the route emerges at the car park at **LE REFRAIN**. The little shelter on the far side has benches, and a wealth of information and photographs relating to the locality.

Le Refrain Hydroelectric Plant

The Refrain Hydroelectric Plant is now totally automatic, and there have been no permanent staff on site since 1980.

161

Prior to that, for many years there was an isolated community living here in the gorge. Men working in the plant would bring their wives and families. The children attended a school on site, which in its heyday had up to 20 pupils – the school closed in 1971. The little chapel, which dates back to these times, stands to the left of the approach road and is now used as a shelter.

Le Refrain (information point) to La Rasse
(7km/4.5 miles, 2hr 15mins, height gain/loss 40m/20m)

Leave the car park along the access road. The main GR5 route continues along this road for the next 2km, but there is an alternative path on the left that threads through the trees parallel to the road for part of the distance. At the road junction at **Carrefour du Refrain** fork left to reach the dam at the **Barrage du Refrain**.

Pass the dam, then a gate and continue along the track close to the edge of the lake. This soon diverts around some equipment, then follows a stony footpath with trees to the right. Some distance further on the path reaches a vertical metal ladder (with a handrail) fixed to the rock face, taking the path up to a higher level.

The route continues along a well-worn footpath through trees and gradually drops back down to river level. Follow this path for several kilometres before passing the ruins of the old farm of Gaillots on the left. A little way beyond, the track curves off to the right and the GR5 takes a foot-path down through trees on the left. This emerges into a rough parking area where waymarks lead right, up the hill. Some steps follow, leading up to the D464.

Go straight across the road and follow the footpath up into woods on the other side. The river takes a broad, sweeping turn here and the path drops down to rejoin the riverbank beyond. Continue for a further kilometre to reach the hotel/restaurant (closed Tue/Wed) at **LA RASSE**. (For the *gîte* at Maison Monsieur go left over the bridge then turn right.)

La Rasse to Châtelot Barrage
(11km/7 miles, 3hr 30mins, height gain/loss 110m/0m)

About a half an hour further on there is another old glass-working site – there was a furnace here at **La Verrerie de la Guepe** until 1820.

Beyond this, 3km from La Rasse, is a signposted path junction where there is a choice of two routes, both leading to the Châtelot Barrage. The main path carries on to the left, signposted GR5 Barrage du Châtelot, and the alternative route, sometimes known as the Sentier Bonaparte, is signposted to the right.

Alternative Route

The alternative route is summarised here, but not described in detail. The simplest alternative is about 1.5km longer than the main route and involves a steep climb out of the gorge. Following the climb the route takes the road to the village of **GRAND'-COMBE-DES-BOIS**, then follows paths to pass the Belvédère de la Grotte de Grenier, dropping down to rejoin the main GR5 route several kilometres before the barrage. This alternative route can be extended to include the village of Le Pissoux, where there is the possibility of refreshments, to then rejoin the main route just before the Châtelot Barrage.

The main route follows the path left, soon passing the Bistrot Bonaparte, open during high summer.

Another hydroelectric station comes into view on the Swiss bank about 3km after passing the junction with the alternative route. The gorge is particularly steep sided here and the site incorporates a funicular for access. Close by is the Abri du Torrat, another accessible shelter.

Some of the most scenic stretches of the Doubs gorge lie ahead in the next 4km leading up to the Châtelot Barrage. The sides of the gorge close in and the footpath is forced to climb up to a rocky ledge beneath an overhang. Beyond this, some special care is needed. The GR5 uses a narrow footpath that crosses a very steep slope high above the river, then the route makes its way back down to river level.

Further on the footpath reaches a junction with a broader path where a returning branch of the alternative route comes in from the right. The main GR5 turns to the left, following the sign to Châtelot.

Not long after, there is a junction that might cause confusion – ahead is a GR waymarked path to Le Pissoux, and to the left is a GR waymarked path to Châtelot. The path to **LE PISSOUX** (café) is part of an alternative route, and the main GR5 turns left here.

This path provides a view of the dam before reaching a T-junction where a right turn is signposted. Follow this track to meet another T-junction where you turn left along an earth vehicle track leading to the car park close to **CHÂTELOT BARRAGE**.

Châtelot Barrage to Saut du Doubs

(3.5km/2 miles, 1hr, height gain/loss 60m/30m)

Take the path down from the car park, going towards the dam. The route passes behind a viewpoint overlooking the gorge. Continue down a flight of steps at the bottom of which a footpath is signposted towards Saut du Doubs. Follow this broad path, which climbs up from the river.

Within 10mins fork down on a narrower footpath to the left which in turn leads to a gravel path. Follow it down to the left to reach a sign at **Moron**. Continue down to join a lakeside track and turn right.

This level track reaches a rather striking feature where two opposite rocky headlands leave a narrow river

passage between. The route leads around the northern headland, passing beneath a rock arch. Beyond, the path climbs through woods. As the sound of a waterfall grows louder, a short diversion along the path dropping down to the left leads to a low-level viewpoint opposite the **SAUT DU DOUBS** falls. Continuing upwards along the original path, the route passes beside a viewing area to the left.

To get to a closer viewpoint, continue on downhill, keeping to the left fork on the way and following the path around to the viewing area by the falls.

Looking across the gorge at Châtelot

The Saut du Doubs

Saut du Doubs to Villers-le-Lac
(6km/4 miles, 2hr, height gain/loss 70m/60m)

Returning from the viewpoint just by the falls, fork left and pass first one, then a line of kiosks, and then a café/restaurant. This leads to the embarkation point for pleasure boats from Villers-le-Lac. From here take the road up to the right, climbing round a hairpin bend. At present the GR5 follows this road up to the crest of the hill, where there is a junction with another road at a place called **Les Vions**. (To reach the *gîte* at Cerneux Billard turn right here, then right again towards Le Pissoux, then left.)

From Les Vions take the road to the left, passing the 'No Entry' traffic signs. Continue downhill, passing a gap in the trees to the left that provides a good view over the sweep of the Doubs below.

This road joins the Route des Combes after about half an hour. Continue ahead to reach a junction with a more major road and turn left downhill along the Rue des Murgers.

This road leads down towards the riverside. Turn right and follow alongside the river towards **VILLERS-LE-LAC** (hotels, *gîte*, campsite, restaurants, cafés, shops). Keep to this road until it reaches a junction with a main road in the town centre, with the road bridge over the Doubs in sight to the left.

The tourist office is to the right, along the Rue Berçot.

SECTION 10

GR5 Villers-le-Lac to Mouthe

(85km/52.5 miles)

Some of the real highlights of the whole walk are found in this long section, including Joux Castle in its eagle's-nest setting, and the spectacular clifftop walk to the summit of Le Mont d'Or.

From Villers-le-Lac the GR5 rejoins the Swiss border after a long, steady climb. The landscape, and particularly the buildings, become noticeably more Alpine, and a series of vertical limestone rocks, the Dames des Entreportes, form an unusual geological feature beside the route. The path then climbs to reach Fort Mahler, a mid-19th-century fort overlooking the narrow valley of La Cluse-et-Mijoux. From the lookout point on the end of the promontory, Joux Castle on its massive limestone outcrop is suddenly revealed – the castle is ideally sited to defend the narrow gorge below.

Further on the route passes Lac de St-Point. Although the shores of the lake are ringed by small tourist resorts with facilities for water sports, it is also a haven for wildlife. The GR5 turns east, entering the winter sports areas of Métabief and Morond, and then runs along the top of 200m-high limestone cliffs giving uninterrupted views over the Swiss Jura. This rugged country around Le Mont d'Or is ideal chamois territory. The actual summit of the mountain is just off route, but easily reached by a short detour. The descent from here is by a gentler slope, passing the source of the River Doubs to reach the little town of Mouthe.

This section does include some high and exposed walking. On the approach to Le Mont d'Or the path runs close to precipitous cliffs, which could present a hazard in poor visibility.

This section can be walked in four days, with a suggested first night at the *auberge/gîte* at Les Cerneux, then overnighting at the one-star hotel at La Cluse-et-Mijoux, and a final night off route at Métabief (hotels and *gîte*).

Accommodation and Food

Km	Cumulative km		
		Villers-le-Lac	Hotels, *gîte*, campsite, restaurants, cafés, shops
3.5			Turn off for Le Chauffaud (*gîte*), 1.5km off route
1.5	5.0	Sur la Roche	*Auberge/gîte*
5.0	10.0	Gros Gardot	Café/bar/restaurants (closed Wed)
2.0	12.0	Meix Lagor	*Auberge* (refreshments)
4.5	16.5	Vieux Châteleu	*Auberge/gîte*, restaurant (weekends only out of season)
3.0	19.5		Turn off for Les Cerneux (*auberge/gîte*), 1km off route
11.0	30.5	Les Alliés	*Gîte*, second *gîte* 2km off route at La Perdrix
12.5	43.0		Turn off for Larmont Supérieur (*gîte*), 1km off route
2.0	45.0	La Cluse-et-Mijoux	Hotel, restaurants, café/bar, baker
1.0	46.0	Joux Castle	Café/bar
6.0	52.0	Chaon	Café/bar/restaurant
5.5	57.5	Malbuisson	Hotels, campsite, restaurants, cafés, shops
6.5	64.0		Turn off for Métabief, 1km off route
		(Métabief)	Hotels, *gîte*, restaurants, cafés, shops
1.0	65.0	Les Hôpitaux-Neufs	Campsite, restaurants, café/bar, shops
3.0	68.0	Le Petit Morond	Bar/restaurant
1.0	69.0	Le Gros Morond	*Refuge*
4.5	73.5	La Boissaude	*Auberge* (refreshments)
11.5	85.0	Mouthe	Hotels, *gîte*, campsite, restaurants, cafés, shops

Alternative Routes

	Montbenoît	Hotel, *gîte*, campsite, restaurant, baker
	Les Fourgs	Hotels, *gîte*, restaurants, café/bars, shops

Contact details for tourist offices and accommodation are in the appendix.

Maps

IGN 1:100,000 sheet 38
IGN 1:50,000, Le Doubs No2 Zone Est (part), No3 Zone Sud

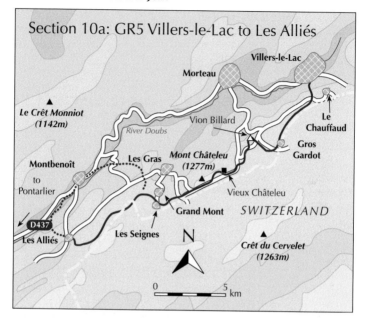

Section 10a: GR5 Villers-le-Lac to Les Alliés

Villers-le-Lac
Morteau
Le Crêt Monniot
(1142m)
River Doubs
Vion Billard
Le Chauffaud
Gros Gardot
Les Gras
Mont Châteleu
(1277m)
Montbenoît
to Pontarlier
Vieux Châteleu
SWITZERLAND
D437
Les Alliés
Les Seignes
Grand Mont
N
Crêt du Cervelet
(1263m)
0   5 km

Villers-le-Lac to Gros Gardot
(10km/6.5 miles, 3hr 15mins, height gain/loss 540m/210m)

Cross the bridge from the centre of **VILLERS-LE-LAC**, near an embarkation point for boat trips to Saut du Doubs. After about 100m turn right along the Rue de la Gare, then left up the Rue du Stade, which is a stiff climb for a minute or two. At the top of the hill various sports facilities surround a seasonal camping site. The road bends to the left past the Salle des Fêtes and reaches a main road at a T-junction. To the left the roadsign is for Morteau, but the GR5

goes right, then right again almost immediately on the D461 towards Neuchâtel.

Just beyond the signs for the edge of Villers-le-Lac go under a large road bridge, then about 100m further on take a minor road up to the left. Although this is marked as a dead end, there is a sign pointing 'vers GR5'. As the road snakes uphill there is a view back over Villers-le-Lac. The road leads across a railway line at a level crossing.

When the road bends sharply to the left just beyond the crossing, the GR5 leaves by a vehicle track to the right, signposted to **Le Chauffaud**. Keep to the main track uphill, ignoring further tracks to the right, still following in the direction of Le Chauffaud. The path enters an open pasture bordered by forest with Alpine-style houses on the slopes.

Farmsteads of the Jura

The farmsteads of the Jura have shallow-pitched overhanging roofs similar to those of their Alpine neighbours. In winter these roofs ensure that rain and snow are carried well away from the base of the walls. Traditionally the walls are further protected by wooden shingles known as tavaillons. In summer, water collected from this large roof area can be a useful resource, as there are few sources of surface water in limestone country.

In response to the extreme cold and deep snow of winter, all of the farm buildings – house, barn and byre – are gathered under one roof. This gives the house the advantages of the heat generated by the livestock and the insulation of the hay and straw storage. It also means there is no need to make a way through deep snow to attend to the animals.

The tuyé, a huge chimney, is used not just for heat but also for smoking meats and cheeses. It has an adjustable cap that allows the smoking process to be regulated, and it is also a source of ventilation, or even entry and exit if windows and doors are blocked by snow.

Further up the hill the path meets a T-junction. Turn right onto a lane that comes out some 10mins later onto the road at the small settlement of **Le Prélot**. Turn right, but almost immediately leave the road by a track

Beyond Villers-le-Lac

to the right signposted to Le Pralot. (To reach the *gîte* at **LE CHAUFFAUD** continue along the road.)

This track crosses open pasture-land, still climbing slightly, with a large old farm coming into sight over to the left. On reaching a lane, turn left. This leads round in front of the farm, which is called **Gradoz Dessus**. Carry on along this road through pastures for nearly 5mins, then look out for a GR cross on an electricity pylon and a sign to the GR5 pointing off the road to the right.

Take the indistinct path going up the edge of a field to enter the woods, becoming narrow and stony between conifer trees, and climbing quite steeply to reach a fence at the top of the hill. Go into the pasture and turn left, following the edge of the forest to reach the high point of this path. Turn right downhill to join a lane at the *auberge/gîte* of **Sur la Roche**. Follow this lane to the right to reach the D447 at a T-junction – some houses are dotted along the road to the left, but the route goes to the right.

After only a few dozen metres leave the road through a small gate to the left. There is a very faint vehicle track across this field and occasional waymarks on isolated trees. After leaving the road the GR5 carries on ahead for a short distance then veers slightly to the left, but the route is not clearly defined. Head for a track that enters the woods beyond the pasture, slightly to the left. Once into the woods join a track going steeply

170

uphill. On reaching an old house with wooden cladding, turn slightly to the right, taking a narrow, rocky path up towards the crest – a mossy, tumbled stone wall runs along beside the path.

As the gradient eases on reaching the crest, the path meets the Franco-Swiss border again, marked by frontier stones.

Cerneux-Péquignot

The border stones here have chevrons on the Swiss side and fleurs-de-lis on the French side, and were erected in 1819. This is two years later than the date on the previous stones (see Section 8, between Abbévillers and Villars-lès-Blamont) because of the particular history of the little village of Cerneux-Péquignot. Negotiations at the Congress of Vienna saw Switzerland laying claim to all the French territory east of the Doubs, but the French were unwilling to give up so much land and negotiated a compromise, and it was finally agreed that only the commune of Cerneux-Péquignot would be ceded to the Swiss. This was entirely against the wishes of the 300 inhabitants, and it was not until 1819, after much discussion, that the frontier stones were set up. Many of the people retained their French citizenship and continued to come into France to vote, but the village has remained a part of Switzerland ever since.

To the right there is quite an open view of the towns in the valley, Villers-le-Lac and Morteau. The route stays fairly close to the crest of the ridge, passing a series of frontier stones, and just beyond a ski lift there is a fenced enclosure around a modern building. Further along the ridge a vehicle track joins the path, carrying on in much the same direction and beginning to descend.

The route crosses a pasture and joins a lane at some farm buildings. The border stones follow a different line here, across the middle of large fields to the left. Beyond there is an open view across the lush green meadows and chalet rooftops of Switzerland, with forests in the distance. Follow the lane past some very large farmsteads and onto the D48 – the GR5 turns right here. The tiny settlement of **GROS GARDOT**, where there are café/bar/restaurants (closed Wed) on both sides of the Swiss frontier, lies a few hundred metres to the left at this junction.

Gros Gardot to Vieux Châteleu
(6.5km/4 miles, 2hr, height gain/loss 240m/130m)

Carry on past a car park on the left and follow the road as it curves to the right. The route leaves on the left just beyond a small wood to go up a gravel vehicle track signposted to Les Feuves. Keep on this track until it reaches the farm of Les Feuves, where it becomes a tarmac lane that swings round some more farm buildings and meets a road. About 50m to the left there is an *auberge* at Le Meix Lagor, but the GR5 goes to the right to very soon join the D447 on a bend. Turn left, passing another path to Le Meix Lagor on the left.

Just after the road has gone through an S-bend the route leaves on a footpath to the right – there is a signpost to Derrière le Mont, 25mins. The path crosses a small stretch of grass then goes to the left along a field boundary. Follow this alongside a tumbledown wall up the hill.

At the top of the field there is a stony footpath with signs to **BELVÉDÈRE DU VION BILLARD**, 100m to the right, and the GR5 to the left. The viewpoint is worth the short detour to look out over a wooded valley with outcrops of limestone cliff and scattered farms. The village of Derrière le Mont is below, and forests spread over the hills into the distance. (There are GR waymarks on the way back from the viewpoint.)

Back on the main footpath follow the sign towards Vieux Châteleu. Keep to the right-hand edge of a field, then cross the next field to reach a large concrete cross. The path continues along the top of the field, with an impressive cliff dropping down beyond the fence on the right, fringed by trees.

In a few minutes the route reaches the D447 again. Turn right along the

171

Derrière le Mont seen from the Vion Billard viewpoint

road and at a point called **Les Cernoniers**, where the road takes a hairpin to the right, leave it for a track to the left towards a small chapel. The track goes between the chapel and an agricultural building into open woodland. A couple of minutes later look out for a red 'GR5' and an arrow on a tree, indicating that the route branches off to the right on a much more minor track. Follow this track, ignoring a first footpath that diverges to the right, and take the right-hand branch of the next fork, along the well-used path. As there is a possibility of going astray on this section, it is worth checking frequently that you are still following waymarks.

The footpath runs parallel to a vehicle track in a broad clearing, merging with the track just before it comes out onto the D447. Turn left towards Vieux Châteleu. A track leaves to the left to a farm called Les Charmottes, which can be seen clearly across the fields, but the GR5 stays on the road. After about 20mins this reaches the *auberge* at **VIEUX CHÂTELEU** (*auberge/gîte*, restaurant – weekends only out of season).

Vieux Châteleu to Grand Mont
(5km/3 miles, 1hr 30mins, height gain/loss 40m/170m)

Immediately beyond the *auberge* the route leaves the road to the right. At the Vieux Châteleu sign the GR5 is directed left up a stony vehicle track towards Grand Mont. A grassy valley drops down to the left, with woods rising up beyond. A few minutes further on the route turns left off the track at a point where it is signposted to Châteleu-loge in 5mins. Leave the track and immediately pass through a stile. There are two paths ahead – a level grassy path goes to the right and a second path heads to the left downhill. Take the left-hand, downhill path through fields and turn right along the bottom of the valley to join a grassy woodland path.

About 5mins later look out for a footpath going up to the left, along-side a fence, to rejoin the D447. Turn right and follow the road downhill, with views of hills ranging into the distance ahead. Pass a farm on the right (Chez Voynot), and at the hamlet of **Nid du Fol** stay with the road when it turns sharply to the left.

Within a short distance this road meets the D404 at a hairpin bend. Turn right, downhill, towards Les Gras. About 200m down this road the route leaves to the left onto a very rough track. It carries on through a field, almost parallel to the road, then enters old conifer forest with tumbled, moss-covered boulders.

Go past a track to the right signposted to Les Cerneux, where there is an *auberge*. The GR5 follows a curve to the left, coming out of the forest, and continues along the forest edge, keeping to the left along the major track when a minor track joins from the right. The village of **LES SEIGNES** is visible ahead, with the limestone edge of Rochers du Cerf beyond. On reaching a road turn right, following the sign towards **GRAND MONT,** then left onto a broad vehicle track signposted to Le Théverot.

Grand Mont to Les Alliés
(9km/5.5 miles, 2hr 45mins, height gain/loss 130m/240m)

The track goes through fields, then woods. Watch out for a GR waymark indicating a turn to the right along a rather overgrown vehicle track. When this joins a more significant forestry track, turn right and almost immediately there is another junction. Turn right again and follow around under an outcrop of limestone to reach a group of farm buildings at **Le Théverot**, where the track comes out onto a road. From here an alternative GR5 route via Montbenoît (summarised below) goes to the right, but the main GR5 route goes to the left, signposted in the direction of Pontarlier.

Alternative Route

The alternative route climbs out of the valley and passes through woods and pastures, crossing the Doubs to reach the village of **MONTBENOÎT** (hotel, *gîte*, campsite, restaurant, baker). The abbey here was founded in the 12th century and embellished in the 15th and 16th centuries, and

inside there is some fine craftsmanship in wood and stone. The capitals of many of the columns are carved with examples of the plants, animals and fish found in this high region of the Doubs. The alternative route leaves Montbenoît by the Pontarlier road, but soon turns south and recrosses the Doubs. It follows the valley for a short distance before climbing over the higher ground and descending to rejoin the main route in Les Alliés.

Almost immediately after the main route leaves Le Théverot, the tarmac comes to an end and a gravel track continues uphill into the forest. Carry on across a large turning circle, with the path becoming rockier as it approaches the base of a cliff. Leaving the woodland the route continues across a pasture with a farm on the skyline to the right ahead. It reaches a signpost pointing up the slope to the right, and at the top of the slope, below the woods, is another signboard pointing left to Côte du Cerf. The farm at **Côte du Cerf** is reached in a few minutes. Turn left through the farmyard to join a gravel track which, once over the brow of the hill, descends through mixed woodland. As it comes out of the woods follow the curve round a clearing and back into trees.

At a signpost to La Ronde des Loups and Fresse, go straight on, ignoring a turning off to the left. Where the main track swings round to the right and becomes a tarmac road, the GR5 follows a track off to the left. This leads through a rough clearing, approaching the hamlet of **Cernet de Doubs**.

The route goes left and downhill round the side of the first house, following the sign towards Les Alliés. This soon leads along the top of a steep slope then curves to the left. At a fork take the lower, right-hand branch and go into a pasture. Turn right, then follow a faint track diagonally across the pasture towards a GR waymark at the bottom. At this point turn right beside a stony streambed. The route

then fords this little stream, and a little later crosses a more substantial stream by a footbridge. Carry on along the waterside towards a track on the right. Cross back over the stream, this time on a concrete vehicle bridge, and continue down a broad vehicle track.

The route stays beside the stream for about 20mins as it descends into a small gorge, quite steep sided at first, but gradually less so. Just after passing a bridge on the left, the track becomes a tarmac lane. The church of Les Alliés comes into view and the GR5 approaches it past the cemetery. The junction ahead is where the alternative GR5 route by Montbenoît rejoins the main route. On reaching this junction turn left towards Passage d'Entreportes.

Les Alliés

The original name of Les Alliés was actually Les Allemands ('the Germans'), but the local people decided in 1915 that naming their village after 'the Allies' would be more appropriate.

Les Alliés to Dames des Entreportes
(5.5km/3.5 miles, 1hr 45mins, height gain/loss 40m/120m)

A few hundred metres out of **LES ALLIÉS** (*gîte*) turn left again, following a GR waymark, down a minor road signposted to La Barillette. This road bends to the right after a small bridge. Follow it as it rises through farmland dotted with large farmsteads and Alpine-style houses.

In front of a farm with a large modern barn (Ferme des Bonjours) the GR5 turns left, still on the road signposted to La Barillette. Just before the next farmstead turn to the right up a gravel track. At a set of direction boards the route goes up onto a slightly higher track on the right.

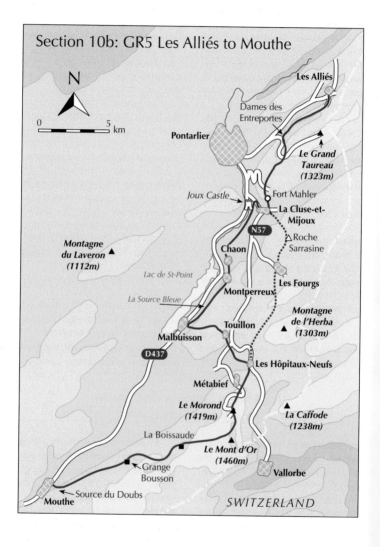

Section 10b: GR5 Les Alliés to Mouthe

N

0   5 km

Les Alliés

Dames des
Entreportes

Pontarlier

*Le Grand
Taureau
(1323m)*

Joux Castle

Fort Mahler

**La Cluse-et-
Mijoux**

N57

Roche
Sarrasine

*Montagne
du Laveron
(1112m)*

Chaon

Lac de St-Point

Les Fourgs

La Source Bleue

Montperreux

*Montagne
de l'Herba
(1303m)*

Touillon

Malbuisson

D437

Les Hôpitaux-Neufs

Métabief

*Le Morond
(1419m)*

*La Caffode
(1238m)*

La Boissaude

*Le Mont d'Or
(1460m)*

Grange
Bousson

Vallorbe

Source du Doubs

Mouthe

SWITZERLAND

Just a few metres further on it veers right again.

The route goes down a grassy clearing and the path is not obvious here. **Watch out for** waymarks on isolated trees and follow from one to the next. Further waymarks can be seen ahead as the path enters trees again. Follow this narrow but clear path through the woods. There may be a wire fence across it at one point, but carry on beyond this, following the waymarks. This reaches a small clearing, then re-enters woods.

About 200–300m beyond the clearing the GR5 follows the path round to the right, ignoring a tiny footpath to the left. Continue down to join a vehicle track diving steeply downhill. This track joins another more major one, still going downhill to the

right. After a short section where the going is awkward because of jumbled stones underfoot, it reaches a road. Turn left along this road, the Chemin des Contrebandiers, and continue past the Ferme des Moines.

At the next farm, the Ferme des Ouillettes, pass between the house and the barn then leave the road to the left, as directed by a signboard. This grassy vehicle track goes uphill behind the barn. **Watch out for** a fork almost immediately, where the main track curves right, but the GR5 follows a lesser track straight ahead uphill. This path leads to the left of a field and becomes a definite vehicle track between the trees. Cross a bridge over a streambed to join a road where the route goes to the left towards **DAMES DES ENTREPORTES**.

Dames des Entreportes to La Cluse-et-Mijoux
(9km/5.5 miles, 2hr 45mins, height gain/loss 210m/230m)

At Dames des Entreportes there is a striking rock formation to the left – a vertical sheet of limestone pierced with openings and with a jagged edge along the top. Opposite the rock the GR5 takes a private road, the Chemin du Morond. (A short alternative GR5 route by the Rochers du Larmont, not described here, leaves to the left at this point.) Further along this road, after the Ferme de la Motte appears to the right, the road crosses a small bridge.

Immediately beyond the bridge the route divides to offer two alterna-

tive routes over the next kilometre stretch. The GR5 *par la route* keeps to the road, but to avoid roadwalking follow the alternative, along the *sentier forestier* to the left.

Follow the track to reach a field. Continue along the track around the outside of the field boundary, first going left downhill, then curving uphill. This leads back up onto the road where the two short alternative GR5 routes rejoin. Turn left, then a couple of hundred metres up the road turn right where there is a sign GR5

Joux Castle and Fort Mahler, seen from Fer à Cheval

par la Grange Ferry. At a fork do not go left uphill on the Sentier Montagnard du Grand Taureau, but take the right-hand, downhill fork which leads into a wide pasture and follows the valley side.

After continuing across this pasture the broad gravel track turns right, with the buildings of Chasal du Creux ahead on the hillside. At a junction the GR5 goes left, still following the valley side. Looking down to the right, in the dip between two forested hillsides, it is possible to see the edge of Pontarlier in the distance.

At the next farm, **Les Jantets** (Jeantets on some maps), go straight through the farmyard and continue the short distance to the road. (The alternative GR5 route by the Rochers du Larmont rejoins the main route here – turn left to reach the *gîte* at Larmont Supérieur). Turn right down the road to reach a car park on the left, and turn left, following signs to Fort Mahler and La Cluse, down a cobbled, tree-lined track. On the way it is worthwhile diverting to the lookout point at Belvédère du Fer à Cheval, less than 1km off route. About 15mins later **FORT MAHLER** (Fort du

Larmont Inférieur), with its rock-cut defensive ditch, comes into view. Access to the fort is not allowed, but following round the edge of the ditch reveals a breathtaking view on the far side. The ground drops away steeply to the valley of La Cluse-et-Mijoux, with Joux Castle standing high on the rocky promontory opposite.

The steps in front of Fort Mahler leading down the valley side have a GR waymark, but are currently blocked off because they are in poor condition. The GR5 now follows a grassy track to the left, then at a T-junction turns right along an earth track and continues to hairpin down to enter **LA CLUSE-ET-MIJOUX**

(hotel, restaurants, café/bar, baker) just behind the church and cemetery.

Alternative Route

An alternative GR5 route turns left along the road in front of the church. This 18km-path passes the viewpoint at **ROCHE SARRA-SINE**, then crosses the open plateau to reach the village of **LES FOURGS** (hotels, *gîte*, restaurants, café/bars, shops) before rejoining the main route at Les Hôpitaux-Neufs.

La Cluse-et-Mijoux to Chaon
(7km/4.5 miles, 2hr 15mins, height gain/loss 200m/160m)

The main GR5 route turns right along the D67, then right again along the N57, where you have to walk along the pavement of the busy main road for over 0.5km in order to cross the railway.

Turn left at a sign pointing to Château de Joux, and follow this quieter road for about 300m before climbing a series of steps to the left, which cuts off the hairpin bends on the approach to **JOUX CASTLE**, where there is a café/bar and a souvenir shop.

Joux Castle

The high point on which Joux Castle stands, overlooking the trade or invasion

route of La Cluse-et-Mijoux, has been fortified for centuries. In the 11th century there was a wooden castle on the site, replaced in the 12th and 13th centuries by one of stone. Louis XIV's architect, Vauban, worked on Joux Castle in the 17th century, and Joffre in the 19th. There are now five successive circling walls, the final one only being added after the Franco–Prussian War of 1870–71.

Despite its apparently impregnable position, the castle has changed hands many times throughout its long history. In 1480 it passed to Louis XI, as a result of bribery and betrayal. In 1507 it was captured by Austrians. In 1639 it was taken by Swedes, then offered by treaty to Spain. In 1668 Louis XIV took Joux unopposed, then it was returned by treaty to Spanish control, then retaken by France in 1674.

In the time of the revolution and the Napoleonic empire it took on the role of a state prison. A 21-day siege in 1814 saw the castle fall to invading Austrians, but negotiations at the Congress of Vienna restored French control.

The castle now contains a museum with a significant collection of weaponry.

From the Joux Castle car park leave by the exit road of the one-way system. After a few hundred metres the road twists to the left. Follow the stony path to the right, signposted GR5 vers Les Angles. This footpath descends through woods to the settlement of Les Angles. Turn right on reaching the road.

Follow the road until it passes over a bridge then turn right. Almost immediately turn left to go up a bank and through an access into a field. Turn right to follow waymarks on occasional trees. This indistinct path veers away from the road towards an electricity pylon near the top of the field. The route enters woodland through an access gap and climbs a steep, rocky path twisting up to the ridge. It runs along the crestline, still climbing, then emerges onto a broad forest track. Turn right here.

For the next half an hour or so the GR5 follows this track as it meanders through the woods, with fairly frequent GR waymarks confirming the route. It becomes a tarmac lane and soon after reaches a road. Turn left towards a large Jura farmstead, Granges Tavernier. At a fork in the road go to the right, and as the road rises over the crest of the hill **LAC DE ST-POINT** comes into view ahead.

Lac de St-Point

The 6km-long Lac de St-Point is the third largest natural body of water in France. According to legend a needy woman carrying a small child sought shelter one night in a flourishing village. The inhabitants sent the pair on their way without help and they found refuge with the hermit St Point. The next morning they looked out to find the valley engulfed in water, with the village submerged. Nowadays a 23km walking trail with interpretation boards completes a circuit of the lake shore.

The road descends towards the D437, but about 100m short of the junction the GR5 goes up the Rue du Centre to the left, with roadsigns to **CHAON** (café/bar/restaurant) and Montperreux. Pass a restaurant, the Auberge des Montagnards, where various regional specialities are served.

Chaon to Malbuisson
(5.5km/3 miles, 1hr 30mins, height gain/loss 40m/20m)

About 100m beyond the restaurant turn left up the Rue Crêt to reach a T-junction with the D44. Cross the road and follow the rough vehicle track that turns to the right and rises above the road, giving a good view over the lake on the right. The track joins a road on a bend. A *belvédère* is sign-posted to the left, but the GR5 goes straight on. At a junction with the Rue des Champs Gauty opposite, turn right into **MONTPERREUX**. Follow this road (D204) through the village, passing an attractive example of a Jura church tower (*clocher comtois*).

The GR5 leaves the D204 by a minor road to the left, the Chemin du Chablet, which enters the Forêt Communale de Montperreux. After a few minutes the tarmac ends and then another track joins obliquely. Continue for about 50m from this junction before taking a track that

forks down to the right. Follow this as it bends uphill to the left, passing a path to the right which leads to **LA SOURCE BLEUE**, a spring just off the route. When the track meets a road, turn right downhill, but only for a short distance.

As the road turns sharply down-hill to the right, with a roadsign to Malbuisson, the route takes a lane to the left, uphill, to meet a T-junction. Turn right and follow the curve round to a small parking area where the route leaves the road obliquely to the left along a grassy track through the forest. Turn left along a road beside some tennis courts at the edge of the village. From here the GR5 carries on at this level, but a right turn goes downhill to the centre of **MALBUISSON** with its range of facilities (hotels, campsite, restaurants, cafés, shops).

Malbuisson to Les Hôpitaux-Neufs
(7.5km/4.5 miles, 2hr 15mins, height gain/loss 100m/30m)

Leave the edge of the village by carrying on straight ahead along a short road between houses. Just before the road becomes a gravel track the route turns sharply to the left, up through a field. Follow the footpath diagonally uphill. There is a single GR waymark on a concrete block, but few confirmatory signs on

the next short section. Continue uphill to meet a broader vehicle track and turn left along it until it reaches a road. Turn right, then almost immediately left at a large information board. (Note that camping is not allowed in this sector.)

The track reaches a crossroads with an old farmhouse on the left.

Keep straight on and a few minutes later pass a track on the right, signposted to Fort St-Antoine 1km away. Carry straight on. Very soon afterwards, when the main track goes straight on, the route leaves by a lesser track to the left. A spur goes off to the left, signposted Vue des Alpes, but the trail swings to the right and the track becomes a stony footpath. At the next junction follow the sign straight on for Touillon. A farm building comes into view, but before reaching it turn right, as indicated by GR waymarks, up a less distinct track. The track curves up to meet the ridge-line ahead and the view into the next valley opens up. On the far side is **MÉTABIEF** (hotels, *gîte*, restaurants, café, shops) and its network of ski lifts.

The GR5 takes a small footpath to the left towards a line of trees, cutting the corner of the track, then follows the track downhill to become a tarmac lane. This lane is called the Rue de la Côte where it passes a farm on the left, but becomes the Rue des Epassages when it meets the village of **TOUILLON**. Follow the Rue Clos du Château then Rue des Etillots to the right. Leaving the village the road descends to a large crossroads with the D45.

Cross over and go through the settlement of **Le Loutelet**, leaving by the Chemin du Miroir to the left. Carry on down the lane, but just before it goes through an underpass take a track up to the right to a level crossing. Do not cross the railway line, which is nowadays just used by tourist trains, but turn right, following a footpath along the side of the tracks. (To reach Métabief follow the lane that soon leaves to the right.) The GR5 continues until it reaches a railway halt at another level crossing. Cross the line here and take a gravel track up into the woods, where it continues parallel to the railway but slightly above it.

Les Hôpitaux-Neufs to Le Morond
(3.5km/2 miles, 1hr 15mins, height gain/loss 430m/0m)

The GR5 rejoins the railway to enter **LES HÔPITAUX-NEUFS** (campsite, restaurants, café/bar, shops) and turns right when it reaches the terminus of the tracks. (The alternative GR5 route by Roche Sarrasine and Les Fourgs comes in from the left.) Cross the road towards the village square and war memorial, then leave by the Rue de la Sablière on the far side of the square, uphill to the right. Just 20m up this road look for a footpath to the right and follow it across a field. It then winds through woods and clearings to reach a track.

Turn right along this broad gravel track and continue along the side of the hill, past picnic areas, to a

Near the summit of Le Morond

T-junction. Turn left, and at the end of the track take the footpath to the right. When it reaches a clearing, note that the GR5 does not follow the path all the way across. About half way up it drops down to the right, towards a GR waymark and an access gap. Cross a pasture diagonally and enter the woods again by an obvious earth track. At the next clearing turn right along the edge of the trees to meet a road (Route du Morond). Turn left here, then follow signs pointing off the road up the Sentier du Morond to the right.

The route continues up the gravel track. Pass a bridge to the right, and about 100m later leave the track to climb up the grassland to the left towards a road cut into the hillside.

The path gets steeper then meets some steps. Climb these and continue through two footpath tunnels. The path turns right immediately below the road cut into the hillside. To the left is a huge, stabilised wall of rock, part of which has been converted into a climbing wall.

After going through a third tunnel, cross the road and go up the side of a ski run. As height is gained on this slope the view back across into Switzerland starts to reveal some impressive peaks, including the dramatically shaped Mont Suchet.

At the top of the ski run take a stony footpath to the left that reaches an information board at a lookout point over the steep valley to the east. The GR5 then crosses the pasture to the right and goes through a tunnel under a ski run to the Chalet du Petit Morond, which has a bar/restaurant. The route joins a gravel track uphill for a short distance, then at the end of the track continues towards a clump of conifers. Amongst the trees the footpath becomes quite steep, but soon reaches the road. Follow this uphill as it swings round to the summit of **LE MOROND**, with its ski buildings.

Summit of Le Morond

The summit of Le Morond has a 360° panorama board. Mont Blanc and many other Alpine peaks are visible from here on a good day. Anyone who is walking the whole GR5 might be interested to see the direction of Nice, 345km (214 miles) away! Nearer to hand it is possible to trace the course of the path as it winds along the crest towards Le Mont d'Or, following the top of the extensive east-facing cliffs.

Le Morond to La Boissaude

(5km/3.5 miles, 1hr 45mins, height gain/loss 40m/240m)

Beyond the information boards follow the signpost indicating Le Mont d'Or. The path goes downhill, curving to the right below a ski information hut, then into woods. At a small col the *refuge Le Gros Morond* is to the right, but the route continues ahead up the opposite slope to meet a gravel track – there is a warning notice about the steep drop beyond. Turn right and follow the track along the cliff top. The next 0.5km of the path gives fine views over the spectacular cliffs below.

Pass the Belvédère des Chamois and reach a field fence. The route keeps to the cliff side of this fence and continues along the path. A few hundred metres before the summit of **LE MONT D'OR** the GR5 turns right, down towards a car park. The summit itself can easily be reached by continuing a little further along the path.

Summit of Le Mont d'Or

Three hundred Alpine peaks are said to be visible from the summit of Le Mont d'Or. The Swiss border is only a short distance away, and it is possible to follow footpaths down into Switzerland and the facilities of Vallorbe. There is a good chance of seeing chamois on this section of the crest, if you can arrange to visit when there is not too much disturbance.

Returning to the GR5, go down through the car park and stay on the road until a line of power cables goes through a broad clearing downhill. Turn left and follow this power line, crossing a track and then a road and passing a farmstead at La Blonay. At the next road the chalet-restaurant **LA BOISSAUDE** is immediately to the right.

The GR5 follows the cliff-top path along the ridge of Le Mont d'Or

La Boissaude to Mouthe
(11.5km/7 miles, 3hr 30mins, height gain/loss 0m/280m)

The GR route still follows the power lines downhill until they turn sharply to the right. At this point follow the path that leaves to the left into the woods. Within a few hundred metres the route comes out onto a road and turns to the right, passing Les Granges Raguin. Very soon beyond this **look out for** a left turn onto a vehicle track, with a sign to Corneau. It runs just inside the woods to a fork where the GR5 goes to the right and crosses a cattle-grid into a pasture. The track winds past a big barn at **Le Corneau** and leads into the forest.

At a turnstile the route meets a T-junction with a track. Turn right and follow this as it twists and turns, with clear waymarking. After going through a narrow access gap the path, scattered with limestone blocks, goes downhill through beech woods. It takes a bend to the left and emerges from the trees. Cross the grass to join a tarmac lane and turn left towards a small stone hut with a GR waymark.

The hut stands in front of the farm of **La Vannode**. Turn right here in the direction of La Bousson, skirting the farm and going down a field. After a large sycamore turn left to follow a wall to the top corner of the field, then turn right for about 200m until the route turns through an access in the wall into the open woodland on the other side.

At the next T-junction the GR5 goes right, and then passes through an

185

access in a wire fence to come out of the woods a few minutes later, just before **GRANGE BOUSSON**.

Go past the farmstead on a concrete track, cross a lane and go into the field opposite. The path here is rather indistinct, and it is necessary to look carefully for the waymarks heading across further fields towards a row of beech trees. On joining another track go to the right, downhill.

A few minutes later the GR5 reaches a tarmac lane at Sapeau Léger, but turns to the right, away from the farm. Within 100m, where the lane takes a sharp bend to the right, take the path off to the left, indicated by a GR waymark on the road surface. Turn left at a T-junction to follow a clearly marked track twisting through the trees until it comes out at a road where the route goes downhill to the right. When this road takes a hairpin bend to the right, take the vehicle track straight ahead, following GR waymarks. This track meets a road at a hairpin bend and the route continues downhill to meet another road.

Turn left here, following signs to Route de la Source and *sentier panoramique*. Ahead is a view of the town of Mouthe, spread out along the valley floor.

Follow the *sentier panoramique* as it twists through the trees and under ski lifts until it meets a well-made footpath at a T-junction. The path to the left goes to a viewpoint looking over the source of the Doubs. The GR5 turns right and descends some steps. At the bottom the **SOURCE DU DOUBS** is to the left.

From the bottom of the steps the GR5 goes to the right to reach a T-junction just in front of a caravan/campsite. To the right there is an *auberge* and a ski lift, but the route goes to the left then turns right just before the river. Follow the footpath into Mouthe along the side of the river.

When the path enters **MOUTHE** (hotels, *gîte*, campsite, restaurants, cafés, shops) turn left and then right towards the church. On meeting the main street (D437) the GR5 turns left past the *hôtel de ville*, but the tourist office can be reached by turning right.

SECTION 11

GR5 Mouthe to Nyon

(65km/40.5 miles)

From Mouthe as far as the Swiss border the route crosses the high plateau, much of which lies within the Haut-Jura regional park and is densely forested. While the first 20km do not involve any significant ascents, beyond Chapelle-des-Bois there is a very steep climb of about 250m to reach the high lookout points of Roche Champion and Roche Bernard, which provide the best places on the route for an extended view over the Jura plateau. From up on this ridge it is possible to appreciate just how much of the land is forested. The plateau is scattered with large farmhouses set within clear areas of grazing, although as time passes the forested area is steadily expanding. Two lakes lying just below the ridge, Lac de Bellefontaine and Lac des Mortes, add to the panorama.

From here the route makes its way to the small resort of Les Rousses, where the lively main street seems very tourist oriented, in contrast with some of the other more traditional villages. Not far beyond, the GR5 passes close to the waterfall at Bief de la Chaille and then rises to reach the Swiss border. Beyond the village of St-Cergue the descent from the plateau begins, and if the weather allows you may be rewarded with a grand sight of the Alps before the path drops rapidly down to flatter country on the final approach to Nyon on the shores of Lake Geneva.

This section can be walked in three days, with suggested stops at Chapelle-des-Bois (hotel and *gîte*) and La Cure (hotels and *gîte*).

Accommodation and Food

Km	Cumulative km		
		Mouthe	Hotels, *gîte*, campsite, restaurants, cafés, shops
7.5		Chaux-Neuve	Hotels, *gîte*, shop (closed Wed, and Sun pm)
4.5	12.0	Castel Blanc	Hotel
9.0	21.0	Chapelle-des-Bois	Hotel/restaurant/bars, *gîte*, shop (closed Sun pm)
4.0	25.0		Turn off for Chalet Gaillard, 1.5km off route
		(Chalet Gaillard)	*Gîte*, refreshments
2.0	27.0	Le Plan Perrat	Rough shelter
12.5	39.5	Les Rousses	Hotels, *gîtes*, restaurants, café/bars, shops
3.0	42.5	Bief de la Chaille	Youth hostel
1.0	43.5	La Grenotte	*Gîte*/refreshments
0.5	44.0		Turn off for Les Jacobeys (campsite), 2km off route
0.5	44.5	La Pile	Hotel/restaurant
1.0	45.5	La Cure	Hotel, *gîte*, restaurants
8.0	53.5	St-Cergue	Hotels, campsite, restaurants, cafés, shops
6.5	60.0	Trélex	Restaurant, shop
5.0	65.0	Nyon	Hotels, range of refreshment facilities and shops

Contact details for tourist offices and accommodation are in the appendix.

Maps

IGN 1:100,000 sheet 38
IGN 1:50,000 Parc Naturel Régional du Haut-Jura
(Both maps cover all but the last few kilometres.)

Mouthe to Chaux-Neuve
(7.5km/4.5 miles, 2hr 15mins, height gain/loss 60m/0m)

Mouthe

The position of Mouthe, at close to 1000m of altitude and sitting at a low point relative to surrounding land, has earned it a unique reputation as 'La Petite Sibérie'. In winter a layer of cold air can accumulate here, resulting in some very low temperatures indeed. It holds the record as the coldest commune in all of France, with a low of −36.7°C measured on 18 January 1968.

Continue along the main street in **MOUTHE** to reach a crossroads at the far edge of town where the D389 is signposted left towards the Vallée de Joux. Turn left down this road, passing a customs building. After 0.5km the road bends to the right and, immediately beyond, the GR5 leaves to the right following a broad track.

Within about 10mins the main track heads off towards the left and the route follows a more minor track that carries on ahead. The path crosses a small wooden bridge then enters woods.

Pass a path on the right to Moulin Cagnard, and about 5mins later a broader track comes down and joins from the left. Follow this to the right for about 50m to reach a small tarmac lane and continue on ahead. The waymarks are infrequent and often just paint marks on the surface of the road.

The lane meets a road at a T-junction where you turn right, although confirming waymarks may still be sparse. Follow the road around the left-hand bend just ahead, and only a short distance later, as the road turns to the right the GR5 leaves obliquely to the left along a vehicle track.

This track leads through woodland and after about 10mins passes a concrete building. Carry on to the edge of the woods. The route leads along the bottom of a broad, shallow valley and crosses to the right of a small stream. Not long after, the track takes a sharp turn to the right and the GR5 carries on ahead, taking a footpath that leaves just on the bend.

The path reaches a lane where Hameau Vuillet is signposted to the right, but the GR5 crosses straight over onto the footpath opposite. A few minutes later, just beyond a stile, ignore the first path that branches up the bank on the right. Keep with the main lower path, despite the lack of waymarks, and about 5mins later the route does lead up to the right – there is a waymark on a rock to indicate this – then crosses a stile into the field beyond. Turn left and follow the fence in the direction of the church of **CHAUX-NEUVE** (hotels, *gîte*, shop – closed Wed and Sun pm).

On entering the village pass the Auberge du Grand Git on the left, then join a minor road and follow this

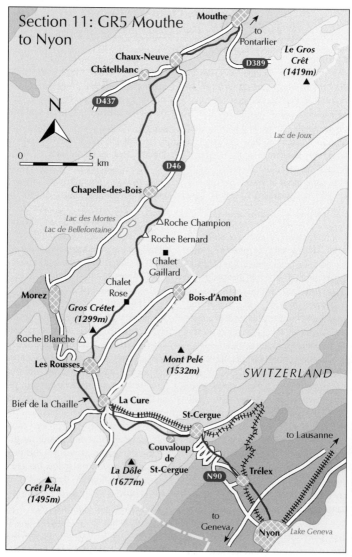

Section 11: GR5 Mouthe to Nyon

Mouthe

to Pontarlier

D389

Le Gros Crêt (1419m) ▲

Chaux-Neuve

Châtelblanc

D437

N

0   5 km

Lac de Joux

D46

Chapelle-des-Bois

Lac des Mortes
Lac de Bellefontaine

△Roche Champion

△Roche Bernard

■ Chalet Gaillard

Morez

Chalet Rose ■

Gros Crétet (1299m)

Bois-d'Amont

Roche Blanche △

Les Rousses

Mont Pelé (1532m) ▲

SWITZERLAND

Bief de la Chaille

La Cure

St-Cergue

to Lausanne

Couvaloup de St-Cergue

La Dôle (1677m) ▲

Trélex

N90

Crêt Pela (1495m) ▲

to Geneva

Nyon

Lake Geneva

around to the right to join the D437. Turn left here, then left again down the Grande Rue. The village shop and a *gîte* are just along here (for *gîte* enquiries apply to the hotel on the corner).

Chaux-Neuve to Chapelle-des-Bois
(13.5km/8.5 miles, 4hr 15mins, height gain/loss 210m/130m)

Follow the Grande Rue out of the village, and immediately after crossing a bridge with metal railings turn right down Le Lernier, a minor road. Follow this road as it rises gently between open pastures. Soon after reaching the top of the rise a signpost directs the GR5 off to the right along a footpath that strikes out up the field and into the woods beyond.

Once among the trees this path swings left and soon follows the top of a broad ridge. After some 15mins it leaves the forest and meets a gravel track at a T-junction. Take this track uphill to the left to a turning circle. The GR5 takes the track to the right, but only follows it for perhaps 30m, when waymarks indicate a turn onto a footpath to the right. This heads downhill, passing a tumbledown wall and a small old building on the right.

A few minutes later this path reaches a T-junction with a forest track where you turn left (there are the ruins of a farm opposite the junction).

The path follows the forest edge, then goes through woods to pass an isolated stone building to the left, facing an open field, and soon afterwards reaches a road. There is a sign to Castel Blanc Hôtel to the right, but the GR5 goes uphill to the left.

The road climbs steadily, passing a side road off to Les Enguenelles. Continue along the road for some distance through woodland, passing a small clearing, then a track to the right to Grande Combe, then another to the right to Pré d'Haut. There is a large clearing soon after where the GR5 leaves the road by branching diagonally off to the right on a path through the woods. Within 10mins the path joins a gravel track and continues ahead along it.

The route through the woods for the next 3km may sound complex, as there are several junctions, but waymarking is good and route-finding should be straightforward.

After following the track for perhaps 10mins the route takes a left fork along a broad downhill track signposted to Chapelle-des-Bois. Only a few minutes later fork left onto a less well-made path that leads to a T-junction with a gravel track. Turn left downhill.

Within 5mins this gravel track curves sharply left, and the GR5 leaves on the right along a muddy track through the woods. On reaching a signpost follow on ahead in the

191

Jura plateau beyond Chaux-Neuve

direction of Chapelle-des-Bois, then the way curves right and within moments joins a rough track coming in from the right. Follow this down to the left.

The track quickly reaches a road. Cross straight over and go down the bank on the opposite side (the direction is confirmed by a signpost indicating Chapelle-des-Bois, Sentier Chemin Jobez).

A short distance along this path a sign points off right to a viewpoint from which there is a fine outlook across the valley – the heavily forested ridge in the distance lies 5km further along the route.

On returning to the GR route the footpath drops down through scattered trees, then goes back into the woods. After a stile the path follows to the left of a woodland edge where a

signpost confirms the route, which follows the main path as it curves to the right and does not take the minor path ahead. Very soon, leave the track on a grassy footpath to the left that leads around the back of farm buildings. Carry on, following the scant remains of a stone wall, past a field trough towards more trees opposite.

The footpath joins a broader track and progresses through the trees, leading out onto a road next to a building with traditional wooden *tavaillons* covering the wall. Turn to the right, down the road, to reach the village of **CHAPELLE-DES-BOIS** (hotel/restaurant/bars, *gîte*, shop – closed Sun pm), passing the *gîte d'étape* on the right. Some more recent building developments are separated by fields from the older part of the village.

Turn right along the Chemin Minon, then left at the junction to reach the village square where there are two café/restaurants.

La Distillerie Michel

Just 1.5km outside the village of Chapelle-des-Bois is La Distillerie Michel, founded in 1888 and still a thriving producer of liqueurs from gentian roots. The plants in question are not the tiny, blue-flowered rockery alpines, but tall-growing yellow gentians that are common in mountain regions throughout much of Europe, and abundant in many of the pastures crossed by the GR5. As they can reach up to 2m high, they need a substantial root system for support. An astonishing 2000 tonnes of roots are harvested in Europe each year, but this wild resource does not appear to be under threat. The roots of one plant can weigh 5kg, and they are collected from the mountain pastures on a 15–30-year rotation interval, to allow regrowth.

The yellow gentian has a long history of use by herbalists, and its bitter-tasting extract is still claimed to counteract a wide variety of ills. When taken as an aperitif or liqueur, it is said to be an effective tonic and stimulant.

Chapelle-des-Bois to Roche Bernard
(4.5km/3 miles, 2hr, height gain/loss 210m/0m)

Turn right and walk along the road, passing the church and the little village shop on the left. Just beyond, turn left along the Chemin des Sources, which winds around behind a building then out between pastures, passing a golf course. A metal cross on the right dated 1639 marks a plague burial site. When the road takes a sharp bend to the right, a sign-post points the GR5 off to the left across a footbridge over a stream.

The rocky track beyond the bridge climbs diagonally across the pasture to enter woods. A few minutes later it crosses a track that comes downhill to a water-supply building. Carry on along the footpath opposite, and within a few hundred metres this joins the track higher up. Continue left along this track.

At a point where a small building comes into view ahead there are some signposts. Follow the route signed to Roche Champion par GR5, uphill. The route goes up through a clearing towards trees, crosses a rough drystone wall and continues upwards.

The path gets steeper and begins a series of hairpin bends up through the trees. When the ground flattens at the top of this section, there is a potential route-finding problem. It is tempting to carry on ahead at the top along a distinct, but incorrect, path that starts to descend, without waymarks. **The correct route actually**

turns sharply to the right as soon as the flat area is reached and follows an earth path. This path is easily missed because there is currently no visible arrow at the turn.

The path contours for some distance, heading to the southwest along the ridge, then reaches another potentially misleading point. Arriving at a small grassy area a path appears to continue up a very rocky section to the left that needs some scrambling. This is a false trail, as there are no waymarks beyond. The actual route continues ahead from the grassy area in front of the rock scramble and drops down slightly, following a clear gravel path.

The path leads on through the trees to a first open lookout area. Continue for just a few minutes to a second lookout area, the **BELVÉDÈRE DE LA ROCHE CHAMPION**. There is an enormous cross here and a superb view over the Jura landscape.

A signpost points the way towards Roche Bernard, 1hr away. The path leaves along the clifftop and within a few minutes the route forks to the right. This little rocky footpath does not follow a direct line here, but meanders along the top of the cliffs, following waymarks and passing close to border stone numbers 183A and 184, then passing a short distance to the right of the next stone.

Within 5mins the route joins a vehicle track at a hairpin bend and continues to the right. A few minutes later **watch out for** a path leading off up to the left. Although a little unclear at first, it skirts a railed-off cleft in the limestone then passes border stone 186.

Beyond, the path reaches a junction and a signpost with handwritten signs. To the left is Chalet Gaillard (*gîte/refuge* and drinks, 30mins), but the route goes to the right. Soon afterwards, at the Croisée des Roches junction, **ROCHE BERNARD** is indicated up a rocky path to the left that leads out onto the viewpoint.

Roche Bernard to Carrefour de la Fontaine

(9km/5.5 miles, 2hr 45mins, height gain/loss 0m/70m)

The path continues along the crest of the ridge, turning right at a waymarked T-junction before reaching the signpost at Les Essarts. Take the left fork here along the broad, stony track, and within 10mins the route is diverted onto a smaller track to the right. A few minutes later a track joins from the left and the route follows down to the right.

This track leads to a substantial triangular clearing at **Le Plan Perrat**. Take the route up to the right towards Chemin Neuf, which becomes a tarmac lane and passes an unlocked shelter.

The next junction is at **Le Chemin Neuf**, where the GR5 is signposted

The Jura landscape stretched out below Roche Bernard

left towards Le Chalet Rose. This leads through the forest for about 20mins to meet the road at **Le Plan des Buchaillers**. Turn right along this road for a little over 1km, and at the Carrefour du Capucin the GR5 turns left along a vehicle track that arrives at the **Carrefour du Plan Pichon**. Turn right at this track junction.

Follow this track until it meets a narrow road at the **Carrefour de la Biche**. Turn right, downhill, and continue along the road for 5mins to reach the **CHALET ROSE** (this is a locked shelter, although it is shown on maps as an *abri*). Leave the road on the left and take a rough vehicle track that soon passes a small quarry. Stay with this track, which reaches the Carrefour de la Fontaine.

Carrefour de la Fontaine to Les Rousses
(5km/3 miles, 1hr 30mins, height gain/loss 0m/120m)

From this point there is an alternative route for the GR5 that may be used from July to November, following woodland paths and rejoining the main route before the Roche Blanche junction. The route described below is the more general route, which follows quiet vehicle tracks and roads.

Carry on along the track for about half an hour to reach a minor road at Combe Sèche. Turn left down the road, ignoring side paths, until you reach the junction of **GROS CRÉTET** about 1km away. The GR5 leaves the road to the right along a vehicle track.

195

A few minutes later the route branches off left along a track signposted to Les Rousses.

At the next junction, to divert to visit the viewpoint of **ROCHE BLANCHE** 20mins away, which is well worthwhile, continue along the track and follow the yellow disc waymarks. To keep with the GR5, turn off to the left along a footpath.

Beyond this junction the waymarks lead through a slightly complicated woodland route on the approach to Les Rousses. The path crosses a track, and later takes a right fork that leads to a steep downhill section, then joins a more major track, following it to the left. The route leaves again almost immediately on the left along a well-marked path.

Pass through a turnstile, drop down through open woodland, then follow the little rocky path to reach a road. Turn right along this minor road to a junction with a major road (D29). Turn

right here, and within a few hundred metres look out for a tarmac track that rises obliquely on the left. Follow this to reach another, quieter road.

The main part of **LES ROUSSES** (hotels, *gîtes*, restaurants, café/bars, shops) still lies ahead – the church can be seen on the crest of the hill in front. To reach it go across this staggered junction by turning left then immediately right, down the Rue du Préchavin. (**Note** If you turn right at the staggered junction you risk confusion with the red and white waymarks of the GR559.)

Follow the road down past a pizzeria on the left. Turn up a steep little path on the left that cuts off the corner and climbs up to rejoin the road. Turn left and follow the road as it curves around to join the main street of the town. Turn left and walk down this street, passing a variety of cafés and shops – the tourist office is at the far end of the main street.

Les Rousses to La Cure
(6km/4 miles, 2hr, height gain/loss 140m/100m)

Continue along the main street until you reach the *mairie* on the left. Turn right down the road opposite and continue between car parks and under a major road. After the underpass turn immediately right, passing a block of shops and offices on the left.

Follow this road around a sharp bend to the left, then turn off right

along the Rue des Entrepreneurs. After 5mins the tarmac ends. Continue ahead along a broad footpath through a mix of woods and clearings.

The path reaches a small road. Cross this and go down the surfaced lane opposite. This passes an isolated house then reaches a signpost at **Le Bonzon**. Carry on straight ahead towards Bief de la Chaille.

Waterfall at Bief de la Chaille

The lane has now become a track and continues through the woods. Carry on for about half an hour to reach a junction at **Sous le Saut** where the GR5 goes straight on. The track then climbs up fairly steeply to meet a road. Turn right and follow the road for a few minutes to reach the **BIEF DE LA CHAILLE** signpost. (A short diversion off route to the right leads down to a shaded little gorge with a waterfall.)

Continue along the road, passing a youth hostel on the right. The road now leaves the trees and the view opens out. (The distant radar dome on the skyline lies on La Dôle in Switzerland.)

Turn off to the right along a minor road with a 'Dead End' sign. This immediately bends left, first passing Les Ecureuils then a series of garages. Follow this road downhill. It turns right and crosses a stream, and imme-diately beyond the bridge turns right once more, but the GR5 carries on ahead along a vehicle track. This leads uphill, passing the *gîte d'étape* of La Grenotte, and at the top of the hill reaches a busy main road (D29). (To reach the campsite at Les Jacobeys, turn right here.)

The GR5 turns left here (but note that GR waymarks also lead to the right for the GR9). Follow alongside this road for about 0.5km, passing the 'Auberge des Piles'. As the main road bends sharply to the left, leave it along a little side road to the right. Follow this road until it rejoins the main road a few minutes later. Continue ahead to reach the major road junction that is now in sight. Cross the busy N5 and go down the road opposite, the D29, into the village of **LA CURE** (hotel, *gîte*, restaurants).

La Cure to St-Cergue
(8km/5 miles, 2hr 30mins, height gain/loss 40m/140m)

Ahead is the French customs post. To follow the GR5 into Switzerland, turn around to the right along the road beside the Swiss customs post, then continue up the busy N90.

La Cure

La Cure is truly a frontier village, part being in France and part in Switzerland. The division does not only apply to the village as a whole – some individual buildings have the border running through them. This is taken to extremes in the Franco-Swiss Hotel Arbez, where one of the rooms has a double bed with the two sides lying in different countries.

The waymarking for the GR changes from here on, with all walking routes in this area waymarked with a yellow diamond. Signposts either use place names or the words *tourisme pédestre*, but there are no references to the GR5.

Follow the main road for about 400m, passing a souvenir shop (where money can be changed). Just after the road bends to the right, look out for yellow diamond signs on traffic signposts to the left. Turn left up this minor road, the Route de la Bouriaz, and within 10mins the yellow signs lead off left along a footpath beside the railway.

The path soon comes down to join the road to the right. Cross straight over the road and take the wide vehicle track that leaves to the right, with a footpath sign for Nyon. Keep to this track as it passes a water-supply enclosure on the right, then twists left to go through woods.

Follow this forest track for about 1km, and just as it becomes a tarmac road turn right, following the footpath sign. This leads through a gate towards a group of buildings. The path reaches a signpost at **La Pile Dessus** that indicates that the path to Nyon is off to the left. Turn left and set off across open pasture in the direction indicated, although there is hardly any real footpath.

After a few minutes this meets a vehicle track at the head of the field. Follow this left, continuing in the same general direction as indicated previously. The track begins to fade, but carry on to pass a yellow arrow on a rock. A signpost then comes into view near to the forest edge. Go towards this sign, which is on a wide vehicle track. Turn left along this track towards La Trélasse. (To the right the signpost points to **LA DÔLE**.)

The track continues through a forest clearing. Pass a ski school on the right and reach a signpost at **La Trélasse**. Continue on the same track in the direction of St-Cergue.

The track first heads towards a main road. On reaching a stone wall, do not go through the gate ahead, but turn right to follow the path that runs parallel to the road and the wall for some distance. Pass a sign for La Givrine, off to the left.

The path crosses a lane and carries on down the hill, following a clearing with tall trees on either side. The route is then directed left, up towards some buildings that form the little settlement of **COUVALOUP DE ST-CERGUE**.

Keep to the more major path as it twists around up the hill and then joins a road just by a junction. The houses of this settlement are up to the right. Cross over to the signpost, which indicates that the St-Cergue path goes straight ahead down a gravel track. Follow this as it heads off down a narrow clearing between conifers. Fork right at a signposted junction in the forest and a few minutes later the path emerges onto a road.

Follow the road downhill, with chalets on both sides, and turn right on reaching a T-junction. A couple of hundred metres further on, leave the road to the left, following a tarmac track into the woods. This leads onto a footpath that crosses a large field, then runs alongside a power line for a while before dropping left to join a road.

Turn right down the road, passing the St-Cergue campsite on the left. When the road meets the N90 at a junction just beyond a recycling point there are two tracks leaving on the right – take the one on the left, the Chemin de la Vieille Route. On the edge of **ST-CERGUE** (hotels, campsite, restaurants, cafés, shops) a signpost with a red/yellow diamond points right along Chemin Jacques Rousseau. Go down here and meet the main road by the Hôtel de la Poste. The tourist office and station are both to the left.

St-Cergue to Trélex
(6.5km/4 miles, 2hr, height gain/loss 0m/540m)

St-Cergue

St-Cergue is one of the Jura villages that maintains the annual 'Désalpe' celebrations that mark the return of cattle from more distant high pastures. The leading cows are decorated with colourful headdresses and driven down through the village street, and the farmers, all in traditional attire, seem to enjoy the occasion. The event usually falls on a Saturday in late September or early October. The street is lined with a variety of stalls and there is a holiday atmosphere.

Turn right and leave the village alongside the main road. Just beyond a hotel/restaurant there are

*The **Désalpe** festivities at St-Cergue, when cows are brought down from the summer pastures*

two tracks leaving the road on the left – the GR5 leaves by the second, steeply downhill. Before leaving the road a short diversion to the layby just ahead gives the chance of a fine view over Lake Geneva and the Alps.

The broad track drops steeply down through the woods. Within 3km it crosses the main road six times, cutting across the various hairpin bends – route-finding is not a problem.

After the last road crossing the track soon emerges onto a minor road. Turn left and follow this quiet road into the village of **TRÉLEX** (restaurant, shop). On entering the village pass the road of l'Acquedaine on the right. Immediately after there is a vehicle 'No Entry' sign on a lane to the left – go down here to the main road.

Trélex to Nyon
(5km/3 miles, 1hr 30mins, height gain/loss 0m/120m)

Cross the main road and go down Coin Greinge. After it curves to the right, turn left down the Route de la Gare, and left again at a water trough onto a small road between orchards. Cross the railway line and follow the little road opposite. Pass the cemetery on the left and take the tarmac track that continues between open fields ahead.

On reaching a crossroads take the track opposite, which leads under a bridge beneath a large, busy road. Beyond this the track joins a road at a corner. Carry straight on here and follow the road as it turns right. Turn left very soon after, following the yellow waymarks to go along a long, straight road, the Chemin de Changins, which is heading directly towards Nyon.

This lane reaches a fork near some buildings to the left. Turn right along the Chemin du Groseiller, which crosses a small stream then leads to a main road, the Route de St-Cergue. Turn left and walk down here towards the centre of **NYON** (hotels, range of refreshment facilities and shops). Stay on this road for about 1km, crossing straight ahead at a major junction with the Route d'Oulteret.

Head initially for the railway station by continuing along to the end of the Route de St-Cergue, then taking the pedestrian way under the railway to reach the Place de la Gare.

Turn left on coming out of the underpass to reach the station – the tourist office is several hundred metres further along this road. To follow the GR5, cross the road from the station and turn right, then almost immediately left into Rue de la Gare. Carry straight on through the pedestrianised area. Turn left along Place Bel-Air and then go down the Ruelle des Moulins almost opposite. This leaves the shop-

The end of the walk, on the shore of Lake Geneva at Nyon

ping area and enters an older part of town, passing the castle.

Follow this alley as it turns left, then turn left at the junction with Rue de Rive, and finally right down Rue de la Colombière.

This brings you to the shore of **LAKE GENEVA**, with the embarkation point for the ferry across the lake just ahead. The GR5 carries on from St-Gingolph on the far side of the lake. Ahead lie a further 660km (400 miles) of the route through the French Alps to reach the end of the path in Nice (see *Walking the French Alps GR5*, Martin Collins, Cicerone).

SHORT WALKS ALONG THE GR5/GR53

Some of the finest stretches of the GR5 and GR53 can be enjoyed as day walks, and the circuits suggested below incorporate some particularly recommended sections of the route.

While the GR5/GR53 is well waymarked, and described elsewhere in this guide, some of the return parts of these circuits may not be so easy to follow without a map. We have highlighted where a separate map would be recommended.

1 Castles of the Northern Vosges
(12km/7.5 miles, 3hr, height gain 440m)

This circuit visits three fine castle ruins.
Map Club Vosgien 1:50,000, sheet 2/8 (useful but not essential)
Start from Fleckenstein Campsite

From the campsite at Étang du Fleckenstein take the small forestry road opposite (signposted Gimbelhof) to reach the GR53 at the Col du Litschhof. Follow the GR53 for 5.5km (see Section 1), passing castles at Loewenstein and Fleckenstein to reach Froensbourg.

Return by going back along the GR53 to the end of the Étang du Fleckenstein, then turn right along the D925 back to the starting point.

2 Haut-Barr Castle
(21.5km/13.5 miles, 5hr 30mins, height gain 710m)

This route explores wooded hills and castle ruins typical of the Northern Vosges.
Map Club Vosgien 1:50,000, sheet 1/8 (recommended)
Start from Saverne

The 9km stretch of the GR53 south from Saverne (see Section 3) passes several castle ruins, perhaps the most striking being Haut-Barr. Continue to the junction at Haberacker. From here the GR531 (blue rectangles) can be used for the return route, passing Ochsenstein and Greifenstein Castles on the way back to Saverne.

3 Mont Ste-Odile
(5km/3 miles, 1hr 15mins, height gain 110m)

This short circuit connects the Mur Païen (a prehistoric wall), the convent at Mont Ste-Odile and the lookout point on Maennelstein.
Map Club Vosgien 1:50,000, sheet 4/8 (useful but not essential)
Start from Mont Ste-Odile Convent (with parking)

Alongside the Mur Païen

From the convent follow the GR5 (see Section 4) south past Maennelstein as far as Kiosque Jadelot. From the *kiosque* retrace your steps for only about 20m to pick up the red disc path to the left to La Bloss. From the junction at La Bloss follow the GR5 past the Mur Païen back to the convent.

4 Gazon du Faing

(23km/14.5 miles, 6hr, height gain 680m)

(With possible shorter circuit of 15.5km/9.5 miles, 4hr, height gain 430m.) This walk follows an impressive section of the GR5 along the crest of the Vosges, returning at a lower level past four glacial lakes. The Route des Crêtes bus service, which runs on Sundays and holidays from May to October, can add some flexibility to walk planning (details from tourist offices).
Map Club Vosgien 1:50,000, sheet 6/8 (strongly recommended)
Start from Col du Calvaire (with parking)

From Col du Calvaire follow the GR5 south (see Section 5) along the crest for about 9.5km. At Haut de Baerenbach (less than 1km before Col de la Schlucht) turn left off the GR5, following the yellow triangle waymarks towards Baerenbach. On reaching the GR531 (blue rectangles) turn left. At Baerenbach go to the left and follow yellow disc waymarks all the way to Lac des Truites (also known as Lac de Forlen), passing

Overlooking Lac Blanc

along the dam at Lac Vert on the way.

At Lac des Truites cross the dam and follow the red disc waymarks towards Lac Noir. After about 25mins, when Lac Noir is in sight below, **watch out for** the red/white/red route crossing the track. To the left is signed Hautes Chaumes, but currently there is no sign to the right, which is where you turn to go down to Lac Noir to join the GR532 (yellow rectangles), which leaves by the road then climbs the bank to the left into the forest. Continue along the GR532 to Lac Blanc, where a detour to visit the *belvédère* overlooking the lake is worth-

while. Leave Lac Blanc by the GR532, which follows the road, then drops off it to the left to climb away from the lake. Turn right on meeting a major forestry track then rejoin the GR5 to reach Col du Calvaire.

Shorter Circuit
Follow the GR5 only as far as Collet du Lac Vert, then take the red disc route down to Lac Vert to pick up the return path (15.5km/9.5 miles).

5 Le Hohneck
(19km/12 miles, 5hr 30mins, height gain 930m)

(With possible shorter circuit of 10km/6 miles 3hr, height gain 430m.)
This excellent circuit gives a good flavour of the Southern Vosges.
Map Club Vosgien 1:50,000, sheet 6/8 (recommended)
Start from Mittlach, west of Munster, or Le Hohneck (summit parking)

From Mittlach take the GR5 south-west (see Section 6) to the Col du Herrenberg. Turn right along the ridge using the alternative GR5 route (red/white/red), passing Le Rainkopf and Le Kastelberg. At Le Hohneck pick up the GR5 again (see Section 5) to drop back down to Mittlach, passing Lacs Schiessrothried and Fischboedle.

Shorter Circuit
Start at Le Hohneck and follow the GR5 only as far as Lac de Schiessrothried, then the GR531 (blue rectangles) up to join the GR5 alternative route near to Ferschmuss, and return along the ridge to Le Hohneck. (**Note** This part of the GR531 includes some rocky sections, crossed with the help of fixed chains.)

6 Le Grand Ballon
(14.5km/9 miles, 4hr, height gain 460m)

This route, crossing the highest summit in the Vosges, gives fine views over the Alsace Plain.
Map Club Vosgien 1:50,000, sheet 6/8 (recommended)
Start from Col du Haag, on the Route des Crêtes

From Col du Haag the GR5 crosses the summit of Le Grand Ballon (see Section 6) then drops down past the Ferme-Auberge du Ballon. Just over 0.5km from here, leave the GR5 and take the blue cross route to the left to Judenhut. Follow this path past Judenhut towards Gustiberg.

About 15mins beyond Lieserwasen **watch out for** a junction where the blue cross path divides. A blue cross sign points off to the right towards Schutzle and Lautenbach, but this is not the route to follow. The path to Gustiberg carries on ahead along the existing vehicle track (still following blue crosses), but the sign confirming this is not prominent.

After passing the farm of Gustiberg continue following the blue cross route towards Lac du Ballon. Go across the dam and take the red/white/red path uphill and through the parking area, then to the left, signed towards Col du Haag. This zigzags upwards. Turn left on reaching the GR532 (yellow rectangles) to return to Col du Haag.

7 Les Échelles de la Mort
(20.5km/12.5 miles, 5hr 30mins, height gain 670m)

This stretch of the GR5 in the gorge of the Doubs includes the ladders at Les Échelles de la Mort, and an excellent viewpoint over the gorge. The suggested return route involves a steep climb out of the gorge.
Map IGN 1:50,000 Le Doubs No2 Zone Est (strongly recommended)
Start from Charmauvillers; alternatively, use parking at Le Refrain

From Charmauvillers follow the road down to Bief d'Etoz. Turn right along the GR5 (see Section 9) and follow it along the gorge for 6km, going down the ladders at Les Échelles de la Mort to reach the car park at Le Refrain.

At Carrefour du Refrain, about 2km beyond the car park, leave the GR5 and follow the road uphill for about 1km. Take a footpath to the right, signposted to Le Bois-de-la-Biche (blue/yellow waymarks). At the signpost at La Douvotte turn right towards Les Échelles de la Mort for less than 100m, then at the next sign-post take the track to the left, uphill. This reaches a pasture just below the hotel at Le Bois-de-la-Biche.

From the signpost in this pasture follow the track to reach the large farmstead at Vaudey (there are occa-sional blue/yellow waymarks).

Join the road (D292) and turn right. After about 3.5km, where the road reaches a junction, turn right and continue to the *refuge* at La Montée. A few hundred metres beyond this the road turns to the left. Take the track leaving to the right, signposted Charmauvillers par le sentier du crête, and follow the blue/yellow waymarks to reach the road at Col de la Vierge. Take the D342 almost straight opposite, then turn along the road to the right after less than 100m, sign-posted to Seud. A small footpath to the right descends back into Charmauvillers.

8 Saut du Doubs

(25.5km/16 miles, 7hr, height gain 400m)

This circuit includes perhaps the finest stretch of the GR5 path along the Doubs gorge, and also passes the celebrated waterfall at Saut du Doubs.
Map IGN 1:50,000 Le Doubs No2 Zone Est (strongly recommended)
Start from The car park at the Châtelot Barrage, reached by road through Le Barboux and Le Pissoux

From the car park go down the steps and follow the GR5 south (see Section 9) to Saut du Doubs. Carry on from the waterfall to the embarkation point for boat trips and take the road out of Saut du Doubs. Leave the GR5, taking a track to the right signposted to Le Châtelard and Le Pissoux. Follow the blue/yellow waymarks and signs to Le Pissoux. From the village carry on

straight on, following signs to Gourdavi. This part of the route now follows the red/white waymarks of the high-level alternative GR5 route. About 10mins beyond Gourdavi watch out for a fork – do not follow the blue/yellow waymarks down to the right, but fork left, still following red/white waymarks. Follow these through Grand'Combe-des-Bois, then continue along the road to reach a signpost to Sur la Côte. Turn right here and drop down the hairpins to rejoin the GR5 main route (see Section 9). Turn right to return along the gorge to the car park.

9 Le Morond and Le Mont d'Or
(12km/7.5 miles, 3hr 30mins, height gain 550m)

This walk includes the impressive clifftop section of the route as it approaches Le Mont d'Or, with extensive views over the Swiss Jura.
Map IGN 1:50,000 Le Doubs No3 Zone Sud (strongly recommended)
Start from Métabief (parking by ski lifts)

Starting from the tourist office by the ski centre in Métabief, walk through the Forum and take the road to the left, the Route du Morond. Walk up this quiet road for about 0.7km and turn right up the GR5 (see Section 10). Follow this for about 4km over Le Morond to reach the cliffs by Le Mont d'Or. A short diversion reaches the summit itself.

To return to Métabief, either retrace your steps or continue through the car park at Le Mont d'Or, following the GR5 until it leaves the road to the left. Stay on the road from here to reach the first junction and turn right towards Le Floçon. Carry on past the parking at Le Floçon, and where the road hairpins to the left, leave by a track to the right, sign-

The cliffs of Le Mont d'Or

posted to Métabief. Almost immediately, curve sharply left to follow a
path to Le Paradis Chalet.

At Le Paradis turn left down the
road and descend to a hairpin to the
left. Leave the road here by a track to
the right, with a sign for the walking
circuit of Les Falaises du Mont d'Or.
Carry on for a short distance and take
the path forking left, signposted to
Métabief. At the next fork follow the
blue/yellow waymarks to the right,
which indicate the route back down
to Métabief.

10 Roche Bernard
(9.5km/6 miles, 3hr, height gain 210m)

(With possible longer circuit of 22.5km/14 miles, 6hr 15mins, height
gain 520m.)
This circuit includes one of the best viewpoints over the Jura plateau.
Map IGN 1:50,000 Parc Naturel Régional du Haut-Jura (useful but
not essential)
Start from Chapelle-des-Bois, between Mouthe and Les Rousses

The 4.5km of the GR5 south from
Chapelle-des-Bois (see Section 11)
includes a steep climb to the ridge of
Mont Risoux, passing the outlook
point of Roche Champion to reach
Roche Bernard. A return route is
possible by retracing the path for a
short distance to the signpost at
Croisée des Roches and turning left
towards Sur les Lacs. This descends
steeply to join a quiet road where
you turn right and return to Chapelle-
des-Bois.

Longer Circuit
Follow the GR5 beyond Roche
Bernard to Plan des Buchaillers.
Take the lane to the left to reach
the village of Bois-d'Amont. Turn
left at the junction of Les
Combettes and follow the Tour
de la Haute-Bienne (red/yellow
waymarks) past Chalet Gaillard
to return to Roche Bernard.

OTHER WALKS IN THE VOSGES

LONG DISTANCE ROUTES IN THE VOSGES

In addition to the GR5/GR53 there are several other long distance routes in the Vosges. The GR531 and GR532 both run north–south, and combining sections of these two routes with parts of the main GR5/GR53 allows many circular trips to be considered. The outlines below are not detailed, but offer ideas that might help in planning a trip. (See map 'Walking in the Vosges', page 10.)

The GR531 – Soultz-sous-Forêts to Masevaux
(281km/174.5 miles, 12–15 days)

The GR531 (waymarked by blue rectangles) provides a varied route through the Vosges range, and a walker who traverses the entire length will see many aspects of the Vosgien landscape. Compared with the more important GR5/GR53, some well-known landmarks are bypassed (such as Le Grand Ballon), but there are many other highlights. The route incorporates the excellent viewpoints on Le Grand Ventron and Le Petit Drumont, and passes through the town of Munster in the valley of the Fecht. (See map page 10.)

The northern starting point of the walk, the village of **SOULTZ-SOUS-FORÊTS** (station, café, shop), can be reached by rail. Only a few kilometres from the German border, this is Maginot Line country, and a surviving part of this network of fortifications can be viewed at the fort of Schoenenbourg 4km away. The fort at Four à Chaux also lies close to the route at **LEMBACH** (tourist office, hotel/restaurants, *refuge*, shops).

Approaching the Grotte des Fées, near Chapelle St-Michel (GR531)

The initial part of the walk leads through low wooded hills, passing Lembach and turning south at Froensbourg castle to reach **NIEDER-BRONN-LES-BAINS** (tourist office, station, hotel/restaurants, campsite, shops). For the next short stretch the route stays out of the forest, keeping to the edge of the plain through the old village of Oberbronn, then rising up to **LICHTENBERG** (hotel, *gîte*, café/restaurants), with its castle. The path then winds through woods to reach **SAVERNE** (tourist office, station, hotel/restaurants, hostel, campsite, shops) by way of the Château de Hunebourg and Chapelle St-Michel.

South from Saverne the route through wooded hills passes yet more castle ruins at Schlosserhöhe and Le Schlossberg, before dropping down to

OBERHASLACH (tourist office, hotels, restaurants, shops) in the valley of the Bruche.

There follows a long stretch with little access to facilities, and a diversion to **STE-MARIE-AUX-MINES** (tourist office, campsite, range of facilities) might be required. The GR531 crosses the GR5 at Champ du Feu, and for some 30km keeps to a line that roughly follows the crest of one of the the other main ridges of the Vosges considerably to the west of the GR5. The route crosses the Col de Ste-Marie, emerging onto pasture over Le Rossberg to reach **COL DU BONHOMME** (hotel/restaurant, *gîte*) and Col du Calvaire.

While the GR5 keeps to the high ground from this col, the GR531 leads down to the village of **ORBEY** (tourist office, hotel, *gîte*, campsites, café, shops), then passes the First World War museum and preserved trenches at Le Linge before reaching the small town of **MUNSTER** (tourist office, station, hotel/restaurants, campsite, shops). Although a large part of this town was destroyed during the First World War, some historic buildings remain, including the ruins of the Gregorian abbey. Nesting storks make good use of the rooftops in the centre of town.

The GR531 then regains the Vosges ridge at **COL DE LA SCHLUCHT** (hotels, café/restaurant).

After a short diversion down to the lake at Schiessrothried the route follows the crest of another wooded ridge for about 20km, passing viewpoints at Le Grand Ventron and Le Petit Drumont. After **COL DE BUSSANG** the path crosses the GR5 route at Col des Perches, then descends to the Doller Valley, passing a string of mountain lakes on the way, to reach **MASEVAUX** (tourist office, hotel, campsite, café/restaurant, shops). Beyond the Vosges the path continues to Leymen on the Swiss border.

The village of Masevaux in the south of the Vosges lies on the GR531 and GR532

Facilities

This list only includes the main facilities along the route (TO = tourist office).

Km	Cumulative km		
		Soultz-sous-Forêts	Station, café, shop
8.0		Soultzerkopf	*Refuge*
6.0	14.0	Lembach	TO, hotel/restaurants, *refuge*, shops
3.0	17.0	Étang du Fleckenstein	Campsite
15.5	32.5	Niederbronn-les-Bains	TO, station, hotel/restaurants, campsite, shops
3.0	35.5	Oberbronn	*Gîte*, campsite, restaurant, shop
6.0	41.5	Offwiller/Rothbach	Restaurant, shops
5.5	47.0	Lichtenberg	Hotel, *gîte*, café/restaurants
7.0	54.0	Ingwiller	TO, station, hotel, restaurant, cafés, shops
11.5	65.5		Turn off for La Petite-Pierre, 2.5km off route
		(La Petite-Pierre)	TO, hotels, *gîte*, restaurants, cafés, baker
17.5	83.0	Saverne	TO, station, hotel/restaurants, hostel, campsite, shops
24.5	107.5	Wangenbourg	TO, hotels/restaurants, *gîte*, campsite, shop
12.5	120.0	Oberhaslach	TO, hotels/restaurants, shops
3.0	123.0	Urmatt	Station, hotels, restaurants, shops
7.0	130.0	Mollkirch	Campsites
12.0	142.0	Rothlach	Turn off for Le Hohwald, 3.5km off route
		(Le Hohwald)	TO, hotels/restaurants, *gîte*, campsite, cafés, shop
5.0	147.0	Champ du Feu	Campsite 1.5km off route, *refuge* 1km off route
3.0	150.0	Col de la Charbonnière	Hotel/*auberge*
18.0	168.0		Turn off for Ste-Marie-aux-Mines, 5.5km off route
		(Ste-Marie-aux-Mines)	TO, campsite and range of facilities

11.0	179.0		Turn off for Col des Bagenelles, 1km off route
		(Col des Bagenelles)	Hotel, refuge, *gîte*, *ferme-auberge*
4.5	183.5	Col du Bonhomme	Hotel/restaurant, *gîte*; turn off for Le Bonhomme, 3km off route
		(Le Bonhomme)	Hotels/restaurants, campsite, café, shop
6.0	189.5	Col du Calvaire	Hotels, *refuges*, café/restaurant
5.0	194.5	Orbey	TO, hotel, *gîte*, campsites, café, shops
11.0	205.5	Munster	TO, station, hotel/restaurants, campsite, shops
8.5	214.0	Schanzwasen	*Gîte* (1km off route)
3.5	217.5	Col de la Schlucht	Hotels, café/restaurant
6.5	224.0	Gaschney	*Refuge*
7.5	231.5	Rainkopf	*Refuge*
14.0	245.5	Col d'Oderen	*Auberge*; turn off for Kruth, 4.5km off route
		(Kruth)	Station, hotels, *gîte*, campsite, shops
5.5	251.0	Col de Bussang	Turn off for Bussang, 3km off route
		(Bussang)	Hotels, campsite, restaurants, shops
7.5	258.5	Rouge Gazon	Hotel/*refuge*
3.0	261.5	Neuweiher	*Refuge/auberge*
6.5	268.0	Sewen	Hotels, restaurants
13.0	281.0	Masevaux	TO, hotel, campsite, café/restaurants, shops

Information Sources

From any Alsace tourist office Alsace camping guide, hotel/restaurant guide
From Haut-Rhin tourist office *Guide des Loisirs* (*gîtes d'étape*, *refuges* in Haut-Rhin)
From Bas-Rhin tourist office Guide to *gîtes d'étape* and *chambres d'hôte*
See also **www.gites-refuges.com**

Maps

IGN 1:100,000 sheets 12 and 31
Club Vosgien 1:50,000, sheets 1/8, 2/8, 4/8, 6/8, and 7/8 (small part only)

The GR532 – Wissembourg to Belfort

(369.5km/229.5 miles, 14–21 days)

The GR532 (waymarked by yellow rectangles) is another alternative north–south route in the Vosges that leads the walker past a different selection of points of interest as it crosses and recrosses the GR5/GR53 and GR531. Particular highlights include many attractive towns and villages, such as Turckheim and St-Amarin, and open views gained from such summits as Grand Brézouard and Le Petit Ballon. (See map page 10.)

The GR532, like the GR53, starts from **WISSEMBOURG** (tourist office, station, hotels, restaurants, cafés, shops). It passes significant remains of the old Maginot Line defences before reaching **LEMBACH** (tourist office, hotel/restaurants, *refuge*, shops), from where it continues past the Northern Vosges castles of Petit Arnsbourg and Lutzelhart, climbing a series of low, wooded hills, followed by brief descents into Philippsbourg and Baerenthal. After heading through **LICHTENBERG** (hotel, *gîte*, café/restaurants) it arrives at **LA PETITE-PIERRE** (tourist office, restaurants, *gîte*, hotels, cafés, baker) in the heart of the regional park of the Northern Vosges.

A further walk through the woods reaches Graufthal, with its remarkable rock-cut houses. The path then leads on out of the forest to the little town of **PHALSBOURG** (tourist office, hotel, youth hostel, restaurants, shops), which has a museum and a fortified gateway.

Beyond here the route continues to the Marne–Rhine canal, where the village and castle of Lutzelbourg can be visited. The path follows a stretch of the canal to pass the St-Louis inclined-plain, which is a boat-lift designed to speed canal traffic past a change of level. After the village of **WANGENBOURG** (tourist office, hotels/restaurants, *gîte*, campsite, shop) the path skirts the side of Schneeberg on the way to the castle ruins at Nideck, then passes through **URMATT** (station, hotels, restaurants, shops) and leads on to the museum at the Second World War concentration camp of Struthof.

The route continues through the villages of **VILLÉ** (tourist office, hotels, restaurants, campsite, cafés, shop) and **LIÈPVRE** (hotels, restaurant, campsite, shops) and climbs over the rounded granite summit of Grand Brézouard, where there are fine views towards Fréland in the valley below. The path skirts the two picturesque glacial lakes of Lac Blanc and Lac Noir, set against steep cliffs, then passes close to the First World War cemetery and museum at Le Linge before reaching the town of **TURCK-HEIM** (tourist office, campsite, range of facilities).

Turckheim

The attractive town of Turckheim has a medieval quarter with traditional timbered houses, three ancient gateways and an interesting and very informative museum recording the trials of the people of Alsace during the Second World War.

Continuing from Turckheim, back in the woodland the castle of Pflixbourg is soon reached. Open pasture forms the approach to Le Petit Ballon, then the route runs below the crest of the main ridge of the Vosges before rising to skirt the summit of Le Grand Ballon.

The village of **ST-AMARIN** (tourist office, station, hotels, restaurants, shops) lies at the bottom of a steep descent through woodland, and the Serret museum has a varied collection illustrating the history of the valley. A further walk over wooded hills reaches **MASEVAUX** (tourist office, hotel, campsite, café/restaurants, shops), then the landscape begins to flatten and open up on the approach to **BELFORT** (tourist office, youth hostel, campsite, range of facilities).

The GR532 continues through this historic town, which has a castle, fort, museums, and a massive stone lion designed by Bartholdi, the designer of the Statue of Liberty. Having left the Vosges the route then curves round through the Territory of Belfort to reach **MULHOUSE**.

Facilities
This list only includes the main facilities along the route (TO = tourist office).

Km	Cumulative km		
		Wissembourg	TO, station, hotels, restaurants, cafés, shops
6.0		Col du Pigeonnier	*Refuge*
3.0	9.0		Turn off for Climbach, 0.5km off route
		(Climbach)	Hotel/restaurants, small bakers
6.0	15.0	Soultzerkopf	*Refuge*
11.5	26.5	Lembach	TO, hotel/restaurants, *refuge*, shops

Km	Cumulative km		
11.0	37.5	Obersteinbach	Hotels, *gîte*, restaurants
17.0	54.5	Étang de Hanau	Campsite
3.0	57.5	Philippsbourg	Hotel, shop
4.0	61.5	Baerenthal	TO, hotel, youth hostel, campsite, shops
8.0	69.5	Reipertswiller	*Gîte*, 1.5km off route
1.5	71.0	Lichtenberg	Hotel, *gîte*, café/restaurants
12.0	83.0	Wingen-sur-Moder	Station, hotel, campsite, restaurant, shop
9.5	92.5	La Petite-Pierre	TO, hotels, *gîte*, restaurants, cafés, baker
8.0	100.5	Graufthal	Hotel, restaurants
9.0	109.5	Phalsbourg	TO, hotel, youth hostel, restaurants, shops
4.0	113.5	Lutzelbourg	TO, station, hotel, restaurant, bars, shops
20.5	134.0	La Hoube	Hotel/restaurant; turn off for Dabo, 3.5km off route
		(Dabo)	TO, hotel, *gîte*, campsite, restaurant, shop
6.0	140.0	Wangenbourg	TO, hotels/restaurants, *gîte*, campsite, shop
20.0	160.0	Urmatt	Station, hotels, restaurants, shops
4.0	164.0		Turn off for Grendelbruch, 1.5km off route
		(Grendelbruch)	Hotels, *refuges*, bars, shops
11.0	175.0	Struthof	Restaurant
4.0	179.0	La Broque	Turn off for Rothau, 2km off route
		(Rothau)	Campsite, hostel
1.0	180.0	Schirmeck	TO, station, hotel, restaurants, cafés, shops
6.0	186.0	Salm	*Gîte*
12.5	198.5	Saulxures	Hotels, campsite, restaurants, café/bar, shops
5.5	204.0	Bourg-Bruche	Hotel/restaurant; turn off for Saales, 3km off route

		(Saales)	TO, station, campsite, and range of facilities
15.5	219.5	Villé	TO, hotels, campsite, restaurants, café, shops
14.0	233.5	Lièpvre	Hotel, campsite, restaurant, shops
22.5	256.0	Le Bonhomme	Hotel/restaurants, campsite, café, shop
5.5	261.5	Col du Calvaire	Hotels, *refuges*, café/restaurant
4.0	265.5	Lac Noir	*Refuge*
10.5	276.0	Labaroche	Campsite
7.5	283.5	Turckheim	TO, campsite and range of facilities
17.0	300.5		Turn off for Osenbach (campsite, shop), 3.5km off route
6.0	306.5	Rothenbrunnen	*Refuge, ferme-auberge*
2.0	308.5	Hilsen	*Refuge*
7.0	315.5	Lac de la Lauch	Turn off for Le Markstein, 3.5km off route
		(Le Markstein)	Hotels, *gîtes*, café/restaurants
6.5	322.0	Grand Ballon	Chalet-hotel, restaurants
6.5	328.5	St-Amarin	TO, station, hotels, restaurants, shops
15.0	343.5	Masevaux	TO, hotel, campsite, café/ restaurants, shops
8.0	351.5	Rougemont-le-Château	*Gîte*, restaurant, shops
18.0	369.5	Belfort	TO, youth hostel, campsite and range of facilities

Information Sources

From any Alsace tourist office Alsace camping guide, hotel/restaurant guide
From Haut-Rhin tourist office *Guide des Loisirs* (*gîtes d'étape, refuges* in Haut-Rhin)
From Bas-Rhin tourist office Guide to *gîtes d'étape* and *chambres d'hôte*
See also **www.gites-refuges.com**

Maps

IGN 1:100,000 sheets 12 and 31
Club Vosgien 1:50,000, sheets 1/8, 2/8, 4/8, 6/8, 7/8

SHORT WALKS IN THE VOSGES

Suggestions for short walks in the Vosges are presented under five walking centres. These have been chosen to give an idea of the variety of the region, and to visit some of its many castles, traditional villages, wooded hills and open summits. These walking centres are marked on the map on page 10, 'Walking in the Vosges', and with each walking centre there are very basic maps showing the general course of the walk.

The walk descriptions are brief, but extra details are given at points where there were particular route-finding difficulties. Where routes follow parts of the GR5/GR53, look in the relevant section of the main walk (sections 1–11) for details. An appropriate walking map is highly recommended.

Niederbronn-les-Bains

The spa town of Niederbronn-les-Bains lies in the regional park of the Northern Vosges. Roman and Celtic springs in the vicinity hint at the ancient origins of the town, and the archaeological museum for the Northern Vosges is situated here.

Map Club Vosgien 1:50,000 sheet 2/8

1 Wasenbourg and Oberbronn
(14.5km/9 miles, 3hr 45mins, height gain 460m)

This walk passes castle ruins at Wasenbourg before returning through Oberbronn, a village with many fine examples of traditional Alsace architecture.

Short Walks from Niederbronn-les-Bains

Walking Routes are shown in red
1. Wasenbourg and Oberbronn
2. Wasenbourg Castle and Breitenwasen
3. Windstein and Philippsbourg

Short Walks from Saverne

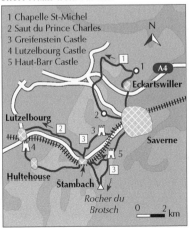

Walking Routes are shown in red
1. Chapelle St-Michel and Saut du Prince Charles
2. The Castles of Greifenstein, Lutzelbourg and Haut-Barr
3. Rocher du Brotsch

Follow the GR53 in the direction of Saverne (see Section 2). Go past the ruins of **WASENBOURG CASTLE** to reach the **COL DE L'UNGERTHAL**.

Cross the road and leave the GR53 to take the second route to the left, following the blue cross waymarks along the Chemin Forestier de la Weissebirke. After about 200m **watch out for** a blue cross waymarked footpath to the left. Take this footpath down the valley, keeping with the main path until you meet the GR531 (blue rectangles), which you follow left to **OBERBRONN**.

Take the road immediately left after the *mairie*, the Rue Gelders, and follow the GR531 back to Niederbronn-les-Bains. This route goes along the road for about 600m then, just after a traffic island, takes a footpath to the left between houses and into the woods. When this path emerges back onto the road, turn left to return to Niederbronn-les-Bains.

2 Wasenbourg Castle and Breitenwasen

(14km/8.5 miles, 3hr 45mins, height gain 380m)

This circuit passes the ruins of the 13th-century castle at Wasenbourg and drops down to return by a level valley track through the hamlet of Breitenwasen.

Follow the GR53 in the direction of Saverne (see Section 2), past the ruins of **WASENBOURG CASTLE**, and carry on to the **COL DE L'UNGERTHAL**. Leave the GR53 by turning right along the road. After about 250m, just before the road bends left, take the vehicle track to the right. This is the start of the blue cross route that leads down into the valley, although at the time of writing there is no waymark at this junction. Go down the track to start following these waymarks.

The footpath zigzags down, then turns right along a track for a short distance, then left onto a waymarked footpath. Where this emerges onto a second track, follow this right for perhaps 200m before following a waymarked path to the left which then hairpins down.

On meeting the track at the bottom of the valley turn right, and from here follow the yellow triangles through **BREITENWASEN** and back into Niederbronn-les-Bains.

3 Windstein and Philippsbourg

(27km/17 miles, 7hr 30mins, height gain 675m)

(With possible shorter circuit of 21.5km/13.5 miles, 5hr 30mins, height gain 760m.)
This circuit visits the 14th-century castle of Nouveau Windstein and the 12th-century castle of Vieux Windstein, then continues to the village of Philippsbourg, which has restaurants and several shops selling locally made goods.

Leave Niederbronn-les-Bains by the GR531 (blue rectangles), taking the Rue de la Vallée (turn right coming out of the **tourist office**, then first right). About 1km up this road leave the GR531 by turning to the left, up the route signposted to Ruines Windstein. From here the route follows red/white/red waymarks for about 5.5km, passing the farm of Reisack and the Restaurant du Windstein before climbing up to the ruins of **NOUVEAU WINDSTEIN**.

Continue ahead to reach the restaurant 'Aux Deux Châteaux' in Windstein – the ruins of **VIEUX WINDSTEIN** are just beyond the restaurant. Take the GR53 in the direction of Niederbronn-les-Bains (see Section 1) as far as **COL DE LA LIESE**.

Shorter Circuit To return to Niederbronn-les-Bains via the lookout tower at Grand Wintersberg, continue on the GR53 (see Section 1) from Col de la Liese (21.5km/13.5 miles).

To continue with the circuit, follow the red disc route from here to Philippsbourg. Pass in front of the Club Vosgien chalet and go along the road to the right, then almost immediately follow the waymarks along a footpath

to the right through a *parcours sportif* alongside the road. This route leads down to **PHILIPPSBOURG** in about 4km. Cross the main road and take the minor road almost opposite towards Baerenthal. At the edge of the village turn left and go along the street parallel to the disused railway.

Follow this lane for about 2km – the route is waymarked with red triangles and signposted to Grand Arnsbourg. Where the lane turns sharply to the left and crosses the river, follow the red triangle waymarks along the track ahead. Very soon after this, leave the red triangle route and take a path forking to the left, with a sign indicating that it connects with the yellow triangle route. Fork left at the next junction and carry on with a lake to the left to meet the yellow triangle route. Follow this to the left along the valley bottom through **BREITENWASEN** and back to Niederbronn-les-Bains.

Saverne

Saverne is a busy town with a wide range of facilities. In the centre you can admire the many fine, timbered buildings that line the Grand'Rue. Nearby, the imposing Château des Rohan overlooks the marina of the Marne–Rhine canal, nowadays popular with pleasure craft. Lying at the edge of the hills, the area contains a wealth of waymarked paths, and several Vosgien castles are within easy reach.

Map Club Vosgien 1:50,000 sheet 1/8

1 Chapelle St-Michel and Saut du Prince Charles

(15.5km/9.5 miles, 4hr, height gain 250m)

This loop to the north of the town passes two places of special note. Chapelle St-Michel sits on a rocky promontory overlooking the plain, with a cave in the cliff below, and the overhanging rock at Saut du Prince Charles lies beside the route on the way back.

Follow the GR531 (blue rectangles) for 5km to reach the Chapelle St-Michel. To do this, go down the Grand'Rue from the **tourist office** to the roundabout, fork left, then turn right along the major road which crosses the rail bridge. Leave this road to the right, along the road to Ottersthal and St-Jean-Saverne (GR531 signpost). Follow the road through Ottersthal and **watch out for** waymarks leading along a minor road forking to the right, beside a roadside cross. Follow the waymarks under the A4 to reach **ECKARTSWILLER**.

In Eckartswiller turn left up the Impasse des Châtaigniers. At the top of this short street do not follow the wider track around to the left, but take a footpath straight ahead (passing a shed in a small flat clearing) to pick up waymarks.

Follow the blue rectangles to reach **CHAPELLE ST-MICHEL**, beyond which is an outlook point, and a steep path beside the chapel leads down to the Grotte des Fées, an impressive rock shelter.

Return from the chapel, past the *buvette* (café), and take the red ring path towards Rothlach. This soon reaches the parking area at the Croix de Langenthal. Follow the red ring waymarks for a further 3km to reach a bridge over the busy A4. Cross the bridge and turn left, following red discs towards Kaltwiller. This very soon reaches the **Rothlach** junction.

Turn left here, but **watch out for** the first junction. Where a path is indicated on the left, towards the Rocher des Faucons, take the red ring path that leaves to the right. Follow this path for about 15mins to reach the **Kaltwiller** junction. From this junction follow the GR53 back to Saverne (see Section 2), passing the overhang known as **SAUT DU PRINCE CHARLES**.

2 The Castles of Greifenstein, Lutzelbourg and Haut-Barr
(26.5km/16.5 miles, 7hr, height gain 730m)

This walk visits three rather different castles: Greifenstein is a hilltop ruin surrounded by trees, Lutzelbourg, on an exposed bluff, gives more open views over the valley, and Haut-Barr is a more celebrated ruin, popular with visitors. Another point of interest is the secluded rock garden at Grotte St-Vit, an unexpected haven high in the forest.

From the **tourist office** go down the Grand'Rue to the canal and turn left along the first towpath. Go under the first bridge, then immediately left up a ramp to cross over the second bridge, and continue along the towpath on the north side. Follow GR531 waymarks (blue rectangles) leading along the towpath, then branch off to the right to climb to the castle at **GREIFENSTEIN**.

Lutzelbourg Castle

Follow the blue rectangles on past the **Grotte St-Vit**. This leads past the turn off to the lookout point at **Rappenfels**, just off route, then zigzags downhill. Turn right on meeting the red/white/red route just above the canal. Follow this path as far as the **Vallée du Stutzbach** then take the blue cross route into **LUTZELBOURG**.

Pass along the main street then turn left to cross the canal and River Zorn on the D38. Turn right on the far side and leave this road to the left. Fork left on a footpath and follow red/white/red signs up to **LUTZEL-BOURG CASTLE** above.

From the castle take the red ring route towards Hultehouse, then follow the red/white/red signs into the village of **HULTEHOUSE** itself. Leave the village by the yellow disc route, signposted Vestiges Gallo-Romains. After passing a Roman sepulchre with information board, the yellow disc route winds down to **STAMBACH**.

Turn right along the main road in Stambach, then take the GR531 (blue rectangles) to the right at the edge of the village. Within a short distance take the red triangle route off to the left, towards Haut-Barr. Follow these waymarks to reach **HAUT-BARR CASTLE** and continue along the GR53 (red rectangles) back down into Saverne.

3 Rocher du Brotsch

(14km/8.5 miles, 4hr, height gain 570m)

In addition to the castles of Haut-Barr, Grand and Petit Geroldseck and Greifenstein, this southern loop passes the outstanding lookout points at the Tour du Brotsch and the Rocher du Brotsch.

Follow the GR53 to the south from Saverne (see Section 3) as far as the **ROCHER DU BROTSCH**.

On returning from the outlook rock, take the second path to the left, signposted as the yellow cross route to Grand Krappenfels (avoiding the other yellow cross path to Cuve de Pierre). Follow these waymarks past **Grand Krappenfels** and on to

Petit Krappenfels. Follow the red/white/red waymarks from here down to **STAMBACH**.

Pick up the blue rectangle waymarks of the GR531 and follow to the north, crossing the canal and climbing up the hill on the other side. The route then leads past the **Grotte St-Vit** and **GREIFENSTEIN CASTLE**, back down to the canal and into Saverne.

Ste-Marie-aux-Mines

With its long history of silver mining, this town has a mineralogical and mining museum and plays host each year to a fair where minerals, gems and fossils are exhibited and traded. Some of the old mine workings are open to the public and there are many tourist facilities, including campsites.

Map Club Vosgien 1:50,000 sheet 4/8

1 Col de Ste-Marie and Échery Castle
(23.5km/14.5 miles, 6hr 30mins, height gain 900m)

This route to the west of Ste-Marie-aux-Mines passes the site of Faîte Castle and the ruins of Échery Castle, which stand high above the valley. There are also numerous fortifications dating from the First World War.

From the **tourist office** go uphill, then take the D48 to the left towards Sélestat. Look out for a narrow lane on the right, the Rue du Champ de la Chatte. Follow the red disc route along here, signposted to Château d'Eau and Col des Bagenelles. Keep with the red disc waymarks all the way to Col de Ste-Marie by following the route steeply uphill to come out at a clearing. Turn right along a track then leave it on a path to the left very soon after. On reaching a lane, turn left.

About 1.5km along this lane follow the road hard right. Note that about 300m beyond this bend there is an ambiguous waymark – keep following the road around the sharp bend to the left. This passes a farm and the road becomes a track. After about 0.5km, where the main track takes a sharp bend to the right, take a minor track to the left, going to the **COL DE STE-MARIE**.

Cross the road and take the GR531 (blue rectangles), which climbs to some First World War buildings and the scant remains of **FAÎTE CASTLE**. Continue along this path for almost 6km, passing Chaume de Lusse, to reach the junction at

Short Walks from Ste-Marie-aux-Mines

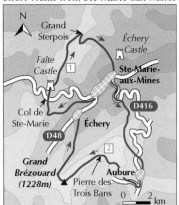

Walking Routes are shown in red
1. Col de Ste-Marie and Echery Castle
2. Aubure and Grand Brézourd

Short Walks from Ribeauvillé

1 Girsberg
2 St-Ulrich
3 Haut-Ribeaupierre
4 Monastery

Walking Routes are shown in red
1. Alsace villages
2. Bilstein Castle and the monastery of Notre Dame de Dusenback
3. The Castles route

Short Walks from Metzeral

1 Kerbholz
2 Kastelbergwasen
3 Lac d'Altenweiher

Walking Routes are shown in red
1. Fischboedle and Le Hohneck
2. Crest of the Vosges and Lac d'Allenweiher
3. Le Petit Ballon

GRAND STERPOIS. Turn right to follow the diagonal blue crosses, signposted to Raleine, zigzagging down for a short distance to reach the yellow disc route.

Follow this to the right towards Ste-Croix and continue down the lane in the bottom of the valley. After about 4.5km along this yellow disc route there is a signpost pointing left to Château d'Échery. A short diversion up the yellow cross route here leads to the ruins of **ÉCHERY CASTLE**. Follow the track indicated, but **be careful to turn off** sharply to the left on a small footpath after only about 100m.

Return to the lane and follow the yellow crosses and yellow discs for about 1km. The lane turns to the right over a bridge, and immediately afterwards take a track to the right towards the Refuge de la Vierge (the waymark is a little way up this track). The yellow cross waymarks are now followed all the way back to Ste-Marie-aux-Mines. Fork left before a water tower and continue up through woods.

After passing the sign for the Forêt Domaniale St-Pierremont, watch for the route – just a few metres after the sign it leaves the track steeply uphill to the right. **Watch out for** the route leaving this path by a tiny footpath to the left only about 50m up this hill.

At the broad junction by the Refuge de la Vierge, take the track to the left to descend into Ste-Marie-aux-Mines.

2 Aubure and Grand Brézouard

(27.5km/17 miles, 8hr, height gain 980m)

This loop climbs up to Aubure, the highest village in Alsace, and then follows a stretch of the GR5 across the summits of Petit and Grand Brézouard. While much of the walk is through forest, there are fine views from the highest ridge.

From the **tourist office** cross Place Keufer opposite and turn left down the Rue Reber. At the roundabout take the minor road that leaves to the right, with a sign indicating the yellow cross route to Aubure (these yellow cross waymarks are now followed all the way to Aubure). Follow the road uphill, turn right where it joins the D416 and continue uphill. Where the road goes around a sharp left-hand bend, take the signed footpath which leaves to the right very soon afterwards.

This path zigzags uphill to cross a track. **Be careful**, as immediately up the bank on the other side you do **not** carry on along the obvious path ahead, but turn sharply right along a footpath – this is easily missed.

Follow yellow cross waymarks for about 2km to reach a track junction where left goes to Petit-Haut and right to Aubure (both yellow cross waymarks). Turn right and continue along this well-waymarked route for 5km to reach **AUBURE**.

Leave Aubure by the road towards Col de Fréland. Follow the red rectangles of the GR5 (see Section 5), which leads over **GRAND BRÉZOUARD**. Beyond this summit

the route drops down to reach a car park where you leave the GR5, taking the right fork. Go down the path in front of the Refuge du Haycot (believed to be out of commission at the time of writing).

Turn right at the next junction, following the red/white/red route signposted for Échery. At a small bothy, La Cabane Verte, the route divides. Take the right-hand branch of the red/white/red path and follow this down the valley into **ÉCHERY** and back along the road into Ste-Marie-aux-Mines.

The footpath above Échery

Ribeauvillé

Ribeauvillé is a small town on the Alsace Wine Route. With its narrow streets of timbered houses and range of shops, it is popular with tourists. It sits right on the edge of the plain, close to vineyards and traditional Alsace villages. The Vosges mountains rise up just to the west, with several castles within easy walking distance.

Map Club Vosgien 1:50,000 sheet 6/8

1 Alsace Villages
(14km/8.5 miles, 4hr, height gain 480m)

This walk leads up into the hills then returns by way of two villages that both reflect the wine-producing traditions of the area. Riquewihr is an old, walled village with many narrow streets and old buildings, and as there is much to explore it is popular with visitors. Hunawihr, the neighbouring village, is quieter, but also has many typical Alsace houses.

From the **tourist office** walk up through the old town to join the GR5 (see Section 5) at the Route de Ste-Marie-aux-Mines. Follow the GR5 just past the Col du Seelacker until you reach a junction where the red/white/red route leaves by a footpath sharply to the left, signposted to Riquewihr.

Turn left down this path, but almost immediately **watch out for** a path off to the left to Riquewihr (red/white/red waymarks) – do not continue on the red/white/red route to Aubure.

On joining a road, go left downhill. After passing a layby and picnic site to the right, branch off left down the Chemin de la Grande Vallée. Where there is a choice of red/white/red routes, take the right-hand path, Riquewihr par le Château. This leads past the ruined tower of **REICHENSTEIN**. Turn left on meeting a lane and carry on into the village of **RIQUEWIHR**.

Go through the gateway ahead to visit the village, but the route turns left in front of this gateway. Where the road

231

bends to the right, take the steps up to the left and turn right along the road at the top. At the next junction take the left-hand of the two roads ahead to follow the route to **HUNAWIHR**.

Enter the village by the Rue de Riquewihr and cross straight over into the Rue du Nord. Follow this round a curve then very soon take the road to the left, signposted to Ribeauvillé. This minor road leads through the vineyards back to Ribeauvillé.

2 Bilstein Castle and the Monastery of Notre Dame de Dusenbach

(14.5km/9 miles, 4hr, height gain 610m)

This is a woodland walk reaching fine outlook points at Bilstein Castle and Rocher St-Jacques, and returning by way of a secluded monastery.

From the **tourist office** walk up through the old town to join the GR5 (see Section 5) at the Route de Ste-Marie-aux-Mines. Follow the GR5 past the Col du Seelacker as far as the junction where a sign indicates the blue disc route to Château de **BILSTEIN**. Follow this route to the castle then return to this junction.

Take the other blue disc route downhill, signposted to La Pépinière. Look out for a footpath to the right leading down to an excellent lookout rock at **Rocher St-Jacques**. Return to the track and follow the blue disc route down to the bottom of the valley.

On reaching the track at the foot of the hill turn right, then very soon left onto the yellow cross route (signposted La Pépinière). Go along the riverside then turn right across a footbridge. Turn right down the road (there is currently no sign) then immediately left at a *maison forestière*. Leave this road by a footpath to the right and follow the yellow crosses and yellow triangles uphill.

On reaching a vehicle track turn right to follow the yellow crosses to Dusenbach. After about 1.5km take the yellow cross path to the right, down the valley to the **MONASTERY OF NOTRE DAME DE DUSENBACH**. Take the blue triangle route, the Sentier Maria Raydt, to the left beside the monastery and follow it back into Ribeauvillé.

Reichenberg Castle

3 The Castles Route
(13km/8 miles, 3hr 30mins, height gain 510m)

The four castles of Reichenberg, Haut-Ribeaupierre, Girsberg and St-Ulrich are within easy reach of Ribeauvillé.

From the **tourist office** go down to the main road and turn left along the Route de Bergheim. Where this turns right, take the road to the left and immediately turn off onto the red/white/red waymarked route signposted to Haut-Koenigsbourg and Reichenberg.

Follow this out of town, then take a left turn uphill, the Sentier Viticole Schlusselstein. After only 30m turn right, signposted to Reichenberg, and continue along this track for about 2km between vineyards. Turn left on reaching a road just below **REICHENBERG CASTLE** and pass the castle, then turn right up a track and fork left on the route to Thannenkirch.

Leave the track to the left, still on the red/white/red route, to the outlook rock of Witzigfelsen.

Note There are two footpaths leaving the rock. Take the small footpath downhill immediately beside the rock (do not return to the main track uphill, signposted to Haut-Koenigsbourg) to drop down to the road and then turn right. Leave the road to the left and follow the red/white/red path up the valley to **THANNENKIRCH**. Continue up into the village then left down the main street, joining the GR5 (see Section 4). This leads past the three other castles on the way back down to Ribeauvillé.

Metzeral

Metzeral is close to the GR5, and with its railway station and range of facilities is a useful stopping-off point from the main route. It is also a good centre for a visit to the area, giving access to a number of walking routes as well as the historic town of Munster 7km along the valley.

Map Club Vosgien 1:50,000 sheet 6/8

1 Fischboedle and Le Hohneck

(18.5km/11.5 miles, 5hr 30mins, height gain 890m)

This walk leads past the lakes of Fischboedle and Schiessrothried, which nestle in wooded glacial cirques, and the route to the summit of Le Hohneck provides excellent views over the steep-sided valley below. However, part of the circuit follows a difficult path which involves rocky sections crossed with the help of fixed chains, and about 800m is climbed between Metzeral and Le Hohneck summit.

Walk along the valley from Metzeral towards **MITTLACH**, taking the quiet road on the north side of the River Fecht. Before reaching the village turn to the right up the Wormsa Valley, following the red rectangles of the GR5. Pass **Lac de Fischboedle** and continue up to **LAC DE SCHIESS-ROTHRIED**. To the left of the lake, by the dam, is a signpost pointing towards Kerbholz and Kastelberg. Follow this path for about 200m then take the GR531 (blue rectangles) which leaves to the left on a footpath (do not continue ahead, following the blue triangle route).

Near the summit of Le Hohneck

The path climbs steeply and a short diversion to the left reaches the *belvédère* at **Spitzkopf**. From the lookout point retrace your steps to the main footpath, then continue along the GR531, which becomes a rocky path where some sections have fixed chains and steps. At the path junction at **KERBHOLZ** turn right to follow the GR531 to the *ferme-auberge* of **KASTELBERG(WASEN)**.

Go up the track from the *ferme-auberge*, but turn off to the right very soon afterwards along a footpath (yellow cross waymarks) towards Collet du Hohneck. The path climbs up and merges with a broader path at a signpost. Continue ahead, following the obvious path around the outside of the cirque which leads to the restaurant on the summit of **LE HOHNECK**.

Descend by the GR5 (see Section 5) to Schiessrothried, then return along the valley to Metzeral.

2 Crest of the Vosges and Lac d'Altenweiher
(22km/13.5 miles, 6hr, height gain 780m)

A high-level walk along the crest of the Vosges involving a height gain of about 800m.

Walk along the valley from Metzeral to the village of **MITTLACH**, taking the quiet road on the north side of the River Fecht. On reaching the village follow the red rectangle GR5 waymarks out of Mittlach in the direction of **COL DU HERRENBERG** (see Section 6). At the col turn right along the ridge following the alternative GR route (red/white/red) – this passes **LE RAINKOPF**. Beyond here, but before reaching the *ferme-auberge* of Ferschmuss, turn right along the yellow cross path towards Altenweiher. This is a complex junction, so be sure to avoid the blue rectangle path back to Rainkopf summit.

Follow the yellow cross path, which soon zigzags steeply downhill. After about 40mins turn left at a T-junction and follow the waymarks to **LAC D'ALTENWEIHER**. Cross the dam and take the footpath that goes downhill on the far side of the stream, below the dam (this is also waymarked with yellow crosses, but they are rather scarce), leading down to a parking area. Go left along the road back into **MITTLACH** then on to Metzeral.

3 Le Petit Ballon

(16.5km/10.5 miles, 5hr, height gain 790m)

This walk climbs 700m up to the summit of Le Petit Ballon (1267m), giving fine views over the Eastern Vosges. **A walking map is strongly recommended**, as the waymarking alone is insufficient.

Leave Metzeral and walk up the D10 to reach **SONDERNACH**. Turn left in front of the *mairie*, following the sign towards Rothenbrunnen. Carry on up the road (do not take the road off to the right across a bridge, which has a roadsign to Le Petit Ballon), and at its end take the track that forks left and follow this, with occasional yellow cross waymarks, up through the forest.

The route zigzags upwards following tracks and paths. The yellow cross waymarks are currently very faded and not all junctions are indicated, but in combination with the recommended map it is possible to follow the route up to the *ferme-auberge* of Ried.

Continue along the track past the *ferme-auberge*. The track becomes a footpath and reaches a T-junction with another track where you turn right, uphill (red diagonal cross route,

but few waymarks). At a signpost beside the *ferme-auberge* of Rothenbrunnen, turn left across open pasture to join the road near to the car park for Le Petit Ballon. Cross the road and turn right up the hill to reach the summit of **LE PETIT BALLON**.

Retrace your steps as far as the signpost at Rothenbrunnen and follow the red diagonal cross route signposted to Metzeral. At a signposted junction take the path towards Metzeral that forks left through a turnstile (do not follow the other red diagonal cross route down the main track to Breitenbach).

Continue down this path for nearly an hour, then watch out for a junction where the route to Metzeral turns sharply left downhill. Follow this, waymarked by red diagonal crosses then by red rings, back down to Metzeral.

OTHER WALKS IN THE JURA

LONG DISTANCE ROUTES IN THE JURA

In addition to the GR5, sections of the GR9, GR59 and several other routes all cross the Jura. There are also five separate GR de Pays circuits which in total cover a large part of the region. Of the many possibilities for long distance routes, two have been chosen for special mention here. The outlines below are not detailed, but offer ideas that might help in planning a trip. (See map 'Walking in the Jura', page 11.)

Along the Crest of the Jura
(61km/38 miles, 3–4 days)

The GR5 only crosses a small part of the French Jura before leaving the high land and diverting towards Lake Geneva. This misses out a ridge of higher summits further south on the plateau. The route suggested here, which is a continuation of the line of the GR5 southwards, allows this crest to be explored. The route has no official title and is made up of a combination of three GRs. It provides fine walking over a series of open summits and includes several excellent lookout points. The starting and finishing points of this walk are easily accessible by rail from Geneva or Geneva airport. (See map page 11.)

From **LA CURE** (station (Swiss), hotel, *gîte*, restaurants) follow the GR5 (see Section 11) until you reach the signpost to La Dôle. Turn right here and follow the route that leads up the ridge, to the summit of **LA DÔLE** (1677m). Join the GR Tour du Léman (Balcon du Léman) at the summit, which forms the basis of most of the rest of the route. From La Dôle it

View south from La Dôle

follows the crest of the ridge back into France and crosses the Réserve Naturelle de la Haute-Chaîne du Jura. After dropping down to the **COL DE LA FAUCILLE** (café/restaurant) it then rises to reach the high point of **LE RECULET** (1719m). About 1km after **GRAND CRÊT D'EAU** (1621m) leave the GR Tour du Léman to take the GRP Tour de la Valserine down into **BELLEGARDE-SUR-VALSERINE** (tourist office, station, hotels, campsite, restaurants, shops).

Facilities
This list only includes the main facilities along the route (TO = tourist office).

Km	Cumulative km		
		La Cure	Station (Swiss), hotel, *gîte*, restaurants
17.5		Col de la Faucille	Café/restaurant; turn off for Mijoux, 2km off route
		(Mijoux)	Hotel, *gîtes*, restaurant, café, shops
11.5	29.0	La Loge	Chalet/*refuge*; turn off for Lélex
		(Lélex)	TO, hotel, restaurants, café/bar, shops
4.0	33.0		Turn off for chalet/*refuge* Curson, 1.5km off route
6.5	39.5	Passage du Gralet	Turn off for Chézery-Forens, 4km off route
		(Chézery-Forens)	Hotel, campsite, restaurant, café, shops
5.0	44.5		Turn off for Menthières (*gîte*), 2km off route
16.5	61.0	Bellegarde-sur-Valserine	TO, station, hotels, campsite, restaurants, shops

Note Wild camping is not allowed in the nature reserve.

Information Sources
From Franche-Comté tourist office *Gîte* guide
From Ain tourist office Camping guide
See also **www.gites-refuges.com**

Maps
IGN 1:100,000 sheet 38 (small part only), sheet 44
IGN 1:50,000 Parc Naturel Régional du Haut-Jura

GR59 – Arbois to St-Amour

(134km/83 miles, 5–8 days)

The GR59 stretches from the Ballon d'Alsace in the Vosges to connect with the GR9 at Yenne, south of Geneva. As a north–south route
from Vosges to Jura, it might be thought of as a rival to the GR5, but
the two routes are very different. The GR59 maintains a more west-
erly course, passing Besançon and Lons-le-Saunier. In general it
avoids high plateau country, and explores the lower-lying *reculées*, a
scenic area of plateau edge and broad, flat, steep-sided valleys that
forms a picturesque and interesting landscape. To the west of the
path the land falls away quickly and vineyards become frequent. This
is the centre of the Jura wine-growing area, with villages clustered
along the edge of the plateau, sometimes sheltering just below
exposed limestone cliffs. These long-established settlements, often
the site of a notable old church or castle, add variety to the trip.

While the GR59 in its entirety would provide a rewarding journey,
the short summary and notes below concentrate on a particularly
interesting 134km-section that includes some of the best *reculée*
scenery and is a good introduction to the area (see map page 11).

Picking up the GR59 at the small
town of **ARBOIS** (tourist office,
station, hotels, campsite, restaurants,
shops), the path heads south.
Vineyards are already becoming a
feature of the lower land.

At **POLIGNY** (tourist office,
hotels, campsite, restaurants, shops)
the path cuts in around the *reculée*,
staying low and leading below the
cliffs. The next stretch passes a clutch
of old winemaking villages:
Passenans, Menétru-le-Vignoble and
CHÂTEAU-CHALON (restaurants,
cafés) then on to **BAUME-LES-
MESSIEURS** (campsite, restaurant,

cafés). All of these villages have their
own particular character, but Baume-
les-Messieurs is one of the most
scenically sited places in the region,
the village houses dwarfed by the
surrounding limestone exposures,
which form steep, rocky outcrops
all around.

On from here the route skirts the
town of **LONS-LE-SAUNIER** (tourist
office, station, hotels, campsite,
restaurants, shops) and leads through
more open country, twisting around
the south of the town and passing
several lookout points. The next
section sees the route winding south,

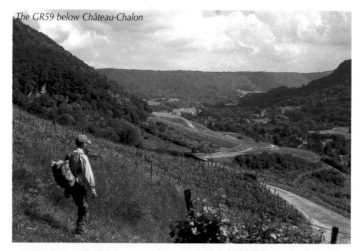
The GR59 below Château-Chalon

on the very edge of plateau country, passing a whole series of small villages, including **ST-LAURENT-LA-ROCHE** (*gîte*), Rotalier and Gizia. The path is for the most part through forest, but there are also open views over the flatter lands to the west.

The route passes within a few kilometres of **ST-AMOUR** (tourist office, station, hotels, campsite, restaurants, shops), where a return rail connection is possible.

Waymarking is currently old, and not up to the same standard as along the GR5, so allow some extra time for route-finding.

Facilities
This list only includes the main facilities along the route (TO = tourist office).

Km	Cumulative km		
		Arbois	TO, station, hotels, campsite, restaurants, shops
11.5		Poligny	TO, hotels, campsite, restaurants, shops

11.5	23.0	Les Bordes	Turn off for St-Lothain (*gîte*, shop), 2km off route
3.0	26.0	Passenans	Hotel, restaurant, café, shop
10.5	36.5	Château-Chalon	Restaurants, cafés; turn off for Voiteur, 2.5km off route
		(Voiteur)	Hotel, shops
15.0	51.5	Reculée de Baume	Hotel/restaurant
4.0	55.5	Baume-les-Messieurs	Campsite, restaurant, cafés
5.0	60.5	Lavigny	*Gîte*
2.0	62.5	Pannessières	Hotel
7.5	70.0	Perrigny	Hotel, restaurant, shops; turn off for Lons-le-Saunier, 3km off route
		(Lons-le-Saunier)	TO, station, hotels, restaurants, campsite, shops
18.5	88.5	Vernantois	Hotel
5.0	93.5	Montaigu	Turn off for Lons-le-Saunier, 3km off route
		(Lons-le-Saunier)	TO, station, hotels, restaurants, campsite, shops
11.0	104.5	St-Laurent-la-Roche	*Gîte*
16.5	121.0	Gizia	Turn off for Cousance, 3.5km off route
		(Cousance)	Station, hotel, campsite, shop
13.0	134.0	L'Aubépin	Turn off for St-Amour, 2.5km off route
		(St-Amour)	TO, station, hotels, campsite, restaurants, shops.

Information Sources

From Franche-Comté tourist office Camping guide, *gîte* guide
See also **www.gites-refuges.com**

Maps

IGN 1:100,000 sheets 37 and 44
IGN 1:50,000 Jura, No1 Zone Ouest

Short Walks from Ornans

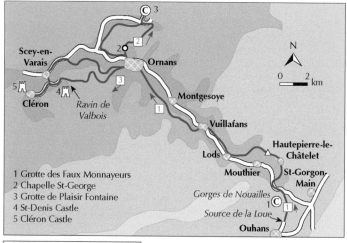

1 Grotte des Faux Monnayeurs
2 Chapelle St-George
3 Grotte de Plaisir Fontaine
4 St-Denis Castle
5 Cléron Castle

Walking Routes are shown in red
1 Source de la Loue
2 Grotte de Plaisir Fontaine
3 Cléron

Short Walks from Baume-les-Messieurs

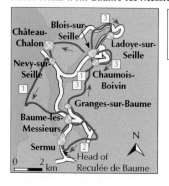

Walking Routes are shown in red
1 Château-Chalon
2 The Reculeé de Baume
3 Cirque de Ladoye

SHORT WALKS IN THE JURA

Suggestions for short walks in the Jura are presented under four walking centres. The French Jura covers a wide area, so this selection is necessarily limited. The choice has been made to cover a range of landscapes and types of walks. The walking centres are marked on the map 'Walking in the Jura' on page 11, and with each walking centre there are very basic maps showing the general course of the walk.

The walk descriptions are brief, with extra details given at points where there were particular route-finding difficulties. Where routes follow parts of the GR5, look in the relevant section of the main walk for details. An appropriate walking map is highly recommended.

Ornans

The small town of Ornans, with picturesque old houses lining the banks of the Louc, makes an excellent base for local walking excursions. The GR590 runs east and west from the village, with several lookout points, castles and caves within walking distance. Ornans is 30km northwest of Pontarlier and could be reached from the GR5 by way of the GR595.

Map IGN 1:50,000 Le Doubs No1 Zone Ouest

1 Source de la Loue
(Basic route 20km/12.5 miles one way, 5hr 30mins, height gain/loss 160m/420m.
Additional 5km/3 miles, 1hr 30mins if using bus to access starting point.)

(Possible shorter circuit of 9km/5.5 miles, 2hr 30mins.)
There is much to see on this walk along one of the best sections of the River Loue. The river's source is at the head of the Nouailles Gorges, and it follows a twisting course along a scenic wooded

245

ravine. The GR passes elevated lookout points and there are several caves nearby, including the Grotte des Faux Monnayeurs, which is accessible from the route.

Buses from Ornans to Pontarlier run several times a day, stopping at the villages of Montgesoye, Vuillafans, Lods, Mouthier and St-Gorgon-Main, allowing some flexibility for planning a walk. Bus timetables are available at Ornans tourist office.

The starting point is the car park at Source de la Loue. This can be reached by taking the bus to St-Gorgon-Main, walking along the D41 towards Ouhans, and then following GR595 waymarks towards the Source de la Loue. (Alternatively, the bus driver may be willing to drop you off earlier, to connect with shorter, signposted footpaths that reach the Source.)

From the car park take the concrete track down to **SOURCE DE LA LOUE**, then continue beyond the Source, following the red/white waymarks of the GR595 signposted to Mouthier. On reaching the D67 turn left and continue down the road for about 1.5km. The **GROTTE DES FAUX MONNAYEURS** is reached by

diverting off the route down a sign-posted footpath to the left. The GR595 climbs up from the right of the D67 to reach **HAUTEPIERRE-LE-CHÂTELET**, and passes some fine viewpoints before descending to meet the river again at **LODS**.

From Lods the GR595 continues along the bottom of the valley through **VUILLAFANS**, where it crosses the river and returns to Ornans.

If you have your own transport, a circular route can be followed from the car park at Source de la Loue by taking the above route until the Grotte des Faux Monnayeurs, then following another branch of the GR595 back along the bottom of the gorge to the Source (9km).

The source of the Loue

2 Grotte de Plaisir Fontaine

(16.5km/10.5 miles, 5hr, height gain 280m)

This route reaches the cave at Plaisir Fontaine and returns by the valley of the River Brème.

From the *hôtel de ville* in the centre of town walk along the road past the **tourist office**. Pass Place Courbet, and shortly after turn right along the Rue des Martinets, signposted towards the *site du château*. The route from here to the cave follows the GR595, but the red/white waymarks are sparse in places.

Fork left along the Rue du Charmont and then follow the red/white waymarks up a lane to the right. The waymarks lead across a road and on to a junction where a sign points to the **CHAPELLE ST GEORGE** and a *belvédère* off to the right. These are easily reached by a short diversion, but the route resumes by following the waymarks left at this junction.

Follow red/white GR waymarks (and also blue/yellow waymarks) along several tracks and paths through woodland towards Grotte de Plaisir Fontaine.

Beyond the woods the route follows a fence line then reaches a track. Turn left and carry on to reach the lane just ahead, then turn right and follow this past a large farm (Ferme de Septfontaines). Some 0.5km along the lane **look out for** a track leaving to the left – there is a signpost for Grotte de Plaisir Fontaine, but little indication of red/white waymarks. Follow this track, which becomes a path, crosses a field and leads into woods.

After the woods the route reaches a track at a T-junction where the GR cross to the right indicates a left turn is needed. Continue to a road (D280) then carry on ahead along it. At a road junction there are signs pointing off right to the **GROTTE DE PLAISIR FONTAINE** – follow the signs up to the cave then return to this junction.

To return to Ornans, cross the road at the junction, taking the track to the left of the stream. Following blue/yellow waymarks, the route leads across two girders over a stream and comes out onto an open field. A signpost points right from here, but the path becomes indistinct. Follow a faint track that cuts across the field to reach a signboard on the other side, pointing down the path towards Ornans.

Follow the blue/yellow markers, eventually signed towards parking on the D67. When this is reached, turn left for a short distance. At a sign about rock climbing (*l'escalade*) a track leaves the road to the left. Follow this – it climbs a little, but keeps roughly parallel to the road and

rejoins it again a short while later. Continue along the road back into Ornans.

3 Cléron
(24km/15 miles, 6hr, height gain 190m)

This walk follows the GR590 to the west of Ornans to reach the village of Cléron. The route passes the nature reserve at Ravin de Valbois, the castle ruins of St-Denis and a riverside *château* at Cléron. The suggested return is by way of Scey-en-Varais, passing the celebrated viewpoint over the Loue at Le Miroir de Scey.

From the *hôtel de ville* in the centre of town walk along the road past the **tourist office**, then turn left at Place Courbet. Cross a footbridge over the river, pass the Fishing Museum and follow the road as it curves to the right around the church. The route passes a bridge to the right and continues ahead along the road close to the river bank.

From here as far as Cléron the route follows the red/white waymarks of the GR590. Continue along the road (D241), passing college buildings, and leave Ornans. The road becomes the Route de Chassagne, and soon after this the GR590 turns left onto a forest track following waymarks.

Follow the waymarked route through woods, crossing the D241. About an hour after this, turn right on reaching the signboard for the **RAVIN DE VALBOIS** nature reserve. Keep
248

with the GR590, passing the ruins of **ST-DENIS CASTLE**. The route follows a path down through the woods and joins a track which then leads onto a quiet road at the Ferme du Pater. Follow this into **CLÉRON**.

To return, retrace the route for about 1.5km. Where the road turns to the right just beyond a ruined farm there is a signboard detailing fishing regulations on the Loue. Leave the road by a blue/yellow waymarked route to the left, beside this sign. Fork right immediately and follow the riverbank footpath. The route merges with a track to the right and continues ahead to reach a footbridge over the river. Cross this to enter the village of **SCEY-EN-VARAIS**.

Veer right through the village to reach the D101. Turn right and follow it to reach the viewpoint at **Le Miroir de Scey** just outside the village. Continue along the road for just over

1km, then take the road to the right that crosses the Loue by a small bridge. Just across the river follow the road and fork left at the first junction. This quiet country road leads back to Ornans.

Baume-les-Messieurs

The village of Baume-les-Messieurs lies in a region of impressive limestone scenery – particularly striking are the broad, flat, steep-sided valleys known as reculées – to the northwest of the high plateau and does not form part of the GR5 (the best long distance route here is the GR59, see 'Long Walks in the Jura' earlier in the book). The land just to the west is well known as the stronghold of Jura wine production, and the area abounds with age-old villages. Château-Chalon, within walking distance, is an attractive example of a fortified settlement.

Map IGN 1:50,000 Jura No1 Zone Ouest

1 Château-Chalon
(25.5km/16 miles, 7hr 30mins, height gain 640m)

The highlights of this walk are the viewpoints over Baume-les-Messieurs, enclosed by a steep-sided valley, and the picturesque Jura village of Château-Chalon, overlooking a sea of vineyards. The route includes several short, steep climbs.

This route follows parts of the GR59 and GR59D, both with red/white waymarks, but although this sounds simple, the waymarking is sparse at points. It is an excellent and rewarding walk, but the account below is only an outline. **A separate walking map is essential**, and allow plenty of time for route-finding.

Leave Baume-les-Messieurs by the road up behind the abbey, signposted to Crançot, and at the first hairpin leave by a footpath straight ahead, signposted to Les Laves. Follow this uphill to rejoin the road and turn right. On reaching a road junction turn left to **GRANGES-SUR-BAUME**, where there is a *belvédère* slightly off route to the left. Continue through the

The hilltop setting of Château-Chalon

village and fork left down the lane signposted to Les Laves.

From here to Chaumois-Boivin the waymarking is currently poor. Follow the lane for about 5mins, passing two tracks off to the left. **Look out for** an indicator waymark warning of a right turn ahead, and go right at the next fork where there is currently no waymark. At the next fork go right and pass a sign to Cabane Gout d'Eau to the left. Turn left on meeting a road. At the next fork, just a few minutes later, follow the main track round to the left, although there are no obvious waymarks.

Follow the waymarks to the left into the farm of Saugiat, then to the right just beyond it. At a T-junction turn right along the road, then almost immediately left following a sign towards Chaumois-Boivin. Follow the

250

road as it curves to the right and passes through the village of **CHAU-MOIS-BOIVIN**.

Take a footpath that drops down to the left, off the road, and descends to the village of **BLOIS-SUR-SEILLE**. Turn left through the village. On reaching a T-junction the GR59 leaves along the track opposite, then takes the path continuing uphill. Keep with the GR59 until **CHÂTEAU-CHALON** comes into sight. On passing a roadside cross it is easiest to stay with the road (D5) into the village.

Return is by following the GR59D to the south. This leaves the village by a grassy track next to the church down through vineyards, then joins a tarmac track that leads downhill into the village of **NEVY-SUR-SEILLE**. (**Note** The GR59D does not enter the village, but the actual route here is currently very hard to locate).

Turn right along the road (D70) for about 0.5km, then left along a small road by the river. GR59D waymarks lead along this road and over a bridge to the right. Turn right then follow the lane. Avoid the private road off to the right, but turn left at the next junction, which has a 'No Entry' sign for vehicles.

Where the lane bends sharply right, continue ahead along the earth track, following waymarks up through the woods. On emerging from the woods turn left to reach a T-junction on the edge of the forest. Turn right and follow the track along the edge of the woods. After about 1km this passes a *table d'orientation*. Continue ahead, still following close to the woodland edge, until you reach a road.

This is a GR path junction. **Caution** – do not follow the GR59 onwards towards Lavigny and Pannessières. Instead, follow the road to the left for a short distance and turn left up a waymarked track signposted towards a chapel. This is the GR59 leading back to Baume-les-Messieurs.

The route soon crosses a road and continues ahead. On meeting another road the route turns right, although waymarking here is currently poor. Follow this road for about 1km to reach a junction. Take the path opposite down through woods.

The path emerges briefly onto a lane by an iron cross, but leaves again immediately by another downhill path. At the next road the route goes left to head back into Baume-les-Messieurs.

2 The Reculée de Baume
(9km/5.5 miles, 3hr, height gain 210m)

This short walk provides some striking views of the limestone scenery around Baume-les-Messieurs. There is a climb of about 200m to reach a viewpoint at the head of the *reculée*.

Leave Baume-les-Messieurs by the road up behind the abbey, signposted to Crançot, and at the first hairpin leave by a footpath straight ahead, signposted to Les Laves. Follow this uphill until it meets the road again, and then turn right. Continue along the

road past the first junction, carrying straight on along the D70. In a few minutes this reaches a T-junction with the D4. Cross straight over and follow the red/white waymarked path that leaves at this point. Within 10mins this path emerges further along the D4.

The village of Baume-les-Messieurs is surrounded by the steep cliffs of the reculée

The route continues along a little footpath that leaves directly opposite on the other side of the road (this may not be immediately obvious.) Turn left on reaching a clearer path at a marker stone. At a fork follow the yellow bicycle route waymarks to the left – the path becomes very narrow then comes out onto a track. Cross straight over and follow ahead to a lane which reaches a road. Turn right to the viewpoint at the **RECULÉE DE BAUME**.

From the head of the Reculée de Baume continue along the lane, which is signposted to Sermu – this return route still follows the red/white waymarks of the GR59. Follow these waymarks straight ahead when the road to Baume leaves to the left. The route leads on through **SERMU** in much the same direction. The road becomes a track, and when this swings off to the left, carry straight on along the more minor track. The route then keeps to the high ground not far from the edge of the *reculée*.

About 1km beyond Sermu the path forks. Take the wider path to the right, which starts to descend steeply, following occasional waymarks. Follow this route downhill, and turn left on reaching a road to return to the centre of Baume.

3 Cirque de Ladoye
(24km/15 miles, 7hr, height gain 660m)

This more extended tour explores *reculée* scenery to the north of the village and involves some quite steep climbs. With your own transport you could start at Blois-sur-Seille to walk a shorter (10km) portion of the route.

Follow the GR59 to **BLOIS-SUR-SEILLE**, as described in walk 1 (Château-Chalon). Take Sentier de Ladoye, which goes along the Montée du Village and turns left up Montée de la Charlotte. At the next junction follow the track opposite, indicated by a walking sign. This leads up to another road (D5) where you turn right and continue into **Granges de Ladoye**. Follow signs through the village to the right, then onto a footpath leading steeply down through the woods to **LADOYE-SUR-SEILLE**. Follow the road back into Blois-sur-Seille.

From Blois-sur-Seille it is then possible to do a further loop by leaving the village by the Rue des Chenevières. Follow this road towards Les Chaumois and La Marre for only a few minutes, then take a footpath to the right. This clearly waymarked path can be followed past two lookout points and back to Blois-sur-Seille.

If you started the walk from Baume-les-Messieurs, it is only necessary to follow this loop as far as **CHAUMOIS-BOIVIN** to rejoin the GR59 and retrace your steps to Baume-les-Messieurs.

Les Rousses

Les Rousses is a small plateau town, popular as a ski resort. It lies close to several long distance footpath routes (GR5, GR9, GR559, Tour de la Haute-Bienne), offering lots of scope for short excursions. The nearby peak of La Dôle, just over the Swiss border, is within walking distance.

Map IGN 1:50,000 Parc Naturel Régional du Haut-Jura.

1 Roche de Lavenna and Roche Blanche
(13km/8 miles, 3hr 15mins, height gain 160m)

This short circuit visits two easily accessible local viewpoints. The outward section follows the red/yellow waymarks of the Tour de la Haute-Bienne and the return uses the GR5.

From the **tourist office** walk along the main street and turn right just after passing the *mairie*, then left on reaching a T-junction. Turn right up the Route du Noirmont, then left along the Montée du Rochat. Take a

Short Walks from Les Rousses

Walking Routes are shown in red
1. Roche de Lavenna and Roche Blanche
2. La Cure circuit and La Dôle summit
3. Belvédère des Maquisards

Short Walks from St-Claude

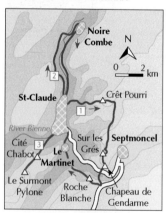

Walking Routes are shown in red
1. The Gendarme's Hat
2. The Bienne Gorge
3. Mont Chabot

signposted track to the right, just before reaching the school. This leads through woods, then goes left across pastureland to meet the road at Vy à Chaton.

Turn right along the road, then very soon after go off right towards the Plage du Rocher du Lac. Follow this track towards Lac des Rousses, but just before the lake turn off left along the waymarked path that skirts the end of the lake, to emerge onto the road beyond. Climb the path into the forest on the far side of the road.

A signpost indicates a side path to the left to the outlook point at **ROCHE DE LAVENNA** – follow yellow/white waymarks, then return to this junction.

Keep following the red/yellow waymarks to meet the GR5 at **Carrefour de la Fontaine**. Turn left and return to Les Rousses along the GR5 (see Section 11), with a recommended diversion to visit the excellent lookout point at **ROCHE BLANCHE**.

Lac des Rousses

2 La Cure Circuit and La Dôle Summit
(21.5km/13.5miles, 6hr, height gain 680m)

(With possible shorter circuit of 8km/5 miles, 2hr, height gain 140m.)
This circuit climbs about 600m to the summit of La Dôle (1677m),
where there is a fine 360° view.

Follow the GR5 south from Les Rousses (see Section 11), passing close to the waterfall at **BIEF DE LA CHAILLE**. Leave the GR5 about 1km beyond the signpost at **La Pile Dessus**. A signpost here indicates that La Givrine is to the left and La Dôle to the right (1hr 30mins distant). Turn

255

right along this track and continue until the buildings on the N5 come into view ahead. On reaching a *tourisme pédestre* signpost turn sharply left uphill, as indicated.

Continue uphill to reach a road, with the 'Couvaloup' restaurant a few hundred metres off to the left. Cross the road, following the track opposite. Follow the main track, which has occasional yellow *tourisme pédestre* waymarks. This leads out of the forest and climbs up to the summit of **LA DÔLE**, visible ahead.

Return by the same route to reach the GR5. Follow this back as far as **LA CURE**, then continue past the French customs post and follow the footpath signs along the Route Royale, a quiet road that leads directly back to Les Rousses.

Shorter Circuit Follow the GR5 from Les Rousses, passing Bief de la Chaille to reach La Cure, then return directly along the Route Royale (8km).

If you have transport, the route up La Dôle can easily be accessed from the parking on the N5 at Les Dappes.

The path up La Dôle

3 Belvédère des Maquisards

(11km/7 miles, 3hr, height gain 390m)

This easy walk to the west of Les Rousses passes a woodland water-fall on the way to an elevated *belvédère*.

Follow the GR5 south (see Section 11) as far as **BIEF DE LA CHAILLE**. Turn right and follow the GR9 to Prémanon. Just after joining this path a short diversion to the left along the side of the stream reaches the waterfall. Keep with the red/white waymarks of the GR9 to reach a road, and follow this to the left to go by way of Prémanon d'Amont to **PRÉMANON**.

Leave the GR9 and take the road to the right towards Morez (D25), following signs towards the Belvédère des Maquisards. Just before the road bends to the right, take the vehicle track that carries on straight ahead, following green/white waymarks. Carry straight on over a road, then at the next road follow straight on. At Plan de la Loge turn left towards Les Maquisards and go straight ahead at the next junction, now following blue/white waymarks. Fork left after about 5mins, passing a signpost with the slightly confusing name of Belvédère des Maquisards, and continue straight on to the main road.

Cross over and take the path slightly to the right up to the **BELVÉDÈRE DES MAQUISARDS**.

From the *belvédère* retrace your steps as far as the signpost Belvédère des Maquisards, then turn left. The route now follows blue/white waymarks to link back with the GR5. Cross straight over the main road and follow the waymarks along a track. Continue through the trees to a clearing with a house visible ahead. Before reaching the house **look out for** a footpath turning sharply back to the left and take this back into the trees. On reaching a very rough track take a footpath almost immediately opposite which climbs the banking and turns left, initially to run parallel to the track.

At the junction called Les Moulins turn left towards Bief de la Chaille and descend to cross the **Pont Perroud**. Across the bridge turn left, still following blue/white waymarks, and climb up the other side of the valley to rejoin the GR5 at **Le Bonzon**. Turn left to return to Les Rousses.

St-Claude

This small but lively town sits in a long, narrow valley and earns a living from a whole range of activities, including diamond cutting and the manufacture of tobacco pipes – tourism plays only a small part in its prosperity – and there is a museum reflecting the town's industries and heritage. Access by rail is possible, and there are many facilities.

Map IGN 1:50,000 Parc Naturel Régional du Haut-Jura

1 The Gendarme's Hat
(20.5km/13 miles, 6hr, height gain 1200m)

(With possible shorter circuit of 17.5km/11 miles, 5hr 30mins, height gain 810m.)
This is an excellent and varied walk that explores the landscapes of the Jura plateau. Folded rock formations are a feature of the circuit, with the Chapeau de Gendarme above the Gorges du Flumen a prime example. However, the walk does include some clifftop paths that could be hazardous in poor weather.

Emerging from the **tourist office** turn right along the road. Walk along the Avenue de Belfort to fork right up to the Place Christin. Take the right fork uphill – Rue Christin. Follow the red/yellow waymarks along this road to reach the signpost at Carrefour de Très Bayard.

The route now follows the red/yellow waymarks of Tour de la Haute-Bienne for some time. Turn right uphill to Le Pontet, then left to reach the eroded rock face at **CRÊT POURRI**. Shortly after this a possible 0.5km

diversion to the left leads to the lookout at **Rocher du Frênois**. The main route continues ahead to reach the road at La Main Mort, where the fingerboard is misleading. Turn right and follow the road over a small bridge.

Beyond this there are three roads – take the middle one, although the waymarking is not obvious. This becomes a track that leads to Col de la Tendue. Turn right here to Le Rafour and right again towards Septmoncel. Pass the signpost at La Loceresse, then within about 10mins

Le Chapeau de Gendarme

look out for a track leaving to the right. This is currently only signed as a snowshoe route, but is also the walking route. (If you reach the Auberge Chantemerle you have overshot this junction.)

Turn right at Sous le Jetalet and cross a field to Sur le Replan, where the route leaves the Tour de la Haute-Bienne. Turn right to follow the yellow waymarks towards Sur les Grés, and within a few minutes the route is signposted off left. At the fork immediately afterwards take the main track to the right. Follow yellow waymarks to the lookout point at **SUR LES GRÉS**, then turn left and follow the path downhill, crossing to the left-hand side of the fence. Where the path splits keep to the right and carry on downhill. Follow the path down the right-hand side of a field, then into woodland at the bottom corner. At the

sign offering a choice of routes to the Chapeau de Gendarme, take the path to the left, then turn right at the next junction to reach the **CHAPEAU DE GENDARME**.

From the rock, drop down to the road. Turn right downhill for just a couple of minutes and **look out for** a small footpath (waymarked by yellow paint marks at the road edge) leaving to the left. Follow this downhill to reach the next loop of the road, turn left for a short distance and take another footpath leaving to the right. At the bottom of this path the route **turns left**.

Shorter Circuit The circuit can be shortened at this point by turning right and going down the road for about 1.5km. A footpath signposted off left just before the Roche Percée leads down the valley back to Le Martinet (17.5km circuit).

To continue with the main route, go up the road for just a few metres then take a footpath to the right into the woods, by a signpost.

On reaching the road turn right uphill to reach **Les Moulins**. Cross the small footbridge to the right and follow the yellow disc path steeply uphill. Within 1.5km it reaches the D25 at **La Cernaise**. Turn right, following the signs to le Martinet and Roche Blanche, and turn right again on meeting a road. Then after about 5mins turn right yet again, following the sign to reach the lookout point at **ROCHE BLANCHE**.

Leave by a small footpath to the left that runs quite close to the cliff edge then drops down by hairpins through woodland, with occasional yellow disc waymarks. At a fork follow the blue arrow to the left, downhill, to reach a road at a small hydroelectric station. Turn left and follow the road to **LE MARTINET**. Turn right at a T-junction and continue to the main road, then turn left and follow the road into St Claude, where signs lead past the cathedral to the tourist office.

2 The Bienne Gorge
(17km/10.5 miles, 4hr 30mins, height gain 150m)

This circuit explores a section of the wooded gorge of the Bienne.

Emerging from the **tourist office** turn right, then fork down to the left towards the *gare* (railway station). Turn off right into the Rue de la Glacière, then left into the Rue du Faubourg des Moulins and cross the bridge.

From the bridge turn right uphill, then take the Chemin des Arrivoires, which forks right, downhill. Follow this down towards the river and divert briefly around a large building. Continue along the footpath by the riverside, marked by occasional yellow waymarks. After about 20mins

the route ahead is blocked by a rock outcrop and the waymarks lead uphill, zigzagging steeply. Avoid the path marked with a yellow cross and continue up to reach first the rail line, then a road.

Turn right along the road and very soon take the minor road off to the right, signposted to Noire Combe. After about 150m take the lane leaving to the right, although there are currently no waymarks. This crosses the railway by a level crossing then becomes a footpath. Where the old track has slumped into the river a footpath leads around the blocked section.

After crossing a small bridge over a (dry) stream there is a fork. Take the major, right-hand path, which soon leads down to an old river bridge. Do not cross the bridge, but follow the signposted route ahead towards Champs de Bienne. This soon leads back onto the lane. Turn right and continue along for about 3.5km.

Follow the lane across the river bridge, and a little further on take the signposted footpath to the right towards Noire Combe. Turn right where this path rejoins the road and walk uphill to pass through the village of **NOIRE COMBE**. On the far side of the village there is a signpost indi-cating several footpaths. Take the lower track straight ahead towards Les Cheneviers, which is the start of the route back to St-Claude along the east bank of the Bienne, and is well marked by yellow waymarks.

After about 1hr 15mins the path leads out into a meadow, and a foot-path sign by an electricity post indicates the route turns left towards Cascade de la Vouivre and St-Claude. The path leads on past the little water-fall to join a track at the Dièle sign. Turn right along this track, and when it joins a road take this downhill to the right.

At a road junction turn right along the Rue Jean Jacques Rousseau and carry on ahead towards the town centre.

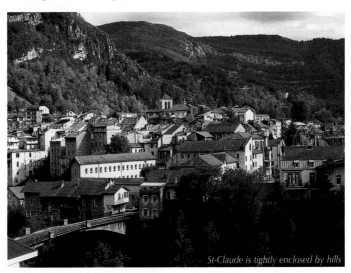

St-Claude is tightly enclosed by hills

3 Mont Chabot
(4km/2.5 miles, 1hr 30mins, height gain 470m)

(With possible extension to 10km/6 miles, 3hr, height gain 670m.)
This short walk is rewarded with a fine view over St-Claude and the
Bienne Valley.

Emerging from the **tourist office** turn left and walk up the Ave de Belfort, then right and along the D436 in front of the cathedral (signposted to Lons-le-Saunier). This soon leads over a bridge. Just 100m beyond the bridge go left up an alley, where a footpath sign indicates Le Surmont Pylone and other destinations.

Only 50m further up **look out carefully for** another footpath sign on the right, pointing up to the right between two close buildings and easy to miss. This footpath climbs steeply, soon leading to an initial lookout at Le Marais, then to a higher point at **CITÉ CHABOT**. Return from here for the 4km walk.

Extended route (10km) Following ahead, this path eventually joins a road at the outlook point at **LE SURMONT PYLONE**. Return by the same route.

APPENDIX: Contact Details

Tourist Offices and Accommodation

General Tourist Information

General tourist information, including a list of all the hotels in a region, may be obtained by contacting the following.

For Alsace there is a general website (**www.tourism-alsace.com**), but brochures are best ordered by contacting the two *départements* below.

For the north of Alsace, Agence de Développement Touristique du Bas-Rhin, Maison du Tourisme, 9 rue du Dôme BP 53, F–67061, Strasbourg, Cedex, 03 88 15 45 80 (**www.tourisme67.com**).

For the south of Alsace, Association Départementale du Tourisme du Haut-Rhin, Maison du Tourisme, 1 rue Schlumberger BP 337, F–68006, Colmar, Cedex, 03 89 20 10 68 (**www.tourisme68.com**).

For Franche-Comté, contact Comité Régional du Tourisme de Franche-Comté, La City – 4 rue Gabriel-Plançon – 25044 Besançon, Cedex, 03 81 25 08 08 (**www.franche-comte.org**).

For the southern part of the long distance route along the Crest of the Jura, contact Comité Départemental du Tourisme de l'Ain, 34 rue Général Delestraint – BP78 01002 Bourg-en-Bresse, Cedex, 04 74 32 31 30 (**www.ain-tourisme.com**).

Web links for gîtes and refuges

www.gites-refuges.com is a useful resource for walking accommodation within France, which can be accessed regionally (by *département*).

Refuges run by the Amis de la Nature organisation usually have restricted opening. Their website (**www.amis-nature.org**) allows contact details for each refuge to be accessed. Select first 'Les Structures d'accueil', then 'Maisons/chalet refuges', then the appropriate *département*.

Similarly, *refuges* run by the Club Vosgien usually have restricted opening. Their website (**www.club-vosgien.com**) allows contact details for each *refuge* to be accessed. Select first 'Conseils', then 'Liste des refuges'.

Note All the hotels listed below are 2 star unless otherwise stated.

GR5/GR53 Route
Section 1

Wissembourg	Tourist office, 03 88 94 10 11
Col du Pigeonnier	*Refuge*, **www.club-vosgien.com** (restricted opening)
Climbach	Hotel, Cheval Blanc, 03 88 94 41 95
	Hotel, À l'Ange, 03 88 94 43 72
Fleckenstein	Camping Fleckenstein (on the *étang*), 03 88 94 40 38
Obersteinbach	Hotel, Alsace-village, 03 88 09 50 59
	Hotel, Anthon, 03 88 09 55 01
	Gîte, 03 88 09 55 26
Windstein	Hotel (1*), Windstein, 03 88 09 24 18

Section 2

Niederbronn-les-Bains	Tourist office, 03 88 80 89 70
	Campsite, Heidenkopf, Route de la Lisière, 03 88 09 08 46
Lichtenberg	Hotel (unclassified), Au Soleil, 03 88 89 96 13
	Gîte, Centre d'Accueil, 03 88 89 96 06
Wimmenau	Hotel, À L'Aigle, 03 88 89 70 41
La Petite-Pierre	Tourist office, 03 88 70 42 30
	Gîte, 03 88 01 47 00
Imsthal	Campsite, Imsterfeld, 03 88 70 42 12
Graufthal	Hotel, Au Vieux Moulin, 03 88 70 17 28

Section 3

Saverne	Tourist office, 03 88 91 80 47
	Youth hostel, 03 88 91 14 84
	Campsite, Rue du Père Liebermann, 03 88 91 35 65
St-Gall	Campsite, Au Paradis Perdu, 03 88 70 60 59
La Hoube	Hotel, Des Vosges, 03 87 08 80 44
Dabo	Tourist office, 03 87 07 47 51
	Gîte, Chalet Refuge, Camping du Rocher 03 87 07 47 51
	Campsite, Camping du Rocher, 03 87 07 47 51
Wangenbourg	Tourist office, 03 88 87 33 50
	Gîte, Refuge du Grand Tétras, 03 88 87 34 34
	Campsite, Les Huttes, Route du Nideck, 03 88 87 34 14
Luttenbach	*Gîte*, 03 88 50 90 62
	Campsite, Camping du Luttenbach, 03 88 50 90 62
Oberhaslach	Tourist office, 03 88 50 90 15
Urmatt	Hotel, À la Poste, 03 88 97 40 55
Col du Donon	Hotel, Du Donon, 03 88 97 20 69

Section 4

Schirmeck	Tourist office, 03 88 47 18 51
Rothau	Hostel, La Claquette, 03 88 97 06 08
	Campsite, Terrain Municipal, 03 88 97 07 50
Champ du Feu	Campsite (off route towards Belmont) 03 88 97 30 52
Chaume des Veaux	*Refuge*, **www.amis-nature.org** (restricted opening)
Le Hohwald	Tourist office, 03 88 08 33 92
	Gîte, 03 88 08 33 47
	Camping Municipal, 03 88 08 30 90
Mont Ste-Odile	Hotel (at convent, 1*), 03 88 95 80 53
Barr	Tourist office, 03 88 08 66 65
	Campsite, Rue de L'Ile, 03 88 08 00 45 (June/Oct)
Mittelbergheim	Hotel, Gilg, 03 88 08 91 37
Andlau	Tourist office, 03 88 08 22 57
Gruckert	*Refuge*, **www.amis-nature.org** (restricted opening)
Scherwiller	Campsite, 11 Rue Faviers, 03 88 92 94 57
Châtenois	Tourist office, 03 88 82 75 00
	Gîte, 03 88 92 26 20
Haut-Koenigsbourg	Hotel, Relais du Haut-Koenigsbourg, 03 88 82 46 56
Thannenkirch	Hotel (3*), Touring, 03 89 73 10 01
	Hotel, Auberge de la Meunière, 03 89 73 10 47

Section 5

Ribeauvillé	Tourist office: from outside France, 03 89 49 08 40 from inside France, 0820 360 922
	Campsite, Pierre de Coubertin, Rue de Landau, 03 89 73 66 71
	Campsite, Des Trois Châteaux, 03 89 73 20 00, (July/Aug)
Aubure	*Gîte*, Les Brimbelles, 9 Route de Ste-Marie-aux-Mines, 03 89 73 91 04
	Camping Municipal La Ménère, 03 89 73 92 99
Col des Bagenelles	Hotel (unclassified), Auberge Renaud-Rautsch 03 89 47 51 74
	Refuge, **www.club-vosgien.com** (restricted opening)
	Gîte, 140 La Hollée, 03 89 47 51 38
Le Bonhomme	Hotel, De la Poste, 03 89 47 51 10
	Hotel, Tête des Faux, 03 89 47 51 11
	Campsite, 10 Rue de la Petite Montagne, 03 89 47 57 50
Étang du Devin	Hotel/*gîte*, 105 Étang du Devin, 03 89 47 20 29, **www.etangdevin.com**

Col du Calvaire	Hotel (unclassified), Les Terrasses du Lac Blanc, 03 89 86 50 00
	Refuge, Tinfronce, 03 89 71 21 94 (restricted opening)
	Refuge, Centre Le Blancrupt, **www.blancrupt.com**
Schanzwasen	Hotel/*auberge*, Schanzwasen, 03 89 77 30 11
Col de la Schlucht	Hotel (unclassified), Du Chalet, 03 89 77 04 06
	Hotel (unclassified), Le Tétras, 03 29 63 11 37
Trois Fours	*Refuge/gîte*, 03 89 77 32 59
Haut-Chitelet	*Refuge*, La Schlucht, **www.amis-nature.org** (restricted opening)
	Refuge, Du Sotré, 03 29 22 13 97
Le Hohneck	Hotel, Auberge au Pied du Hohneck, 03 29 63 11 50
Schiessrothried	*Refuge*, Vosges Trotters de Colmar, **www.gites-refuges.com** (restricted opening)
Metzeral	Hotel, Aux Deux Clefs, 03 89 77 61 48
	Hotel, Pont, 03 89 77 60 84
Alternative Route	
Le Rainkopf	*Refuge*, **www.club-vosgien.com** (restricted opening)

Section 6

Mittlach	Hotel (unclassified), Val Neige, 03 89 77 61 12
	Camping Municipal du Langenwasen, 03 89 77 63 77
Hahnenbrunnen	*Refuge*, Touring Club Mulhouse, 03 89 77 63 17 (restricted opening)
Le Markstein	Hotel, Wolf, 03 89 82 64 36
	Hotel (unclassified), Auberge du Steinlebach, 03 89 82 61 87
	Refuge Du Treh, **www.amis-nature.org** (restricted opening)
	Gîte, Chalet Le Point, 03 89 82 63 35
	Gîte, Maison d'Accueil, 03 89 82 74 98
Le Grand Ballon	Club Vosgien Chalet-Hôtel du Grand Ballon, 03 89 48 77 99
Molkenrain	*Refuge*, **www.amis-nature.org** 03 89 37 32 52 (restricted opening)

Section 7

Thann	Tourist office, 03 89 37 96 20
	Gîte, Cercle St-Thiébaut, 22 Rue Kléber, 03 89 37 59 60
	Campsite, Stade Municipal, 03 89 37 96 20 (July/Aug)
Bourbach-le-Haut	Campsite, 03 89 38 82 59 (July/Aug)
Rouge Gazon	*Auberge*/hotel/*gîte*, 03 29 25 12 80

Boedelen	*Refuge*, **www.club-vosgien.com** (restricted opening)
Ballon d'Alsace	Grand Hôtel du Sommet, 03 84 29 30 60
Plain de la Gentiane	*Refuge*, Quand Même, **www.amis-nature.org** (restricted opening)
Auberge Stalder	*Gîte*, 03 84 27 13 95
Giromagny	Tourist office, 03 84 29 09 00
	Gîte, Relais du Randonneur, Rue des Casernes, 03 84 27 14 18
	Campsite, Le Paradis des Loups, Rue Maginot, 03 84 29 05 11
Évette	*Gîte*, Le Malsaucy, 03 84 29 21 84

Section 8

Héricourt	Hotel (unclassified), Le Lion Rouge, 03 84 46 18 89
	Hotel (unclassified), L'Aquarium, 03 84 56 80 80
Vandoncourt	*Gîte*, Des Aiges, 1 Rue des Aiges, 03 81 37 86 94

Section 9

St-Hippolyte	Tourist office (mid-June/mid-Sept), 03 81 96 58 00
	Campsite, Les Grands Champs, Rue Baumotte, 03 81 96 54 53
Fessevillers	*Gîte*, 03 81 44 41 34
Goumois	Hotel (3*), Taillard, 03 81 44 20 75
	Hotel, Moulin du Plain, 03 81 44 41 99
	Gîte, Refuge de la Forge, 03 81 44 27 19
	Campsite, La Forge, 24, Chemin de la Forge, 03 81 44 27 19
Le Vaudey	*Gîte*, Le Boulois, 03 81 68 68 38 or 03 81 44 04 46
Bois de la Biche	Hotel, 03 81 44 01 82
La Rasse	Hotel, 03 81 68 61 89
Maison-Monsieur	*Gîte*, Switzerland, 0041 (0) 32 968 60 60
Le Cerneux Billard	*Gîte*, Le Cernembert, 03 81 68 01 85

Section 10

Villers-le-Lac	Tourist office, 03 81 68 00 98
	Gîte, Le Clos Rondot, 03 81 68 08 33
	Campsite, Rue du Stade, 03 81 68 00 98 (mid June to mid Sept)
Le Chauffaud	*Gîte*, Les Tavaillons, 03 81 68 12 55
Sur la Roche	*Auberge/gîte*, 03 81 68 08 94 (may be inclusive of meals)
Vieux Châteleu	*Auberge/gîte*, Auberge du Vieux Châteleu, 03 81 67 11 59
Les Cerneux	*Auberge/gîte*, Les Gras, 03 81 68 81 81 (may be inclusive of meals)

Les Alliés	*Gîte*, Accueil nordique des Alliés, 03 81 46 31 97
	Gîte, La Perdrix, 03 81 38 10 36
Larmont Supérieur	*Gîte*, Refuge du Larmont, 03 81 46 61 07
La Cluse-et-Mijoux	Hotel (1*), Du Château de Joux, 03 81 69 40 36
Malbuisson	Tourist office, 03 81 69 31 21
	Campsite, Les Fuvettes, 03 81 69 31 50
Métabief	Tourist office, 03 81 49 13 81
	Gîte, Chez Cousin, 27 Rue du Village, 03 81 49 23 99
Les Hôpitaux-Neufs	Campsite, 17 Rue de la Poste, 03 81 49 10 64 (June/mid-Sep)
Le Gros Morond	*Refuge*, **www.clubalpin.com/fr**
Alternative Route	
Montbenoît	Tourist office, 03 81 38 10 32
	Gîte, La Grosse Grange, 06 82 48 64 25
	Campsite, La Grosse Grange, 06 82 48 64 25 (Jul/Aug)
Les Fourgs	Tourist office, 03 81 69 44 91
	Gîte, Les Granges Bailly, 03 81 69 40 62

Section 11

Mouthe	Tourist office, 03 81 69 22 78
	Gîte, Art et Randonnée, 23 Rue de la Varée, 03 81 69 21 69
	Campsite, La Source du Doubs, 03 81 69 24 74
Chaux-Neuve	Hotel, Du Grand Git, 03 81 69 25 75
	Hotel, Pays Nature, 03 81 69 16 09
	Gîte, Du Passant, 10 Grande Rue, 03 81 69 16 09
Castel Blanc	Hotel, Le Castel Blanc, 03 81 69 24 56
Chapelle-des-Bois	Hotel, Les Bruyères, 03 81 69 21 71
	Hotel, Les Mélèzes, 03 81 69 21 82
	Gîte, La Maison du Montagnon, 03 81 69 26 30
Chalet Gaillard	*Gîte*, Forêt du Risoux, 03 84 60 94 13 (may be inclusive of meals)
Les Rousses	Tourist office, 03 84 60 02 55
	Gîte, Le Grand Tétras, 705 Route des Rousses d'Amont, 03 84 60 51 13
	Gîte, L'Ancolie, 03 84 60 33 80
Bief de la Chaille	Youth hostel, 03 84 60 02 80
La Grenotte	*Gîte*, 03 84 60 54 82
Les Jacobeys	Campsite, Le Danico, 03 84 60 78 74
La Pile	Hotel (1*), Auberge des Piles, 03 84 60 00 44
La Cure	Hotel, Arbez Franco-Suisse, 03 84 60 02 20
	Gîte, Des Tuffes, Route de la Faucille, 03 84 60 02 95

St-Cergue   Tourist office, 0041 (0) 22 360 13 14
                      Camping Les Cheseaux, 0041 (0) 22 360 18 98
Nyon   Tourist office, 0041 (0) 22 365 66 00

Long Distance Routes in the Vosges and Jura
Use the information sources included with the route description for accommodation.

Short Walks Centres
Niederbronn-les-Bains See Section 2
Saverne   See Section 3
Ste-Marie-aux-Mines   Tourist office, 03 89 58 80 50
                      Camping du Fenarupt, 03 89 58 54 80
                      Camping les Reflets du Val d'Argent, 03 89 58 64 83
Ribeauvillé   See Section 5
Metzeral   Campsite, Sondernach (1.5km from Metzeral),
                      Ferme-Auberge du Salzbach, 69 Rue de Buhl,
                      03 89 77 70 55
                      Campsite, Mittlach (3km from Metzeral), see Section 6
Ornans   Tourist office, 03 81 62 21 50
                      Campsite, Le Chanet, 9 Chemin du Chanet, 03 81 62 23 44
                      Campsite, Mambouc, Rue du Stade, 03 81 62 21 50
Baume-les-Messieurs   Camping Municipal de la Toupe, 03 84 44 63 16
Les Rousses   See Section 11
                      Campsite, Les Jacobeys, see Section 11
St-Claude   Tourist office, 03 84 45 34 24
                      Camping Municipal du Martinet, Le Martinet, 03 84 45 00 40

Other Useful Contacts
Stanfords   Mapsellers, 020 78361321, **www.stanfords.co.uk**
Amazon (French site) Suppliers of Club Vosgien maps, **www.amazon.fr**
Club Vosgien   Publish maps and guides to the Vosges, **www.club-vosgien.com**
French Regional Parks **www.parcs-naturels-regionaux.tm.fr**
SNCF   French railways, **www.sncf.com**

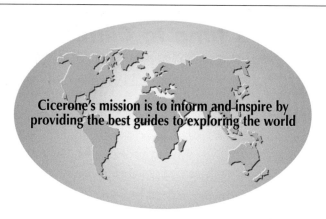

Cicerone's mission is to inform and inspire by providing the best guides to exploring the world

Since its foundation over 30 years ago, Cicerone has specialised in publishing guidebooks and has built a reputation for quality and reliability. It now publishes nearly 300 guides to the major destinations for outdoor enthusiasts, including Europe, UK and the rest of the world.

Written by leading and committed specialists, Cicerone guides are recognised as the most authoritative. They are full of information, maps and illustrations so that the user can plan and complete a successful and safe trip or expedition – be it a long face climb, a walk over Lakeland fells, an alpine traverse, a Himalayan trek or a ramble in the countryside.

With a thorough introduction to assist planning, clear diagrams, maps and colour photographs to illustrate the terrain and route, and accurate and detailed text, Cicerone guides are designed for ease of use and access to the information.

If the facts on the ground change, or there is any aspect of a guide that you think we can improve, we are always delighted to hear from you.

Cicerone Press
2 Police Square Milnthorpe Cumbria LA7 7PY
Tel:01539 562 069   Fax:01539 563 417
e-mail:info@cicerone.co.uk   web:www.cicerone.co.uk

CICERONE